HARPER TORCHBOOKS / The Academy Library

HARPER TORCHBOOKS / The Science Library

(*continued on next page*)

HARPER TORCHBOOKS / The Cloister Library

(*continued on next page*)

PLATE I.

(*Photographic Reproduction by A. Frisch, Berlin, W.*)

GALLIO INSCRIPTION FROM DELPHI.
(Letter of the Emperor Claudius.)

PAUL

A Study in Social and Religious History

ADOLF DEISSMANN

Translated by William E. Wilson

HARPER TORCHBOOKS / The Cloister Library

HARPER & BROTHERS, NEW YORK

περὶ ψυχῶν ἀνθρώπων τὸ ἔργον

PAUL, A Study in Social and Religious History
First edition published 1912
Second edition, revised and enlarged, published 1927
First HARPER TORCHBOOK edition published 1957

227

Library of Congress Catalogue card number: 57-7533
Printed in the United States of America

UNIVERSITATI MANCUNIENSI

εὐχαριστήριον

PREFACE TO THE SECOND EDITION

THIS new edition of my ' Paul '[1] (published in German in 1925) represents a thorough revision of the first edition, which had been out of print for many years both in German and English. Amongst the additions are discussions concerning the principles essential to the cult and its various types, concerning the history of primitive Christianity regarded as a developing cult, and concerning the essential nature and types of mysticism.[2] The peculiarity of the Pauline Christ-mysticism has been brought out altogether more sharply than before. I hope that this may serve to clear away some of the manifold misunderstandings to which my interpretation especially of Christ-mysticism has been exposed. I hope to be able to continue the discussion of Pauline problems in a book of ' Pauline Studies,' already long in hand, which will be published by J. C. B. Mohr, Tübingen. I take this opportunity of thanking my dear friends Mr. Lionel R. M. Strachan and Professor William E. Wilson for their careful work as translators.

ADOLF DEISSMANN.

BERLIN-WILMERSDORF,
PRINZREGENTENSTRASSE, 6, *January*, 1926.

[1] *St. Paul. A Study in Social and Religious History*, translated by Lionel R. M. Strachan, London, 1911. Since the issue of that work the chief lines of my interpretation of Paul's religion were given in my Selly Oak Lectures, 1923, published under the title: *The Religion of Jesus and the Faith of Paul*, translated by William E. Wilson, London, 1923. A Swedish edition was issued, Stockholm, 1925, a Japanese, Tokyo, 1926.

[2] [Here and almost always in other places throughout the book the English word ' Mysticism ' translates the German ' Mystik ' *not* ' Mysticismus ' (see below, p. 147 ff.).—W.E.W.].

PREFACE TO THE FIRST EDITION

An Anatolian, Paul, a man of the ancients, a *homo novus*, rising from the mass of the insignificant many, heeded by no man of letters among his pagan contemporaries, yet destined to be a leading personality in the world's history ; a *homo religiosus*, at once a classic of mysticism and a most practical man of affairs; a prophet and dreamer, crucified to the world in Christ, yet for ever memorable as a citizen of the world and traveller in it, and still moulding the world at the present moment—such is the man whose outlines I have been seeking to portray.   After long years devoted to the study of the ancient records of Paul and their modern interpreters, it was my rare good fortune to find a new teacher to supplement those to whom I shall always look up with gratitude, the old teachers at home. This new teacher is in no sense academic : paper and paragraphs are unknown to her ; all that she teaches she dispenses with generous hand in the bright sunshine and open air—she is in fact the world of the South and East, the world of Paul.   If the western stranger approach this mistress but reverently beneath the olive-trees, she will gladly, and with a mother's joy, speak to him of her great son.

Two journeys to the East, in 1906 and 1909, enabled me to realise the long-cherished hope of seeing with my own eyes the places where the primitive gospel was preached and Paul's life-work was done.   With some small exceptions I visited all the places of importance in the primitive history of Christianity, and I think I may say that I gained a general impression of the structure of the Pauline world which to me personally has increased in value and effect from year to year.   There is no need to labour the point; the advantages of such journeys to the student can only be ascertained by actual trial. If the traveller goes in a teachable spirit, and leaves at home all conceit of his own superior civilisation, he will learn to see things in their true relief and to view them from the proper distance. He sees what light and shade are, and the meaning of heights and depths. His appreciation of simplicity and wild spontaneous growth, and of things not yet harmonised and conventionalised, becomes keener; wondrous problems of classification and division suggest themselves; the extremes of contrast between the modern book-culture of the West and the ancient non-literary culture of Anatolia become tangible. Ill fares it, on the other hand, with our painful inheritance from the scholar's study—the microscopic ingenuity, inexorable, and overweening in its ignorance of the world, which rules straight lines with wooden ruler and cuts out boldly with scissors of steel. Even Doctor Bahrdt[1] returning to Giessen, would not say again to the Four Evangelists:

> Become like one of ourselves I implore you,
> Spruce, dapper, sleek—or they'll ignore you.

Summing up the effect of my travels upon myself, I may say that the good germs of an historical appreciation of Paul, which I owed to my teachers and my own studies, underwent new growth in the apostle's own field and beneath the rays of his sun, but that many

---

[1] [Karl Friedrich Bahrdt (1741-1792), a notorious Professor of Theology at Giessen, whose 'New Revelations of God in Epistolary and Narrative Form,' an attempted modernisation of the New Testament, was satirised by Goethe in a 'Prologue' (1774), in which occurs the couplet:

> 'So müsst ihr werden, wie unser einer,
> Geputzt, gestutzt, glatt—'s gilt sonst keiner.'

—L.R.M.S.]

rank shoots that had sprung up in the shade of the
school walls withered under the same beams. Never
for one moment, however, have I experienced the ' dis-
appointment' which has come to be characteristic of
the newspaper writer of letters from abroad. The New
Testament and the prophets whose souls are vibrant in
the Sacred Book, have become greater to me than
before.

Therefore beside the Paul who has been turned into
a western scholastic philosopher, beside the aristo-
cratised, conventionalised, and modernised Paul, now
suffering his eighth imprisonment in the paper bondage
of 'Paulinism,' I would fain set the Paul whom I think
to have seen at Tarsus, Jerusalem and Damascus, in
Antioch, Lycaonia, Galatia, Ephesus, and Corinth, and
whose words became alive to me at night on the decks
of Levant shipping, and to the sound of birds of passage
winging their flight towards the Taurus—alive in their
passionate emotion, the force of their popular appeal,
and their prophetic depth. I mean Paul the Jew, who
in the days of the Cæsars breathed the air of the
Mediterranean and ate the bread which he had earned by
the labour of his own hands ; the missionary whose
dark shadow fell on the glittering marble pavement
of the great city in the blinding glare of noon ; the
mystic devotee of Christ who, so far as he can be comprehended historically at all, will be understood not as
the incarnation of a system but as a living complex of
inner polarities which refuse to be parcelled out—con-
tending forces the strain of which he once alluded to
himself in writing to the saints at Philippi :—[1]

I am in a strait betwixt the two.

I have a word to add concerning what I regard as
an important conception strongly urged in the following
pages. The whole development of early Christianity—

[1] Phil. i. 23, συνέχομαι ἐκ τῶν δύο.

to which Adolf Harnack has lately applied the term
'double gospel,' i.e. the gospel of Jesus and the gospel
of Jesus the Christ—appears to me to be an advance
from the gospel of Jesus to the cult of Jesus Christ,
that cult deriving its sustenance and its lines of direction from the gospel of Jesus and the mystic contemplation of Christ. This view, which regards the apostles
as devotees of a cult (not of course to be confused with
an established religion), seems to me to do greater
justice to the essential nature of Primitive Christianity
than any other that has been formulated. No other
excludes altogether the possibility of mistaking the development of primitive Christianity for something in
the main doctrinal. The emphasis which I have laid
on the development of the gospel into the cult is nothing
'recent' on my part, as William Benjamin Smith[1] seems
to assume (meaning, I suppose, subsequent to the publication of his 'Prechristian Jesus'). It goes back many
years, and will even be found in my writings before the
appearance of Smith's book, the hypotheses and presuppositions in which, by the way, do not commend
themselves to me.

My sketch of Paul is founded on eight lectures
which I delivered in German by invitation of the Olaus
Petri Trustees at the University of Upsala in March,
1909, and which were immediately published in a
Swedish translation.[2]

ADOLF DEISSMANN.

BERLIN-WILMERSDORF,
   19 *July*, 1911.

---

[1] *Der Vorchristliche Jesus*, 2nd Ed., Jena, 1911, p. xxvii.

[2] *Paulus. En kultur- och religionshistorisk skiss*, Stockholm, 1910,
2nd Ed., 1918.

TRANSLATOR'S NOTE

On the title page of every book by Professor Deissmann issued to the English-speaking public we have come to expect to see the words 'Translated by Lionel R. M. Strachan.' Unfortunately Mr. Strachan was unable to give the time necessary to preparing a second edition of *Paul*, and I was asked to undertake it instead.

There have been many additions and alterations, and these are not confined to the two considerable subjects mentioned in the Author's preface, the discussion of cult and mysticism, but are also to be met with in smaller modifications on almost every page. The present is therefore in the main an independent translation, though in making it I have constantly referred to the excellent translation made fourteen years ago by Mr. Strachan, and have not infrequently availed myself of his renderings; for which help and for his courtesy to me in the matter I offer my hearty thanks.

At the Author's desire, both on the title page and throughout the book, the name of the Apostle stands alone without the prefix 'St.' He has been much impressed by the reasons given by Dr. Peake in the preface to his *Commentary on the Bible* for the omission of this title (*op. cit.*, p. xiii).

I cannot close without expressing my thanks to Professor Deissmann for his kindness in promptly answering all my questions concerning renderings, and for invaluable help in reading the proofs.

WILLIAM E. WILSON.

Woodbrooke, Selly Oak,
Birmingham, 1926.

CONTENTS

CONTENTS

PLATES

THE PROBLEM AND THE SOURCES

CHAPTER I

THE PROBLEM AND THE SOURCES

Two names contain in themselves the primitive history of Christianity : the names of Jesus and Paul.

Jesus and Paul—these two do not stand side by side as first and second. From the broadest historical standpoint Jesus appears as the One,[1] and Paul as the first after the One, or—in more Pauline phraseology— as the first in the One.

Consciousness of His own personality—this is the living force in Jesus from which proceeds that soul-stirring movement which has continued to work among mankind through the centuries down to the present day. This consciousness is self-supported : Jesus stands in history linking heaven and earth together, but He stands in lonely majesty and might : He himself alone.[2] Paul needs some foundation. What Paul is, he is in Christ.[3]

But compare Paul with the others. Then Paul is spiritually the Great Power of the Apostolic Age : he laboured more,[4] and not only laboured more, but created more than all the others.

Therefore the others recede behind him, and therefore the historian, as he surveys the beginnings of Christianity, sees Paul as first after Jesus.

[1] The expression is Pauline, Rom. v. 17, 19. Cf. 1 Cor. viii. 6, and other places.

[2] John vi. 15, αὐτὸς μόνος.

[3] Phil. iv. 13.   [4] 1 Cor. xv. 10.

3

Visible though it be to a great distance, the historic personality of Jesus is not easy for research to grasp; the personal interval is too immense, and the hieroglyphics of the gospels have not all been deciphered. Paul stands nearer and is more easily accessible to us.

Paul indeed is regarded to-day by many as gloomy as well as great. But the darkness is largely due to the bad lamps in our studies, and the modern condemnations of the Apostle as an obscurantist who corrupted the simple gospel of the Nazarene with harsh and difficult dogmas, are the dregs of doctrinaire study of Paul, mostly in the tired brains of gifted amateurs.

If, however, we place the man of Tarsus in the sunlight of his Anatolian home and in the clear air of the ancient Mediterranean world, among the simple people of his own social class, what before pained our eyes like faint and faded pencil sketches, becomes suddenly plastic, alive with light and shade like some mighty relief of ancient date.

Not that we can completely restore this relief. We shall only gain fragments; but they will be important fragments, essential fragments, from which we can reconstruct, at least hypothetically, the proportions and lines of the whole, if we have learnt to view fragments not as scraps but as integral parts.

That is exactly the task of the modern investigation of Paul; to come back from the paper Paul of our western libraries, from the Germanised, dogmatised, modernised, stilted Paul, to the historic Paul, through the labyrinth of the 'Paulinism' of our New Testament Theology to gain contact once more with the actual Paul of ancient days.

The research in the nineteenth century on Paul is both by its thoroughness and the magnitude of its production one of the most imposing achievements of the scientific study of religion. But taken altogether it has been most strongly influenced by interest in Paul, the theologian, and in the 'theology' of Paul. Alongside the enormous discussion of literary questions, especially about the genuineness of the Pauline epistles and their relationship to the 'Acts of the Apostles,' it is chiefly the so-called 'System[1] of Pauline Theology,' or 'Paulinism' that three generations have wrestled over.[2]

But with this doctrinaire direction the study of Paul has gone further and further astray. It has placed one factor which is certainly not absent from Paul, but is in no way the historically characteristic, theological reflection, in the foreground, and has only too often undervalued the really characteristic traits of the man, the prophetic power of his religious experience, and the energy of his practical religious life. The doctrinaire study of Paul has left, moreover, a great riddle unsolved: the open question how far the 'Paulinism' of its discovering was the seat of those

[1] Naturally much turns on the question, what one means by *System*; no one should overlook the carefully weighed sentences of Arthur S. Peake in *The Quintessence of Paulinism*, Manchester, 1917-1918.

[2] A remarkable scientific parallel to the doctrinaire study of Paul is the doctrinaire study of Plato in the nineteenth century, cf. Paul Wendland, *Die Aufgaben der platonischen Forschung*, Nachrichten der K. Gesellschaft der Wissenschaften zu Göttingen, Geschäftliche Mitteilungen, 1910, 2 Heft: 'It may now confidently be said that the comprehensive exposition of the system, however indispensable it may be on didactic grounds, is, from the scientific point of view, a wrongly stated and therefore an insoluble problem' (p. 97). 'A system can be worked out with certainty only in the case of thinkers who have employed the form of the systematic didactic treatise. The same problem must fail, or is only approximately soluble in the case of Plato, Paul, Luther (p. 98), and Goethe, whose writings are not in the least adapted to systematic exposition' (p. 99). There follows then a polemical protest against Zeller's presentation of Plato.

vital forces which must have had a missionary effect, because they carried away the simple people of the Mediterranean world. I am afraid that the people of Iconium, Thessalonica and Corinth would all of them have shared the fate of Eutychus of Troas,[1] if they had been compelled to listen to the paragraphs of modern 'Paulinism' dealing with 'Christology,' 'Hamartiology,' and 'Eschatology.'

Paul at his best belongs not to Theology, but to Religion.

Paul, of course, had been a pupil of theologians and had learnt to employ theological methods; he even employed them as a Christian missionary. But for all that the tent-maker of Tarsus ought not to be classed along with Origen, Thomas Aquinas and Schleiermacher: his place is rather with the herdsman of Tekoa, and with Tersteegen, the ribbon-weaver of Mülheim. Paul the theologian looks backward to Rabbinism. Paul the religious genius gazes into the future history of the world.

Paul is essentially first and foremost a hero of religion. The theological element in him is secondary. naïveté in him is stronger than reflection; mysticism stronger than dogmatism; Christ means more to him than Christology, God more than the doctrine of God. He is far more a man of prayer, a witness, a confessor and a prophet, than a learned exegete and close thinking scholastic.

To show that this is so, is, I consider, the object of this sketch. There is to be no attempt to plumb the depths of the manifold problems concerning the external facts of Paul's biography. Even the questions of

---

[1] Acts xx. 9 ff. The excellent Eutychus, a warning to all who sleep in church, must certainly have been one of the very few people who could manage to fall asleep while Paul was speaking.

chronology [1] and literary criticism must give place to the chief task of displaying the character of the man in the light of social and religious history.

For the task so set, the question of sources becomes comparatively simple.

In the wider sense of the word the sources for displaying the character of Paul in the light of social and religious history are the documents of the ancient Mediterranean world at the time of the great religious change. Especially valuable is the testimony to the social environment of Paul presented to us in the records of the middle and lower classes [2] to be gleaned from the great mass of recently discovered letters and papyri.

Sources in the narrower sense are primitive Christian documents, first and foremost Paul's own letters, then the Book of Acts by Luke, but also everything else which in any way bears a reflection of the personality of Paul. I think chiefly of the Johannine writings in which there pulses the warm life-blood of Paul's devotion to Christ. John is the oldest and the greatest interpreter of Paul. [3]

The problem of sources, in so far as it applies to the letters left by Paul, has become complicated, not

[1] The chief chronological problem only is discussed in the appendix.

[2] Compare my book, *Licht vom Osten. Das Neue Testament und die neuenteckten Texte der hellenistisch-römischen Welt*, 4. völlig neu bearbeitete Aufl., Tübingen, 1923. An English translation of this edition is in preparation and will be issued by Messrs. Hodder & Stoughton, Ltd., under the title *Light from the Ancient East*.

[3] In these lines is indicated the result of a great and important piece of research, which has busied me for decades. Critics who think they can set aside my thesis with a superior wave of the hand, would be better advised to test it by carefully working over the material themselves.

indeed by its own means, but through a fatal vicious circle in which the study of Paul has often moved. Because the personality of Paul has been transferred from the naïve to the premeditated, from the religious to the theological, his letters also have been transposed from the unliterary to the literary class, and by the help of these literary letters the attempt has been made to represent the Apostle as a literary man and a dogmatist.

The letters of Paul thus share with their writer the fate of being frequently misjudged. I do not refer to single cases of exegetical misunderstanding, but to a false valuation as a whole. Their intimate peculiar character—their soul—has been misunderstood. They have been regarded as treatises, as pamphlets in the form of letters, in any case as literary productions, as the theological works of the primitive Christian dogmatic theologian.

This momentous misunderstanding, that the Apostle's letters have been rooted up and laid in the herbarium, is to some extent excused by the fact that in Paul's time in cultured circles the letter was actually employed as a form of literary production.[1] The literary letter, to which to distinguish it from the real letter we shall give the technical name 'Epistle,' was throughout the whole of the later period of antiquity one of the favourite forms of literary art. We find the epistle not only amongst Greeks and Romans, but also amongst the Hellenistic Jews; it was afterwards much favoured by the Christian *literati* of the ancient Church and even to the present day plays a great rôle in our modern literature. But it is in essential characteristics

---

[1] For what follows cf. the discussion 'Prolegomena to the Biblical Letters and Epistles' in my *Bible Studies*, 2nd Ed., Edinburgh, 1903, pp. 1-59.

something other than the letter, and if we wish to form a just historical estimate of Paul's letters we must seek to understand them as unliterary letters as distinguished from literary epistles.

What then is a Letter? And what is an Epistle?

A letter serves separated people instead of conversation. It is an 'I' that speaks to a 'you.' Individual and personal, only intended for the person or persons addressed, it is not destined for publication,[1] even by custom and right it is protected from publication. It is private. The real letter is unliterary, just as is a receipt or a lease. It concerns only the one who has written it, and the one who is to open it, whether the addressee intended be a single person or a family or other circle of persons. Its contents are as varied as life itself. The letter may be trifling, commonplace, passionate, kindly, trivial, wearisome, and it may reflect human fate or family tragedy, moving the souls of writer and recipient to mountain heights or to abysmal depths.

It is otherwise with the epistle. It is a literary artistic form, like the drama, the epigram, the dialogue.

[1] The vexed question, letter or epistle, finally turns on the intention of the writer. Heinrich Wölfflin has therefore rightly distinguished the unliterary letters of Albrecht Dürer from his 'books,' using almost the same formulæ that I have used in regard to Paul: 'In addition to the books, fragmentary writings have also been presented, which were never intended for publication, letters and diaries . . .' (*Albrecht Dürers schriftlicher Nachlass* . . . , edited by Ernst Heidrich, with an introduction by Heinrich Wölfflin, Berlin, 1918, p. 359). That great numbers of the real letters of great men have later on, like Paul's letters, come to be classed as literature, cannot alter their original nature. All literatures contain documents which in origin and intention were unliterary. Indeed it might even be said, the more of such unliterary developed documents that a literature has rescued, the higher it itself stands and by so much less does it as a whole give the impression of being a manufactured and only literary product.

The epistle has only the outer form of a letter ; apart from that it is the opposite of the real letter. It intends to interest and influence a public, or even the public. Since to be published is in its very nature, it uses the personal note only to preserve the illusion that it is a ' letter.' If the letter is private, the epistle is a marketable article. It does not go forth to the world as a single sheet of papyrus like the letter, but from the very first it is reduplicated by the slaves of the bookseller in the great city ; it is intended to be bought, read and discussed in Alexandria, in Ephesus, Athens and Rome.

Thus the epistle is distinguished from the letter just as the historical drama is distinguished from a piece of actual history, or a Platonic dialogue from confidential conversation ; just as the conventional unctuous Life of a saint differs from the account in which by word or pen the eye-witnesses picture to their co-religionists the martyrdom, with phrases halting from emotion, or from the protocol which gives in the briefest and most businesslike manner the details of the action against the confessor,[1] without a thought of producing literature. Epistle and letter are distinguished like art and nature, like the conventionalised and the natural growth, like the premeditated and the naïve.

Certainly there are midway between letter and epistle also mixed types, letter-like epistles and epistolary letters, that is to say naïve epistles, lightly dashed off, and unnatural, tortured letters lacking in naturalness and originality. But the existence of these

[1] For this distinction (also for the understanding of the gospel accounts of the passion) cf. the exceedingly important contributions of Ulrich Wilcken, *Zum alexandrinischen Antisemitismus.* Abhh. der philos.-hist. Klasse der Kgl. Sächs. Ges. der Wissenschaften, Bd. 27, Nr. 23, Leipzig, 1909.

intermediate species does not set aside the fact of, and the importance of, the distinction between letter and epistle. And the question in particular still remains to be settled : in which of the two groups are the letters of Paul to be placed ?

Here the ancient world offers us a wealth of material for comparison. Real unliterary letters have, for example, come down to us from Epicurus and Cicero ; but besides these we have in hundreds of examples actual original private letters written in the Hellenistic-Roman period by Egyptian men and women on papyri and potsherds.[1] There is no room for doubt that these are real letters, and their formal peculiarities, such as præscript, religious wishes at the beginning, formulæ of greeting and other details have made possible quite a new insight into the ancient letter.

On the other hand, we have a wealth of literary letters in the prose epistles for example of Lysias, Aristotle, and Seneca, as also of the poetical epistles of Horace and Ovid ; and a point of especial importance for our problem of sources is that even before Paul the epistle form had entered the literature of Hellenistic Judaism, as the examples of the Epistle of Aristeas which deals with the origin of the Septuagint and a pamphlet against the worship of idols, the self-styled ' Epistle of Jeremiah,' indicate.

It would therefore in itself be not in the least impossible that Paul also might have written epistles, and should therefore be classed as a man of literature —the more so, because in the New Testament alongside the letters of Paul there are other texts which appear to be letters, yet are undoubtedly to be described as

[1] Cf. the selection in *Licht vom Osten*, 4th edition, pp. 119-193, and the other collections of letters there (p. 119) noted.

literary epistles : perhaps the clearest case is the Epistle
of James.

And yet, when once the significance of the distinction between unliterary and literary production is
known and acknowledged, there can be no doubt of the
unliterary character of Paul's letters.   Unfortunately
we are all far too deeply embedded in the merely
literary, and even Christianity, become literary, has far
too great a respect for rows of folios.   Therefore the
liberation of Paul's letters from the literary class is
easily felt by one and another as a form of depreciation.
And for all that, through this very liberation, the
historical (and religious) value of those pages is extraordinarily increased.   Here also we may assert 'That
a quite unusual power of expressing character at first
hand dwells in these things ' [1]

A mere comparison of the formulæ of Paul's letters
with the corresponding peculiarities of the Payprus-
letters of the same time makes the unliterary character
of the Pauline documents clear.   That these texts were
the outcome of a definite situation, which could not be
repeated, and, referring only to this peculiar situation,
are not productions of literary art but of real life, is
obvious on a more exact interpretation of the letters
themselves.   In some cases this is clearer, in others
not so striking, though in the end not to be gainsaid.
Documents unfold themselves to us, documents of the
early apostolic cure of souls, intimate between man and
man, relics of the propaganda of religion, of the missionary work of the Apostles, of the guidance of their
churches, 'survivals' in the sense of the technical
language of historical research.[2]   Paul wrote these

[1] Wölfflin in the work already quoted on Dürer's unliterary letters.
[2] A heathen parallel of exceptional value has lately come to light.
The letter (see translation and explanation in *Licht vom Osten*,
p. 121 ff.) of Zoilos, the worshipper of Serapis, to the Egyptian

PLATE II.

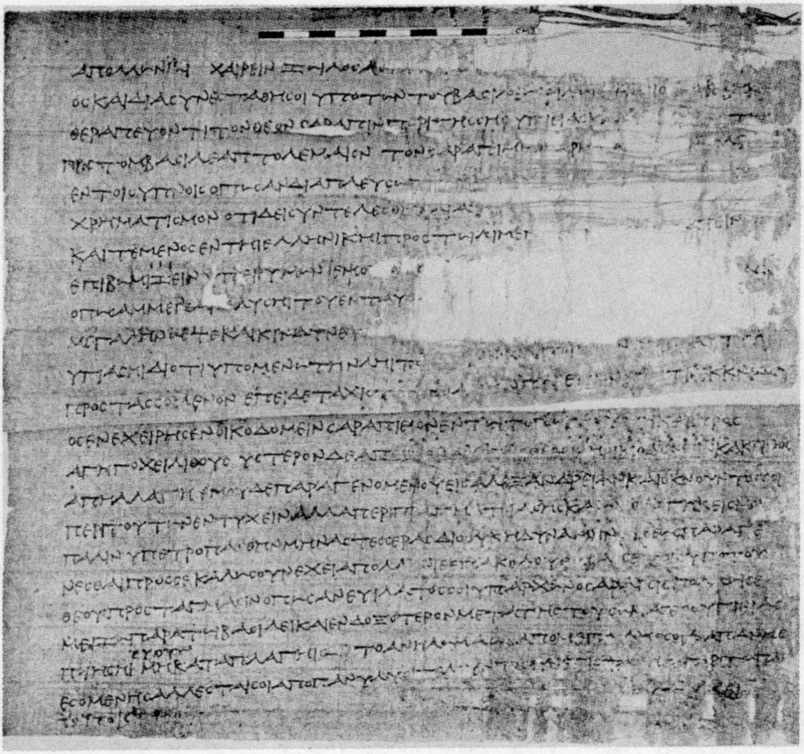

FRAGMENTS OF A LETTER RELATING TO ANCIENT CULT-PROPAGANDA.

(Letter of Zoilos, the worshipper of Serapis, to the Egyptian Finance-Minister, Apollonius, Alexandria, 258-257 B.C. A Papyrus fragment from Philadelphia (Faiyûm). Size of the original 30 × 31·5 cm. (i.e., approximately 10 × 10½ inches), now in the museum at Cairo. Reproduced from Deissmann's *Licht vom Osten*, 4th ed., p. 406.)

(*Front.*)

PLATE III.

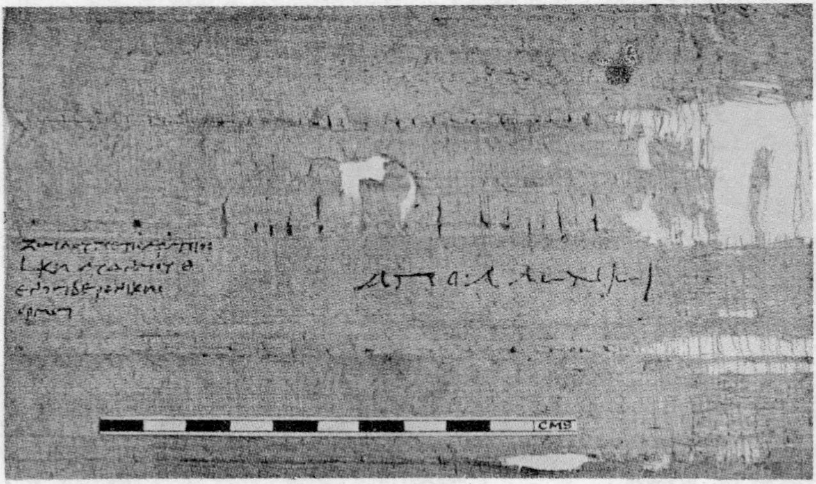

FRAGMENTS OF A LETTER RELATING TO ANCIENT CULT-PROPAGANDA.

(The letter of Zoilos. Alexandria, 258-257 B.C. From Deissmann's *Licht vom Osten*, 4th ed., p. 408.)

(*Back.*)

pages, or in many (perhaps in most) cases[1] dictated them to the pen of a companion,[2] amid the storm and stress of his wandering life, which was so rich in deeply-moving experiences. He then sent them in a single copy by the hand of trusty messengers to the place of their destination over land and sea, from Ephesus to Corinth, from Corinth to Rome, and to Ephesus, without the great world or even Christendom as a whole knowing at the time of their existence.

That after centuries some of these confidential letters would still be in existence Paul neither intended nor anticipated. His glowing faith never reckoned on coming centuries. Spanning apostolic Christendom, like the sultry sky of thunderous weather, was the hope that the present age of the world was hastening to its close, and that the new world of the kingdom of God was just about to appear. Such a hope does not thirst for earthly fame

---

Finance Minister, Apollonios (258-257 B.C.). Here also we have not in the least a literary production, but a 'survival' of religious propaganda. Here I give a reproduction in reduced size of the whole unparalleled document (front and back on Plates II. and III.) and for the rest refer the reader to my commentary in the above mentioned work.

[1] 2 Thess. iii. 17; Gal. vi. 11; Col. iv. 18; 1 Cor. xvi. 21; (2 Cor. x. 1?); Rom. xvi. 22. In all these places either the amanuensis is mentioned or Paul stresses the fact that he writes the last words of the letter with his own hand.

[2] That these letters were spoken letters is a point of view which has not yet received sufficient attention. One ought to ask in many places: Was this spoken loudly or softly, did Paul smile when he said it, or was he quivering with passion, did he strengthen or weaken the sense by some quick gesture? All questions that at first sight seem unanswerable, yet by the penetrating co-operative work of judicious interpreters some approach to answers no doubt can be found. Thus, too, one may much more easily learn to distinguish the different types of Paul's spoken style, from the simple businesslike style right up to the psalmlike and psalm-making fervour of the religious confession of faith.

of authorship, it reaches out longingly after the new, the heavenly.

It was to prepare for this new thing that Paul was working, and the letters he sent out also served this end directly or indirectly. Their subject is always problems of the individual soul or of the Christian community in a definite peculiar situation. The letters are simply the substitute for conversation by word of mouth, and, as has been already pointed out, it is of great importance to think of them as spoken (dictated) and to seek to reproduce the modulations of their living, unliterary words, so as to discover where Paul is smiling, where he is angry, where, to the horror of his later Atticist commentators, he falls halting into *anacolutha*, or where prophetic fervour wings his words. Paul wishes to console, to reprove, to punish, to strengthen ; he defends himself against his enemies, settles questions in doubt, speaks of his experiences and intentions, adds greetings and messages of greeting ; all this, too, mostly without any careful arrangement, unconstrainedly passing from one thing to the other, often indeed jumping. The longer letters, too, show clearly the often abrupt change of mood while he was dictating.[1]

Some of Paul's letters have certainly been lost. The Corinthians, for example, allowed Pauline letters, for which we would gladly give in exchange to-day the whole of the polemical literature of our theological journalists, to be destroyed,[2] and that must have been

---

[1] On this point see Erich Stange, *Diktierpausen in den Paulusbriefen*, Zeitschrift für N.T. Wissenschaft, 18 (1917), p. 109 ff., and (reference from W. Michaelis) E. Iliff Robson, *Composition and Dictation in N.T. Books*. The Journal of Theological Studies, vol. 18, July, 1917, p. 288 f.

[2] In 1 Cor. v. 9 ff. and 2 Cor. ii. 3 f., vii. 8 f., letters of Paul are named, whose contents can in part be reconstructed. A letter from the Corinthians to Paul has also been lost (1 Cor. vii. 1).

the fate of others of Paul's letters also, even in ancient times.

Be that as it may, after the Apostle's death, as people began to gather together scattered leaves from his hand and to copy them, it was possible still to rescue more than a dozen fairly comprehensive letters of Paul. And gradually, although from the first unliterary, this collection began to attain literary standing, they even became a part of the canonical *Corpus* of the Holy Scriptures of Christendom. And thus it is that the letters of Paul have come into our possession with the venerable halo of canonical dignity. It is as if ancient precious stones were given to us in a costly setting; the setting is so rich that our attention is diverted from the stones themselves. But take away the setting, and the diamonds will only shine the more clearly in their own true brilliance.

To regard Paul's letters as unliterary takes nothing essential from them, rather it restores to them their original fire. And whoever has seen the sacred flame glowing in these jewels has noticed that they are genuine precious stones. Covered with dust and disfigured with doctrinaire additions, several letters of Paul appeared unpauline; and many an investigator, led to questioning because of the immense contrasts in their spiritual values, has rejected a part of the letters as not genuine.

If the non-literary character of Paul's letters is fully considered and they are continually compared with the undoubtedly genuine confidential letters of other great men (some of them just as rich in contrasts) all foundation for most of the objections to the genuineness of individual Pauline letters will be removed.

Here and there the delusion is still current that a Biblical scholar's scientific reliability is to be assessed according to the number of his critical verdicts of 'not genuine.' It is as if the fame of Bentley had made many adopt false standards, and the extant letters of Paul have innocently had to suffer over again in the nineteenth century a good part of the martyrdom of the historic Paul :—

> Thrice was I beaten with rods, once was I stoned, thrice have I suffered shipwreck.[1]

The common notes of interrogation made in the study, while perhaps applicable to literary epistles, are almost always unilluminating in the case of unliterary letters ; I have especially in mind the second letter to the Thessalonians and the so-called letter to the Ephesians. Difficulties remain only with regard to the epistles to Timothy and Titus, and perhaps even here they are not so great as some specialists think. In these letters what seems conventionalised, stiff and unletter-like, is perhaps in part an inheritance taken over by Paul from the communal experience of Hellenistic Judaism and only slightly adapted to his purpose, in part post-Pauline addition. As these letters, however, give but little characteristic material for our task of displaying the character of the Apostle Paul in the light of social and religious history, it is not necessary in discussing sources to enter upon the problem of their genuineness —a question upon which I have as yet reached no final conclusion.[2]

Other difficulties, such for example as are presented by the letters of the imprisonment, may perhaps be made easier by a revision of old ways of putting

---

[1] 2 Cor. xi. 23 ff.

[2] In the following pages I shall only quote them in cases where they confirm impressions already made by the certainly genuine letters, or in illustration of typical facts of Paul's world. For the study of the Pastoral Epistles the original work of P. N. Harrison is of extraordinary value : *The Problem of the Pastoral Epistles*, London, 1921.

questions. It is, to mention only one case, by no means impossible to place the letters of the imprisonment altogether or in part in an imprisonment at Ephesus, or in several periods of imprisonment in Asia.[1]

[1] This hypothesis, put forward by me in 1897 (cf. *Licht vom Osten*, 4th Ed., p. 201) has since then been carried further by a great number of specialists and is gradually gaining assent. Cf. M. Albertz, *Ueber die Abfassung des Philipperbriefes des Paulus zu Ephesus*, Theol. Studien u. Kritiken, 1910, p. 551 ff.; Benjamin W. Robinson, *An Ephesian Imprisonment of Paul*, Journal of Biblical Theology, vol. 29, part ii. (1910), p. 181 ff.; Friedrich Westberg, *Zur Neutestamentlichen Chronologie und Golgathas Ortlage*, Leipzig, 1911, p. 84 ff.; Kirsopp Lake, *The Critical Problems of the Epistle to the Philippians*, Expositor, June, 1914, p. 481 ff.; Ernest W. Burch, *Was Paul in Prison in Ephesus?* Bibliotheca Sacra, July, 1914; Ludwig Albrecht, *Die Briefe des N.T. und die Offenbarung des Johannes*, Bremen, 1914, p. 158 f.; Benjamin W. Bacon, *Again the Ephesian Imprisonment of Paul*, Expositor, March, 1915, p. 235 ff.; E. W. Winstanley, *Pauline Letters from an Ephesian Prison*, Expositor, June, 1915, p. 481 ff.; M. Jones, *The Epistles of the Captivity: where were they written?* Expositor, Oct., 1915, p. 289 ff.; Paul Feine, *Die Abfassung des Philipperbriefes in Ephesus*, Beiträge zur Förderung christlicher Theologie XX., Gütersloh, 1916. Cf. also his *Einleitung in das Neue Testament*, 2nd Ed., Leipzig, 1918, p. 142 ff., 3rd Ed., 1923, p. 148 ff.; C. R. Bowen, *Are Paul's Prison Letters from Ephesus?* American Journal of Theology, 1920, p. 112 ff., 277 ff.; J. J. Woldendorp, Nieuwe Theol. Studien 3 (1920), p. 147 ff.; Heinrich Appel, *Einleitung in das Neue Testament*, Leipzig, 1922, p. 48 ff.; P. L. Couchoud, *Revue de l'Histoire des religious*, 1923, p. 8 ff.; W. Tom, *Heeft Paulus te Efeze gevangen gezeten?* in Geref. Th. Tijdschrift, Bd. 24, 1923-1924, pp. 451-460, 500-513; F. Hielscher dates the epistles to the Philippians, Colossians and Philemon from an Ephesian imprisonment in *Forschungen zur Geschichte des Ap. Paulus*, Cottbus, 1925, p. 92. The finely balanced Excursus at the end of the new *Philipperkommentar* by Martin Dibelius (Lietzmanns Handbuch, 11, 2nd Ed., Tübingen, 1925) is also important, p. 75 f., cf. also p. 55; In Otto Schmitz 'Neutest. Forschungen' there recently appeared: Wilhelm Michaelis, *Die Gefangenschaft des Paulus in Ephesus und das Itinerar des Timotheus. Untersuchung zur Chronologie des Paulus und der Paulusbriefe*, Gütersloh, 1925. I have not yet been able to look into some of the studies that have appeared since 1914. I have also

The chief evidence for the essential genuineness of
the letters of Paul that have come down to us is the
circumstance, impossible to invention, that each letter
portrays him as the same character, each time in a new
light and giving a new impression, or even with great
changes of impression in the same letter. It is no
unalterable cold marble statue of 'Paulinism' that we
see each time; rather it is ever the living man, Paul,
whose very speech and gesture we hear and see, here
smiling gentle as a father and tenderly coaxing to win
the hearts of his foolish children—then, thundering
and lightening in passionate anger, like Luther, with
biting irony and sharp sarcasm on his lips. Another
time his eye shines with experience of the seer and his
mouth overflows as he witnesses to the grace he has
known, or his thought loses itself in the tortuous maze
of a religious problem, and his soul trembles under a
load of trouble, or he draws from the harp of David a
gracious psalm of thanksgiving. It is ever the same
Paul in ever new attitude, and where apparent contradictions can be noticed, even there it is the same man,
Paul, with all the polar contrasts of his nature, to which
the words might be applied :

> . . . no book excogitate am I
> But man, made up of contrariety.

He who would most easily learn to know the intimate character of Paul's letters must not begin with

dealt with one particular point : *Zur ephesinischen Gefangenschaft des
Apostels Paulus*, in *Anatolian Studies*, presented to Sir William
Mitchell Ramsay, edited by W. H. Buckler and W. M. Calder, Manchester, 1923, p. 121-127. Further, cf. also Otto Stählin, *Die altchristl.
griech. Litteratur* (S.-A. aus *Handbuch der Klass. Altertumswissenschaft*, 6th Ed.), München, 1924, p. 1144, and the extraordinarily acute
Pauline Readjustments by T. W. Llynfi Davies, Expositor, June, 1924,
p. 446 ff., especially p. 449 f. and 456. Davies puts Ephesians,
Colossians and Philemon (not Philippians) after Ephesus.

the Epistle to the Romans, which now stands at the head of the *Corpus Paulinum*. Romans, which, because of the circumstances of its composition, is the least letter-like and the most epistolary letter of the Apostle,[1] has, owing to its prominent place in the canon, and through the enormous influence—even literary influence—which it has thereby exerted, tended greatly to strengthen the tendency to regard Paul's letters in general as literary epistles. But it is not fitted to be the starting-point for the formation of our conclusions.

It is better to begin with the Epistle to Philemon. This is the shortest, as it is also the most letter-like of Paul's letters, written upon a single sheet of papyrus, just like numbers of Greek letters of the same date now known to us from Egypt.[2] In it there is nothing of the doctrinaire and literary. If one regards this precious leaf as a tract on the attitude of Christianity to slavery, he misses his way not only in historical criticism but also in human taste. It is turning people into ideas and making a book out of a confidential letter : Paul is depersonalised into Christianity and the slave Onesimus has become 'slavery.' Besides, everything is really so perfectly simple. The slave, Onesimus, had run away from his master, Philemon, who lived

[1] See below p. 23.

[2] A good parallel as regards form is for example the letter of the soldier Athenodoros to his 'Sister' Selbeina (Egypt, beginning of third century A.D.), in the collection of papyri of the Neutestament. Seminar at Berlin, published in *Griechische Texte aus Aegypten*, edited by Paul M. Meyer, I. *Papyri des Neutestamentlichen Seminars der Universität Berlin*, II. *Ostraka der Sammlung Deissmann*, Berlin, 1916, No. 20 (p. 82 ff.) with facsimile. The letter is almost to a line the same length as Philemon and gives a clear picture of what one of the smaller Pauline epistles must have looked like outwardly. Compare the facsimile in above-mentioned work.

at Colosse in the interior of Asia Minor. In the
great port of Ephesus, which could be reached in a few
days journey[1] he no doubt hoped to be able to hide,
but was there probably arrested,[2] and in prison learnt
to know Paul who was, so I think, at that time also
imprisoned in Ephesus. Paul converted this man to
the Gospel and sent the runaway back to his master
(possibly having undertaken to the prison authorities
to pay his ransom).[3] The little letter, which he gave
him to take with him, pleaded for forgiveness and
friendly reception for the 'unprofitable.'[4] This letter
is an instantaneous picture of the primitive Christian
cure of souls ; the whole charm of a characteristic
personality is poured out over these few Pauline lines :
Christian feeling is combined with Greek refinement and
the tact of a man of the world. Though a prisoner, Paul
writes with perfect quietness,[5] a happy cheerfulness

[1] To-day one can reach Ephesus from Colosse in one day, travelling
on horseback, or in case of need by rail ; in 1909 I myself made
the journey from Ephesus to Laodicea, which lies close to Colosse,
and back in two days (March 13th and 15th).

[2] Runaway slaves were not infrequently followed with a warrant
for arrest, and the authorities were obliged to try to imprison them.
We still possess in Paris Papyrus No. 10 an original warrant for the
arrest of two runaway slaves out of the time of the Ptolemies (*Notices et
extraits*, 18, 2, p. 177 ff.). A large reward is offered for the capture of
the runaways, and the authorities are to give information as soon as
they hear where they are hiding.

[3] Cf. in *Licht vom Osten*, 4th Ed., p. 281 f., the explanation quoted
from O. Eger.

[4] So Paul says in Philemon 11 playing upon the name Onesimus
(= profitable).

[5] For the contrast read the woeful whining captive letter of the
imprisoned Egyptian of the time of Ptolemy, a particularly valuable
parallel to Paul's imprisonment letters (in the Flinders Petrie Papyri
III, No. 35a and b and 36a). Contact with the outer world was undoubtedly easier for the prisoner in those days than it is in our day.
Compare the smuggled letters offering bribes mentioned in Chapter
II., also Matt. xi. 2 and xxv. 36, and the prisons of Anatolia to-day : a

beams from his eye, he opens the treasures of his
confidence, he appeals to brotherly feeling and to the
love of the Saviour and knows that these powers are
irresistible. Here there is no trace of triviality in
dealing with a matter in itself trivial, no word is wasted,
a strong, and yet elastic soul reveals itself to a confidential friend.

The little letter which has come to us as the sixteenth chapter of Romans, was written in a similar
frame of mind. This leaf is most probably originally
not an organic part of Romans, but a separate letter of
the Apostle to a Christian congregation in Ephesus,
recommending to them Phœbe, a Christian woman of
Cenchreae. Here also Paul speaks confidentially in a
truly letter-like way. Like many a papyrus letter of
that time and numerous letters of the South and East
even to-day, this contains almost nothing but separate
greetings, but each greeting has its own personal tone,
and the whole is full of allusions to common work and
common suffering. Paul, the great martyr and the
great worker looks out upon us from this single leaf of
a letter, the Paul who knew men and was the living
centre of his own circle. Then in one place there
breaks through glowing indignation against those who
corrupt the Gospel, and at the end his faithful friends
hear a full chord from the Harp of Paul, the Psalmist.

visit to the jail at Konia (Iconium) on March 6th, 1909, showed us
very plainly what a large amount of intercourse the prisoners had
through the grating in the door with their friends who had come to
see them. Thus it is understandable that we possess quite a number
of other letters written in imprisonment: especially interesting are
those that come from imprisonment in a temple, for example the
letter of the Egyptian Ptolemaios to Damoxenos (Serapeum 160 B.C.),
contained in the Paris Papyrus No. 51, and newly published by U.
Wilcken in *Archiv für Papyrusforschung*, 6, p. 204 ff. A collection of
prison letters from antiquity would be a charming piece of work.
The oldest is probably that published by A. Ungnad from the time
of Hammurapi (Cp. D.L.Z., 1915, Sp. 353).

First and Second Thessalonians are also genuinely letters. The first especially is full of moving allusions to personal experiences. On the whole written with a certain quietness, in spite of polemical expressions, they let us recognise what we may call the average type of Paul's letters.

The beginning of Galatians is entirely dictated in a spirit of holy indignation. It is understandable how this letter with its lightning and thunderbolts especially captivated our German Reformer. Paul here had to justify himself before the Christians of Galatia deep in the heart of Anatolia against wicked slanderers, who were trying to rob him of the confidence of these young believers by casting doubt upon his Apostolate and stigmatising his Christianity, free from legal bonds, as apostasy. But for all that Paul writes no dogmatic treatise, but a letter of fiery defence, in which he afterwards also strikes other notes. With the whole fervour of his heart he woos the Galatians back to their old love. The character of the Apostle in its most diverse sides is clearly stamped upon it.

First Corinthians begins much more quietly than Galatians. Paul expresses himself about a number of abuses in the Corinthian Church, and thus the letter gives us a deep insight into the wisdom of its author in the cure of souls. Here also there is no lack of sharp polemic, corroding irony and prophetic indignation, but in general Paul is more restrained. He spares the church, where he can, and he appreciates its high and noble witness. In the midst of the desolating confusion of the Corinthian parties, the strife about the denarius, the quarrel between the enlightened and the weak Christians of the Hellenic-Roman capital, the noise of ecstatic fanaticism, he brings in a sublime figure, so mighty, so noble and chaste that it would have been worthy a Phidias, Agape, Love, which reveals the deepest mystery of the nature of God and of His Son, and binds the sons of God together in a great brotherhood. And after that Paul makes his confession of faith in the living Christ, which deeply moves us by its fervour, and witnesses to his hope of immortality. Then changing the great for the small he begins chatting about his plans and his cares.

Perhaps the most personal of the 'greater' Pauline epistles is Second Corinthians. It is as a whole also the least well known to us, just because it is so entirely letter-like, so entirely a personal confession, full of allusions which we cannot now fully understand. Paul begins in deep emotion ; for God has once again graciously saved him out of a terrible risk of death. Therefore the beginning of this letter is filled with inexpressible thankfulness ; but this tone is varied by others, especially by a sharp polemic against legal-minded Christians, who also in Corinth had scattered their seed of slander. Again, as in Galatians, Paul lays bare his inner and outer life for his Christian brethren to see, and especially Chapters XI. and XII. are documents of irreplaceable value for the Apostle's history.

The least personal of the longer letters of Paul is Romans. But even it is, if the intention of the author is the deciding factor, a real letter, not a literary epistle. No doubt there are lines in it which could also be in an epistle, and it might be called an epistolary letter. But in spite of that it is a letter and no book. The idea that it is a compendium of Paulinism, in which the Apostle set down his dogmatic theology and ethics, that characteristic idea beloved of many a Pauline scholar of earlier day, at the very least implies great misunderstanding. Undoubtedly Paul wanted to teach the Roman Christians and he did it in part through the means of contemporary theology. But he does not contemplate the literary public of his day as his readers,

nor yet Christendom in general and later generations ;
he addresses himself rather to a little group of people
living in one of the more modest quarters of Rome, of
whose existence the general public was scarcely even
aware.   It is unlikely that copies of the letter were sent
to the assemblies of Christians in Ephesus, Antioch and
Jerusalem : he only sent this message to Rome.   That
this letter is less animated by personal expressions than
the other Pauline epistles, is explained by the circumstances of its writing : Paul was writing to a church
not yet personally known to him.   The small space
given to personal details does not suggest that Romans
has an epistolary-literary character, but is the natural
consequence of the letter-like unliterary situation in
which it was written.

The situation was similar at the time of writing the
letter directed to Colosse and Loadicea, in the valley of
the Lycus, the so-called ' Epistle to the Ephesians ' sent
at the same time as the letter to Philemon.   These
churches also Paul did not yet know through personal
acquaintance, therefore here also the personal element
is less prominent than the objective.   The peculiar
solemnity of the language is striking—a solemnity of
tone suggesting both liturgical worship [1] and meditation,
which moreover is not unknown in certain parts of
other letters of Paul.   As regards the contents, the
great development of Christ-mysticism, elsewhere only
referred to because already well known, is unmistakable.   A great part of the critical difficulties, found in
the contents of this epistle, disappears when Paul
becomes known to us also from the undoubtedly
' genuine ' letters as the great Christ-mystic.[2]

---

[1] Cf. below, p. 106 f.

[2] The old theses, so greatly used in discussions about genuineness,
that the teaching of the Apostle was contained in the four chief
epistles (the very phrase is itself a *petitio principii*) was an act of

Philippians,[1] on the other hand, is thoroughly letter-like and most strongly personal.   It was directed to a church especially closely connected with the Apostle, which had just given the prisoner a great proof of its love.   Paul thanks them for that, and peculiarly moving and most genuinely personal notes quiver through its lines, and allow us to recognise the personality of the writer, so rich in contrasts, in all the freshness of its nature.

Thus every letter of Paul is a picture of Paul, and therein lies the unique value of the letters as sources for a historical account of their author.   There can be but few Christians of later days, for whose inner lives we have such thoroughly undesigned sources of information.   Even the confessions of Augustine with their literary appeal to the public, cannot stand comparison with Paul's letters.[2]   And there were probably exceedingly few people of the Imperial age of Rome whom we can study so exactly as we can Paul through his letters.

It is quite obvious that a man who, as a contemporary and occasional companion of Paul, describes the Apostle from outside, could not reach the truth that Paul reaches as unconsciously in his letters he draws a picture of himself.   How colourless is the picture of Bismarck by Moritz Busch over against Bismarck's own picture in the contemporary letters to his wife !   But on that account the presentation of

violence.   Unconsciously the way of settling many a question about social and political matters has been derived from this : and now what is it good for ?

[1] My investigations in *Anatolian Studies* (see above, p. 18) refer to this epistle.

[2] The older I grow the more the fact that this wonderful book was written for publication disturbs me.

Paul by Luke in Acts is an indispensable supplement
to the letters of Paul. In some details it is to be
corrected by the letters of Paul, but in many others,
surely it rests on good tradition.[1] In opposition to the
thesis that Luke put aside the testimony of Paul's
epistles in favour of a movement for union, which
sought to mediate between the conflicting parties, of
the Apostolic Age, I assert with confidence that Luke
simply did not know our Pauline epistles. When Luke
wrote they had not yet been collected and published.
What Luke knew of Paul, he gained from other
sources. Some things no doubt he had heard Paul
tell of himself, as, for example, the striking story of his
flight from Damascus in a basket,[2] which the Apostle
perhaps often laughingly related with variations in
detail. Other material, and that certainly his best,
came from his own observation, which he recounts, in
his 'we' portions, just in the style of the antique
description of a sea voyage.[3] And it is a great service
that he has pictured for us Paul as above all the man
of action, Paul the wanderer, who passing through the
ancient Mediterranean world, preached to that world
the living Christ.

We must now seek to gain a picture of this Mediterranean world, which is the world of Paul, for out of
it he sprang and for it he spent his life.

[1] Adolf Harnack's *Studies of Luke* are a sound reaction against the
methods of the torturing Inquisition. The same applies to the works
of Eduard Meyer.

[2] Acts ix. 24 f. That Luke did not get this story from 2 Cor. xi.
32 f. is pretty certain, for with his predeliction for potentates he
would never have forgotten to mention the Ethnarch of King
Aretas.

[3] Cf. e.g. the 'we' account of an Egyptian Admiral (*c.* 246 B.C.)
of his sea voyage to Syria (in the Flinders Petrii Papyri) published by
L. Mitteis and U. Wilcken in *Grundzüge und Chrestomathie der
Papyruskunde*, I. 2, Leipzig, 1912, p. 1 ff.

THE WORLD OF PAUL

CHAPTER II

THE WORLD OF PAUL

Sailing on the Russian pilgrim steamer southwards along the west coast of Asia Minor, past the silent shore of Ephesus and the bare rocks of Samos, through the Archipelago of the Sporades, after twenty-four hours one reaches Rhodes. And if we then take an easterly course we can, after barely thirty-six hours' journey along the south coast of Asia Minor, come to anchor in the roads of the Cicilian port Mersina.[1]

A noble landscape, never to be forgotten, stretches out before us, while from the port the barges are rowed out to unload the ship. The light of the Anatolian morning sun quivers upon the waves and gleams on the

[1] We made this journey, March 16th-19th, 1909, on the Russian pilgrim steamer 'Korniloff' of Odessa bound for Palestine, stayed in Mersina and visited, as well as Soli-Pompeiopolis, Tarsus twice (on March 20th and 21st). The following observations were in the main made then; but a few date from our Anatolian journey in 1906. On pilgrim ships where one may often be the only 'educated man' amongst hundreds of Serb and Russian peasants, Oriental Jewish working people, Armenians, Turks, and Arabs, one learns ten times as much about the condition of the people of the East at the present day (and in ancient times) as on the great Levantine steamers, which even on the waves of the Mediterranean do not let us out of our cage of European civilisation. Only, the obscurities of the learned university man must be put aside in order to come in contact with those people. Caspar René Gregory has some good remarks about small ships, *Zu Fuss in Bibellanden* (*Das Land der Bibel*, II., 6), Leipzig, 1919, p. 8 f. I have left the opening sentences above and the note essentially unaltered, although the route Odessa—Palestine is probably not yet in order again.

oars of the gaily clad Turkish boatmen as they rise out of the water. The brilliant white of the distant houses of Mersina greets us, and we see the domes and minarets of the places of worship, while the flags of the European consulates and of the Turkish authorities flap in the breeze. At the eastern end of the city white steam-clouds arise, and the puff of the locomotive comes over the waves to us. Mersina is the starting-point of the railway track which crosses the broad and fruitful Cilician plain to Adana.

And this Cilician plain [1] stretches out, then, behind the city, green and luxuriant into the distance, here and there interspersed with soft rolling hills crowned with ruins, till at last it is called to a halt by the great foot-hills of the Cilician Taurus, which rise up defiantly to heaven, and cut up the horizon into fantastic shapes. The contours of this immense mountain range are so wildly thrown about, that it is not easy to follow them, and, while the eye rests on the sunny snow of the glaciers, we dream albeit vaguely of primeval catastrophies and the age-long work of the elements, which produced this landscape, long before the hand of man ploughed the land or plied the loom, and before the knee of man bowed before the powers of the world above.

Far away in the East the ridge of the Syrian Amanus mountains, coming from the South, meets the Taurus, and it is a singularly moving experience to see from the ship in the evening after sundown the Amanus range and the snow-crowned peaks of the Taurus in wondrous Alpine glow looking out across the plain and the sea, while an Arab singer sings a passionate farewell to a company of young people embarking.

[1] Cf. especially Franz X. Schaffer, *Cilicia ; (Ergänzungsheft*, No. 141, *zu Petermanns Mitteilungen*), Gotha, 1903, p. 20 ff.

Entering the Cilician plain in March and coming from the interior of Asia Minor or from the west coast one seems to have skipped several weeks ; spring is so far advanced. The fig-trees, which in Ephesus and the Meander valley are thrusting forth their first bright green shoots, have here already large leaves that shine delightfully in the sun ; the asphodel, which still blooms luxuriantly in April on the Plains of Troy and over the ruined heaps of Ephesus, is already withering in the fields of Soli-Pompeiopolis, a ruined city lying by the sea close to Mersina, and the anemones, which delighted us in their first glory of colour in the Meander valley and at Ephesus, have already bloomed in January on the Cilician plain. Even the poplar of Asia Minor, which with its slender silvery stem enters into sisterly rivalry with the minarets that form the characteristic emblem of Anatolia in city and village, is here further advanced, far further than in Konia or Angora ; and by the grey old pillars of Pompeiopolis the luxuriant blossom of the Judas-tree blazes a deep red. Snow scarcely ever falls on that plain. All through the winter the garden supplies the household with its green produce.

Later on the cornfields and cotton plantations yield heavy harvests in rich luxuriance, but then inexpressible sultriness weighs down upon the fields and fever rages up and down the country. As in March, 1909, after some time spent in wandering along the routes of Paul's missions in the interior of Asia Minor and on the west coast, we travelled on the Adana railway through the glorious wheat-growing district of the plain, towards Paul's city, Tarsus, we never dreamt that millions of grains from these ears of corn would not reach the threshing floor : but a few weeks later a fever, more terrible than the worst malaria, broke out on the sultry Cilician plain, and decimated the population as far as

Antioch in Syria—the religious and national fanaticism
of companies of Mohammedans goaded on to murder,
to whose fury thousands of Armenian Christians fell
victims.[1]   And while the surging waves of the streams,
Cydnus and Sarus, swollen by the spring carried away
the bodies of the murdered by hundreds to the sea and
the Cilician earth daily drank anew the blood of martyrs,
there out in the fields the corn perished on its stalks or
was trodden down and burnt in the blind fury of the
persecutors.

To us that journey presented more peaceful pictures,
and it did not enter into our minds that the sultry
brooding heat of that plain has for century upon
century gathered up passions into the soul of the
people, which when the spark came would blaze forth
in fire and burning, in threatening and slaughter.[2]

Our thoughts on that occasion on that broad Cilician
plain were singularly moved by an indescribably wonderful spectacle, a piece of Paul's world, more genuine
certainly than was the first building we entered shortly
afterwards in his own city—the railway-station with
its bilingual (Turkish-European) sign 'Tarsus.'   High
in the air were immense squadrons of storks, coming
from over the sea.   They were the storks of Asia
Minor and Europe on their way northward from Africa
in the south.   They had come down the valley of the
Nile and up the valley of the Jordan over Syrian
Antioch;[3]   then they had probably flown across the

[1] Cf. the letters of Mrs. Helen Davenport Gibbons, *The Red Rugs
of Tarsus, A Woman's Record of the Armenian Massacres of 1909*, New
York, 1917.   Mrs. Gibbons, with her husband, Dr. Herbert Adams
Gibbons, stayed in St. Paul's Institute in Tarsus while I was visiting
the city.

[2] Acts. ix. 1, ὁ δὲ Σαῦλος, ἔτι ἐμπνέων ἀπειλῆς καὶ φόνου.

[3] March 20th, 1909.   On one of the next days (March 25th) we
observed near Antioch a great synod of storks engaged in eating, and
on the Pass of Bailân a part of the course of flight of this squadron.

bay of Alexandretta and were now equipping themselves for the flight over the Taurus, some detachments getting provisions in the broad wet fields, others beautifully manœuvring in the air, while other legions were already making a steady and quiet course for the passes of the Taurus.

Who pointed out the road for these birds? It is the road of the great kings of the East, the road of Alexander and Cæsar, the road of the Crusaders and of the Mohammedan army. Did the man-made road follow the immemorial track of the birds? Did we not hear in the rustle of their wings over the lonely Cilician plain the eternal rhythm of travel? And did we not find there, where the pavement of an old Roman road goes through a wheat field by Antioch alongside the modern road, the way taken by a Cilician traveller, who of old time had travelled from Syria in the south northward over the Taurus and over land and sea from Asia Minor in the east to Europe and the west?

The impression, that the Cilician plain has from the most ancient times been a centre of international intercourse, comes to one even more clearly in Paul's city, Tarsus. Indeed there is but little of the ancient Tarsus remaining above ground, but when the natives dig for ancient hewn stones anywhere about the old city walls, near Paul's gate, they discover pieces of terra-cotta and coins of Paul's time. And above all, the geographical situation for international intercourse remains genuinely the same as in the age of the great change of religion. Just as even to-day on the Cilician plain the two civilisations of Islam, the Turkish and the Arabian, meet, so also in ancient times that country was the threshold of two civilisations and the bridge between two worlds.

From the highest point of the modern city, perhaps from the castle-hill of ancient Tarsus, you look out over

the great plain on all sides and, turning towards the
south, where at times you catch a gleam of the sea, you
have to your left, behind the blue heights of Amanas
and the last outlying portions of the other Syrian ridges
hidden in the glimmering haze, the world of Semitism.
Behind and to your right stretches the endless chain of
the Taurus, more majestic than ever when seen from
Tarsus, with the pass, famed in history, the Cilician
Gates, and behind that lies the world of Hellenistic-
Roman civilisation. Anything coming from Syria and
from the Jordan and making for Ephesus and for
Corinth must pass through those gates, unless it is
borne along the western shore over the waves of the
Mediterranean. Through these gates went the sword-
blades of Damascus and the balsam of Jericho, through
these gates the Logos travelled—He who became man
in Galilee, and again became Spirit for the whole world.

Two young Anatolians who had been educated in
the excellent St. Paul's Institute, the American College
in Tarsus, were our guides through their native city.
As we sat there with them dining in a small inn, one
of them wishing to say something pleasant, praised our
German philosophy and said to me, full of pride in his
own learning, 'You have Kant.' I replied to him, in
no conventional phrase, but completely filled with the
thought of that figure, which had become a living
presence to me on the lonely Cilician plain beneath the
squadrons of migrating birds and on the castle-hill of
Tarsus facing the Cilician Gates : 'You have Paul.'

And truly it is so : that Tarsus has its Paul, and
that Paul came from Tarsus is no chance happening.
The world Apostle came out of a classical centre of
international intercourse, and his home itself was for
him as a child a microcosmos, in which the forces of
the great ancient cosmos of the Mediterranean world
were all represented.

The Mediterranean world the world of Paul! The Apostle himself once gave its boundaries through Jerusalem in the east, through Illyricum, Rome and Spain in the west,[1] while in the north lived the Sythian[2] and Barbarian[3] and to the south the marvellous mountain of Sinai in Arabia raised its head.[4] He who wishes to understand this world of Paul,[5] must not begin with the preconceived idea that it falls apart into two halves, on this side Semitic, on that Græco-Roman. The fact of a relatively high degree of unity, at least in the civilisation of the coast lands of this world, ought rather to be taken as our starting-point.

Paul indeed was acquainted also with a good part of the interior of Asia Minor, and in 2 Corinthians[6] the list of tribulations on journeys through 'perils in the wilderness' and 'in cold' reflects probably mainly what he had experienced in the interior of Asia Minor.[7] In

---

[1] Rom. xv. 19-24.   [2] Col. iii. 11.

[3] Col. iii. 11; 1 Cor. xiv. 11; Rom. i. 14.

[4] Gal. iv. 25.

[5] For geography in the widest sense we are indebted for the best to the great works on the Mediterranean Sea by Theobald Fischer and Alfred Philippson. For the ancient topography of Paul's world to the works of Sir William M. Ramsay. Excellently adapted for an introduction to the subject is the masterly sketch by Theobald Fischer in K. Baedeker's *Das Mittelmeer*, Leipzig, 1909, pp. xxiii.-xxxii. Valuable for our special study is Alphons Steinmann's *Die Welt des Paulus im Zeichen des Verkehrs*, Braunsberg, 1915.

[6] 2 Cor. xi. 26 f.

[7] The change of weather is there in the different elevations often sudden. On a March day in 1909 we had towards evening, at the summit of a Phrygian mountain pass, a violent snowstorm, and next day at noon we were passing a garden of peach trees full of pink blossom. Paul's journeys ought not to be studied without recognising the different elevations of the places he passed through. That Tarsus, Ephesus and Corinth have no elevation worth mentioning and that Syrian Antioch is only 262 feet above sea-level, Jerusalem, on the other hand, is 2587 feet, Damascus 2266 feet, Pisidian Antioch 3936 feet, Iconium 3368 feet, Lystra about 4034 feet : these facts are of importance for the understanding of Paul's world.

the same way 'perils of robbers'[1] probably refers to
the interior of Anatolia.[2]

In coming to a correct judgment about the districts
in which Primitive Christianity made its way the contrast between the interior of Asia Minor and the coastal
regions of the Pauline world[3] must be borne in mind.
The plateau of the interior has a very low rainfall and
the cold winter of the Steppes ; the west has a heavy
winter rainfall and a genuine Mediterranean climate with
Mediterranean vegetation. The inner 'isolated plateau
has almost the character of the interior of Asia,' the west
of Asia Minor (with the neighbouring coast lands), on the
other hand, is ' an Ægean country with contours as varied
as Greece and closely connected with the sea both by
nature and history.' But for all that an 'easy and
extensive intercourse' between the two regions was
possible. To see Angora after Ephesus, or Konia after
Tarsus is to have the contrast between the two regions,
and also their close contact, indelibly clear to the eye.

Now though the lines of Paul's journey routes lead
through hundreds of miles of 'the upper country'[4] over
the mountains of the interior of Asia Minor, yet more

---

[1] 2 Cor. xi. 26.

[2] Even down to our own times it must be admitted that the
formerly flourishing coast lands of Western Asia Minor offered many
a lurking-place for robber-bands, and were in some places dangerous,
especially for native travellers. Cf. the descriptions by Alfred
Philippson in *Reisen und Forschungen in Kleinasien*, I. Heft (Petermann's Mitteilungen Ergänzungsheft, No. 167), Gotha, 1910, p. 6 ff.
The district about Miletus gave us a drastic commentary on 'perils of
rivers, perils of robbers' as on an April evening of 1906, having lost
our way, we rode through the swamps of the Meander after sun-down
and the day following at Didyma were in the house of a Greek who
had just been shot by robbers (see 2 Cor. xi. 26).

[3] I base my remarks here upon the concise characterisation of this
contrast which Alfred Philippson has given in *Reisen und Forschungen
im Westlichen Kleinasien*, I., p. 20.

[4] Acts xix. 1. τὰ ἀνωτερικὰ μέρη.

frequently they cling to the roads of the coastal region
or to the mariners' routes, even twice or thrice covering
for long distances the same track. In the main the
Apostle's world is to be sought where the sea breeze
blows. The coast world of Cilicia, Syria, Palestine,
Cyprus, Western Asia Minor, Macedonia, Achaia, and
beyond these that of the further west, that is Paul's
world.

The heart of this Pauline world is, however, undoubtedly the wonderful region which may be called
' Ægean ': The circle, Ephesus—Troas—Philippi—
Thessalonica—Corinth—Ephesus, saw the greatest
work of Paul. The New Testament reflects this fact
quite clearly in that all the Pauline letters which have
been rescued for the canon, were either destined for
this Ægean circle, or were written within its confines.

The world of Paul is a cosmos—in the truest sense
a world. Offering from its high towering lordly peaks
endless perspectives over the green luxuriant plains
and the sunlit sea, and here, as also in wild gorges and
rustling groves, arousing in the spectator a sense of the
divine awe, it enabled men to grow up in light and air
—men of wide open soul who were able to interpret
the voices of heaven and the riddles of hades. Thanks
to the deep indentation of the seaboard with its numberless safe inlets, and to its islands which serve as
piers of the bridge carrying the road from east to west,
it became the mother of navigation and international
intercourse, turned into travellers the best and boldest
of the men of its immemorial cities, the heroes, artists,
merchant princes, students, singers, and prophets, and
thereby enabled that civilisation to be created which we
all inherit to-day.

If anyone, who is no professional geographer, would

characterise this world of Paul with a single concrete
formula, he might call it the world of the olive-tree,
and with that phrase he would also be within what is
known to us of Paul's own observations. For in
Romans[1] he compares the Gentile world to a wild olive-
tree, though indeed with quite another application.

The world of Paul the world of the olive-tree!
The traveller of to-day, who fares southwards from the
Teutonic North, remains at first for some time in his
own world; the print on the ticket alters indeed a little,
the papers on sale at the stations are different; but
there is no passing into another civilisation. But then
there comes a moment when on a sudden North is
changed into South. That is the instant, when travelling towards Marseilles, the first olive-tree is seen in
the Rhone valley a little south of Valence and north of
Avignon. Many a northerner has failed to recognise
this olive tree, mistaking it for an old willow, deceived
by the similarity of the trunk and its silver grey foliage.
Others like to see in the orange-tree, laden with golden
fruit, the typical tree of the south and east. But that
does not apply in ancient times; the orange-tree is a
relatively later importation. The fig-tree also cannot
be taken as the characteristic tree of the south, for it
flourishes in the open in Heidelberg and Oxford, and
even in Norderney and Heligoland. Rather that first
olive-tree at Avignon with its gnarled trunk and its
solemn gloom is the South and is the Levant.

From the ancestors of this tree blessing distilled
upon the peoples. In the eye of history an enormous
amount of humanising civilisation stands crowned with
the olive branch. The tree of Homer, the tree of
Sophocles, the olive is the living symbol of the unity
of the Mediterranean world, it is the tree also of the

[1] Rom. xi. 17.

Bible, both of Old and New Testament. In the names *Mount of Olives* and *Gethsemane* (that is *oil-press*) as also in the title and name *Messiah, Christ* (*the Anointed*) the olive-tree has influenced the deepest thoughts and the most holy words of our sacred tradition. Without the provision of olives, moreover, Paul's journeys would be inconceivable ; the fruit of the olive-tree will have played the same rôle on his sea-voyages that it does to-day on the Levantine steamers and sailing vessels, especially for the sailors and deck-passengers. A handful of olives, a piece of bread, and a drink of water—the Levantine traveller requires no more than that !

The world of Paul the world of the olive-tree ! There is a map showing the distribution of the olive in the Mediterranean world.[1] When I first saw it, without noticing its title, it appeared to me to be a map of the Jewish or primitive Christian dispersion. As a matter of fact, the zone of the olive-tree and the region covered by the Jewish dispersion under Imperial Rome[2] are almost exactly coincident ; and we might perhaps call the Jewish Dispersion itself by the name by which one of the many synagogues of the imperial capital was called : *Synagogue of the Olive-Tree.*[3] Paul also compared the Jewish race to an olive-tree.[4] But the olive-tree zone almost exactly coincides also with the map of Paul's missionary journeys, if we leave out Tunis,

---

[1] In Theobald Fischer's work *Der Oelbaum. Seine geographische Verbreitung, seine wirtschaftliche und kultur-historische Bedeutung* (Petermann's Mitteilungen Erganzungsheft, No. 147), Gotha, 1904. In the map of Paul's world included in the first edition of *Paul* (1911) the zone of the olive-tree is marked in green, following Fischer. On this subject see also Sven Hedin's *Jerusalem*, Leipzig, 1918, p. 38.

[2] Cf. the ring of about 143 cities (marked blue in my map of 1911) encircling the Mediterranean where the Jewish dispersion was to be found in the imperial period.

[3] Συναγωγὴ Ἐλαίας, *Corpus Inscriptionum Græcarum*, No. 9904.

[4] Rom. xi. 17.

Algeria, and Morocco ; the almost entire lack of olive-trees in Egypt is remarkable, and there, too, we have no trace of Paul having travelled. Almost all the important place-names in the history of Paul are to be found in the zone of the olive-tree : Tarsus, Jerusalem, Damascus, Antioch, Cyprus, Ephesus, Philippi, Thessalonica, Athens, Corinth, Illyricum, Rome (Spain). This world of Paul is relatively uniform, in the first place, in its climatic and other outward conditions of civilisation. The contrasts in vegetation seen by us between Cilicia and Ephesus [1] or between Antioch and Corinth do not weigh very heavily against this. In all this great civilised world the means of livelihood, especially for those in humble circumstances, were probably everywhere much the same as regards food, clothing, housing, and work.

And politically the Imperium Romanum had stamped a uniform impression upon this and even upon the whole ancient world. Alexander and his successors had indeed done much in preparation. The centuries of international politics before Paul, that stretch from Philip and his great son to the Cæsars, are clearly reflected in many newly given Greek city-names, which re-echo through the Pauline tradition : *Antioch* in Syria and *Antioch* in Pisidia, *Seleucia* in Syria and *Attalia* in Pamphylia, *Laodicia* in Phrygia and *Alexandria* (*Troas*) in Mysia, *Philippi* and *Thessalonica* in Macedonia, *Nicopolis* in Epirus, *Ptolemaïs*, *Cæsarea* (*Stratonos*) and *Antipatris* in the Syrian and Palestinian coastal region—each of these names is a monument of that political history which had worked towards the unification of Paul's world.

The importance of this political unity of the world for the coming world-religion has long been recognised.

---

[1] See above, p. 31.

When you stand before the walls of the temple of Augustus in Angora (Ancyra), the capital of ancient Galatia, which Paul indeed probably touched at, you have before your eyes in a somewhat remote part of the Pauline world a classical witness of that political unity of the world—a witness which Paul himself may have seen—in the Latin and Greek text there preserved of the summary of the events of his reign composed by the Emperor Augustus himself.

Although this Monumentum Ancyranum is written in two languages, the conclusion does not follow that in Paul's world Latin was as much an international language as Greek. Greek was the language of intercourse, especially amongst the people of the great cities, to whom in his world he made his appeal, as the fact that his letter to the Christians at Rome was written in Greek most clearly indicates.[1] Greek had penetrated deeply into Syria and Palestine ; in particular the great cities, the special field of Paul's work, were strongly under Greek influence, both as to language and general culture. In Palestine, indeed, Aramaic was the living language of the people, and Paul spoke it.[2] For all that we must recognise that in New Testament times Greek was widely used by the common people in Galilee, Transjordania and Jerusalem. But at Antioch in Syria Hellenism became predominant, and the greatest difficulty which in other cases is presented to the missionary, that of mastering the language, and thereby the psyche of the heathen, scarcely existed for Paul in his world. As from childhood onwards he had been a Jew to the Jews, so also he was a Hellenist to the Hellenists,[3] because the tongue and soul of Hellenism had come to him with the air of Tarsus.

---

[1] The inscriptions of Roman Jews in the Catacombs, which in the great majority of cases are in Greek, point to the same fact.
[2] Acts xxi. 40.   [3] 1 Cor. ix. 20 f.

Finally the world of Paul is uniform also as regards a broad undercurrent of common popular religious beliefs and forms of expression. The naïve geocentric view of earth and heaven is common to all both in east and west. Everyone recognises a here below and there above, the divine must come down from heaven to earth and humanity must rise from earth to heaven. Throughout this whole world of Paul from east to west and from west to east there were current tales many centuries old of visible manifestations of divinity, of the deception and wickedness of demons, of a divine power become human, which overcomes the powers of darkness. And in this whole world of Paul we see a great journeying of Pilgrims, who desired to wash away their sins and to satisfy their need at the great holy places. The Jew of the Dispersion travelling from the west to Jerusalem meets the pilgrim of Ephesus and the sick man on his way to the shrine of Asclepius of Epidaurus possibly on the same ship, and each extols the miracles of his God with believing fervour.

Such is the world of Paul, washed by the same waves, blessed by the same sun, and viewed from within also no chaos of alien bodies brought together artificially by force, but an organism of great compactness.[1]

The reason why this compactness of the Mediterranean civilisation has so often been disregarded, is a doctrinaire attitude similar to that which we have frequently noted in connection with the study of Paul. The culture of the world of Paul has been far too much identified with its literary culture. And certainly, the comparison of the Græco-Roman literature of the first century of Imperial Rome with the earliest written

---

[1] On the unity of civilisation in the East cf. the important observations of E. Littmann, D.L.Z., 1910, col. 164.

records of Jewish-Rabbinic wisdom of Paul's day
shows a striking contrast, a contrast which extends
not only to literary method but to mental and spiritual
attitude. This may be made clear by means of a
parallel. Compare to-day—perhaps the analogy is not
too daring—the lecture of an Islamic teacher in a Mosque
at Damascus, with the teaching note-book of a modern
Italian historian. These are two worlds which are
utterly separated from one another. But if instead we
compare an artisan or street hawker of Damascus with
a man of the same calling in Naples, then it is men of
very similar mental structure that stand before us.

Students of antiquity have for long taken their idea
of the ancient world from ancient literature. But
literature is only a part of the ancient world, and itself
only preserved in fragments, reflects only fragments of
the culture, for the most part, of the upper classes.

Thus then the picture of Paul's world was drawn
almost exclusively with the aid of literary sources,
and became a gloomy background, the better fitted for
displaying the brilliant light of Christianity. The
Gospel had entered a world decadent, morally corrupt
and religiously bankrupt. So many have learnt and
taught, unconsciously also influenced by the polemical
superlatives of the Fathers of the Church, because in
the literature of the period they have only heard the
loud voices which speak of denial, dispair, mockery and
unbridled lust. Because other voices are silent it has
no doubt been supposed that they never have spoken.
And Paul himself seemed particularly liberal with
the gloomy colours in painting a picture of his world,
when in Romans and elsewhere [1] he portrayed the
depravity of his surroundings with the intensity of a
preacher of repentance.

[1] Rom. i. 24 ff. Cp. elsewhere, especially the frequent lists of vices
in his letters.

But the simple truth was forgotten that neither a single phenomenon nor a complex civilisation can be described by a single formula. The world of Paul has its deep shadows, that is quite obvious; but it also has its bright light, that ought to be just as obvious. In the same letter to the Romans which draws that picture of the sensual life of the great city, there stands that tremendous word about the law, which is written in the heart and is active in the conscience of the Gentiles who are without the law.[1]

And now, especially through the great archæological discoveries of the nineteenth century, we have found again parts of the world of Paul which make it possible for us to set the light alongside the shadow. Not only have huge ruins of the great cities of Paul's world been brought to light again through the excavations in Asia Minor and Greece—especially impressive are the uncovering of Ephesus by British and Austrian investigators and the recovery of the cities Pergamon and Miletus, as well as of the great religious centre Didyma, by German research—but in those unliterary texts written on stone, papyrus and potsherd,[2] which now lie in thousands in our museums, the voices of the unliterary people of Paul's world, though apparently silent for ever, have again become audible. In letters, wills, certificates of marriage or divorce, accounts, and receipts, records of judicial proceedings, dedications, epitaphs and confessions of sins, these people stand before us laughing and scolding, loving and mean, malicious and kindly.

The chief value of these new discoveries, it seems to me, lies in this, that besides giving highly important material for the study of language, law and the social

---

[1] Rom. ii. 14 f., . . . τὸ ἔργον τοῦ νόμου γραπτὸν ἐν ταῖς καρδίαις αὐτῶν.

[2] Cf. above, p. 7, note 2.

history, they show us living people much as they naturally were, because entirely free from literary pose and altogether in the workaday clothes of their calling. That the fragments most interesting as human documents come from Egypt depends upon the climate of that marvellous country. Papyrus leaves could not lie buried for two thousand years in Asia ; but in Egypt that is possible. We are, however, certainly within our rights in regarding the spiritual and other facts derived from these human relics of Hellenistic-Roman Egypt for the most part as typical for the world of Paul.

The study of these unliterary documents for what they can show us of the souls of their writers is not yet finished and for long will continue to offer a great field of work ; but already it can be asserted that the old picture of that ancient world morally and religiously degenerate is precisely through these documents proved to be a caricature.

Of course, they also give evidence for the more gloomy sides of Paul's world ; we have amongst the papyri, for example, documents referring to unchastity,[1] bribery,[2] robbery, violence, theft,[3] exposure of children,[4]

---

[1] A large number of papyri throw light on the subject of prostitution, which is referred to also in a number of allusions in Paul's letters.

[2] Compare the letter of complaint against an Egyptian official of the Imperial period who had accepted bribes. Pap. class. Philol. I. No. 5 (Archiv für Papyrusforschung, 4, p. 174). Also the edict of the Egyytian Præfect Tiberius Julius Alexander, A.D. 68, censuring the bribery of officials (Archiv, *loc. cit.*). There are even preserved several letters of the second century B.C., in which a certain Peteyris (in all probability a prisoner) seeks to obtain his liberty ' by promising baksheesh,' as Wilcken appropriately puts it ; he promises 5 talents of copper, then 15 talents (Archiv für Papyrusforschung, 2, p. 578 f.). Also the much discussed passage Acts xxii. 28 is probably

[*For continuation of footnotes see next page.*

and unbridled impudence.[1] And unfortunately it cannot be said that such documents ceased to be written in the Christian period in Egypt.[2] But nevertheless on the whole the brighter colours are clearly seen. The family life of the middle and lower classes is seen here by no means in an only unfavourable light. But above all a strong religious emotion and marked aptitude for religion are to be seen in these people.[3] Paul's world was in no sense religiously bankrupt. Also the religious syncretism and the migrating of Gods from east to west and west to east have now for long been recognised as proofs of strong religious feeling. In Paul's speech on Mars Hill witness is borne to the Athenians that they are very religious ;[4] and this verdict may be safely generalised for the whole of the world of Paul ; and from the standpoint of the history of religion we may adopt Paul's statement—the fruit of generous intuition —that the age of the sending of Jesus Christ was the age of Pleroma (fulfilment),[5] the fitting time divinely ordained for the coming of salvation. How important

---

[1] Cf. the letter of the naughty boy, Theon, to his father, Theon, Oxyrhynchus Papyrus, No. 119 (2nd-3rd cent. A.D.), *Licht vom Osten*, 4th Ed., p. 168 ff.

[2] Cf. e.g. Oxyrhynchus Papyrus, No. 903 (4th cent. A.D.), which reflects an anything but happy Christian marriage.

[3] On this point the numerous religious inscriptions are most instructive.

[4] Acts xvii. 22, κατὰ πάντα ὡς δεισιδαιμονεστέρους ὑμᾶς θεωρῶ.

[5] Gal. iv. 4, ὅτε δὲ ἦλθεν τὸ πλήρωμα τοῦ χρόνου, ἐξαπέστειλεν ὁ θεὸς τὸν υἱὸν αὐτοῦ.

---

to be understood from this point of view : Claudius Lysias refers with satisfaction to the great expense in bribery that had gone to obtaining his citizenship. It is no use objecting solemnly that the citizenship was not purchasable. Compare also Acts xxiv. 26.

[3] Cf. the innumerable letters of complaint in the Papyri.

[4] Cf. Oxyrhynchus Papyrus, No. 744 (June 17th, 1 B.C.), *Licht vom Osten*, 4th Ed., p. 134 ff., and the *Berliner Griechische Urkunde*, No. 1104 (Alexandria, 8 B.C.).

within the whole picture of Paul's world was the special
phenomenon of Hellenistic Judaism dispersed everywhere needs only to be noticed : one glance at the
map [1] is enough to show what the Jewish Diaspora
meant.

From what has been said it follows that the world
of Paul can be reconstructed with more ample materials
than were available for previous generations of scholars,
who worked with literary materials almost alone.   And
now it is possible to ask about that portion of the world
out of which Paul himself sprang, I mean about the
social class of Paul.

The older study of Paul with its one-sided interest
in its bloodless, timeless paragraphs of the ' Doctrine '
or the ' Theology ' of Paul did not trouble itself about
the problem of the social class of Paul.   It was meeting
with the spectre of the modern social question that first
awoke an interest in social affairs of the past—an
interest which deepened with time.   And with many
I believe that the question to what social class Paul
belonged is an important special problem of the general
theme 'the world of Paul.'

To understand a man we need to know the class out
of which he sprang and with which he associated himself.   Not that a man is simply a product of his environment to be mechanically calculated.   Both the genius
and the babbler can have their home in a palace as well
as in a hovel.   The individuality of the man, most of all
the special something in the great man, is a mystery
which does not reveal itself—not even when we have a
complete knowledge of outer circumstances.

But just because we do not believe ourselves able
to analyse the inner contents of a personality by studying
its outer circumstances, we are in a position to appreci-
ate without prejudice everything that can be actually

[1] Cf. above, p. 39, note 1.

ascertained by the study of the environment. If such study cannot enable us to see into the heart of a man, it can at least teach us to interpret the lines and callosities of his hand, or to understand this or that interesting trait in his countenance. Truly we would not like to be without the information that Jesus sprang from an artisan household in a country district, and that Luther was the son of a miner and the grandson of a peasant. So let us follow up the traces which hint at the social class to which Paul belonged.

It appears to me to be certain, that Paul of Tarsus, although his native city was a seat of Greek higher education, was not one of the literary upper classes, but came from the unliterary lower classes and remained one of them. The inconspicuous remark of Acts,[1] that Paul was a tentmaker and in Corinth worked as such in the tent-making household of Aquila and Priscilla, has a special importance in this connection. The tentmaker Paul ought certainly not to be thought of as a learned writer of books, who to refresh himself from his brain work would sit for an hour or two working as an amateur at the loom. Nor ought he to be disfigured with the bombastic-comical title 'tent-manufacturer,' as though the artisan missionary was a disgrace to a Christianity become respectable. Rather he was a simple man who as a journeyman worked at his trade for wages, which were the economic basis of his existence.

There are several places in the epistles where Paul testifies with pride, that as a missionary he had earned his whole living by working with his hands.[2] The pious idlers of Thessalonica[3] were bluntly snubbed by the man

---

[1] Acts. xviii. 3, ἦσαν γὰρ σκηνοποιοὶ τῇ τέχνῃ.

[2] 1 Thess. ii. 9; 2 Thess. iii. 8; 1 Cor. iv. 12 and the whole of chap. ix.

[3] 2 Thess. iii. 10 f.

who worked 'day and night,'[1] that he 'might not be chargeable to anyone.'[2] The great importance of the thought of wages with Paul becomes more understandable when we recognise that this popular sphere of illustration was specially natural[3] to a man who worked for wages, for whom wages were not of grace but of right.[4] And the picture of the tent 'not made with hands' that we are some day to receive from God,[5] is doubly impressive in the mouth of a tent-maker. The mention by the Apostle of 'large letters'[6] also is best explained as a reference to the clumsy, awkward writing of a workman's hand deformed by toil ; and this also throws light on the fact that Paul preferred to dictate his letters ; writing probably was not particularly easy for him, and he may perhaps have dictated many of his letters while himself working at his tent-making.

In the East of to-day the ancient handicrafts continue to exist in many of their characteristic features. Observations which can, for example, be made in the interior of Anatolia, are instructive. When in one of the bypaths of the *Bazar* at Damascus we see a dyer stretching down into his vat with his long blue-stained arms, we are reminded that we have seen exactly the same thing somewhere else ; yes, indeed, it was in Pompeii, where close on two thousand years ago the workmen of the same trade as this dyer stood at the same dye-vat and with the same blue-stained arms dragged the same woollen yarn out of the dye-bath. Thus, too, the old weaver whom we saw in the neighbourhood of 'Paul's gate' making a coarse cloth on his poverty-stricken primitive loom, might at least give us

---

[1] 1 Thess. ii. 9 ; 2 Thess. iii. 8. [2] 2 Thess. iii. 8.

[3] Certainly no thoroughly worked out ethics of wages is to be deduced from this. Cf. *Licht vom Osten*, 4th Ed., p. 266 f.

[4] Rom. iv. 4. [5] 2 Cor. v. 1, οἰκίαν ἀχειροποίητον.

[6] Gal. vi. 11, ἴδετε πηλίκοις ὑμῖν γράμμασιν ἔγραψα τῇ ἐμῇ χειρί.

the suggestion of how the workshop of an ancient
weaver used to appear.   Probably the melancholy beat
of the ancient loom will not be heard much longer in
Cilicia.   In the great modern cotton-spinning mill at
Tarsus, English machinery of a quite other technical
age had long been whirring even before the war ; and
the students of primitive forms of human industry will
have to hasten with their apparatus to record the
manual dexterity and the rhythm of the ancient
handicrafts still conserved in the East.

It would, however, be a mistake to call the artisan
Paul a 'proletarian' in the sense which that word has
to-day.   The very fact that he was born a Roman
citizen shows that his family cannot have lived in
absolutely humble circumstances.[1]   As a free-born man
also his social standing was higher than that of the
many slaves in his churches.   And the language of
the Apostle also enables us to arrive at a better understanding on this question.

A careful investigation of the vocabulary of Paul's
Epistles[2] has proved that Paul did not write literary
Greek ; if further the relation of his style to Atticism
be studied, it is still clearer that he made no attempt
to write according to accepted Greek standards.   These
observations confirm our thesis that both as regards
his home circumstances and the place he occupies in
history he stands below the educated upper classes.
But even though his vocabulary is that of the people
and the tone of every-day speech is predominant in his
letters, yet his unliterary language is not vulgar to the degree that finds expression in many contemporary papyri.
On the ground of his language rather Paul should
be assigned to a higher class.   It is certainly, when all

[1] Acts xxii. 28.
[2] Theodor Nägeli, *Der Wortschatz des Apostels Paulus*, Göttingen,
1905.

is said and done, extraordinarily difficult to solve the problem of social classes of antiquity;[1] even in an attempt to discover Paul's social standing we are conscious that we can only feel our way forward. But anyone who recognises the general scope of the problem, will at least admit that we have drawn a relatively clear line, in placing Paul below the literary upper classes and above the purely proletarian lowest classes.

If finally it is asked, to which side of this middle position the Apostle tends, the answer is : by birth and education, by sympathies and circumstances of life, he belongs far more to the middle and lower classes than to the upper class. He is no social climber forsaking his own class. As a missionary chiefly working amongst the unliterary masses of the great cities Paul did not patronisingly descend into a world strange to him : he remained in his own social world.

Now we turn to the study of his human personality so far as its features are to be discovered : this will show us how Paul, in his origin and nature akin to the unliterary classes of his world, did not sink from sight in the confused mass of the submerged, but, rooted in that mass, as greater than it, arose a leader.

[1] Cf. *Licht vom Osten*, 4th Ed., p. 6 f.

PAUL THE MAN

CHAPTER III

PAUL THE MAN

CONCERNING the outward appearance of Paul the man, there is no reliable tradition. We are like the Christians of Colosse and Laodicea who had 'not seen' his 'face in the flesh.'[1] His Jewish origin, of which he was proud,[2] was no doubt visible to the people of Ephesus and Corinth. And the Paul of the letters which have come down to us was a man who had already passed the fifth decade of his life; he speaks of himself in one place as 'Paul, the aged.'[3] An ancient description of him in an apocryphal book[4] depicts him as by no means an imposing figure, and recollecting the numerous confessions of bodily weakness that run through his letters,[5] we may perhaps conclude that on the whole that description was correct, that in fact Paul was not distinguished by outward advantages of stature and countenance.

There are neither pictures nor busts of Paul; that goes without saying: who in that day would have thought of recording his face for the future, when the countenance of the Master Himself even had not been

---

[1] Col. ii. 1, ὅσοι οὐχ ἑώρακαν τὸ πρόσωπόν μου ἐν σαρκί.

[2] 2 Cor. xi. 22; Phil. iii. 5; Rom. xi. 1.

[3] Philemon 9, ὡς Παῦλος πρεσβύτης—if here πρεσβευτής (cf. Eph. vi. 20) ought not to be read, cf. R. Steck, *Prot. Monatshefte*, 1914, p. 96 ff., even in that case the letters would probably have been written by a man of between forty-five and fifty-five years.

[4] *The Acts of Paul*, 3. On this point compare the suggestions of Erwin Preuschen, ZNTW, 2 (1901), p. 187 ff., which if they do not fully explain the matter are at any rate well worth considering.

[5] 2 Cor. xii. 9 and xiii. 4, etc.

immortalised? Even if the old Jewish horror of pictures had not prevented it, the whole attitude of mind
of primitive Christianity was far too much dominated by
the coming age to be able to think of the interest which
future generations on this earth might feel in the outward features of the Saviour and his Apostles.[1] Just
as little did the artists in marble and colour, who portrayed so many of the Cæsars, the imperial ladies, the
generals, and leading literary men press their services
upon Paul. Who at that time in the official world had
taken any note of the obscure travelling preacher?

The Christ-cult was in the time of Paul a secret
affair of humble unknown people in the back streets of
the great Mediterranean cities. When Paul chanced to
write that the faith of a Christian church was known
'throughout the whole world'[2] he of course means in
the amiable[3] hyperbole, dear to the ancient Oriental,
the microcosmos of the Christian 'world,'[4] not the great
official world.[5] And when, as reported by Luke,[6] he
emphatically states that the facts of his Christian life
did not take place 'in a corner,' this apologetically

---

[1] It is this that makes impossible the early dating by some American scholars of the much-discussed chalice of Antioch.

[2] Rom. i. 8, ἐν ὅλῳ τῷ κόσμῳ, cf. Col. i. 6 ; 1 Thess. i. 8 ; cf. Clemens
Romanus, 1 Cor. v. 7, and with it Friedrich Pfister, *Der Reliquienkult
im Altertum*, Giessen, 1909, p. 267. Moreover, the popular hyperbole
of the 'whole world,' Lk. ii. 1 and Acts xi. 28, ought not to be pressed.

[3] It is a hyperbole of hatred, on the other hand, when it is charged
against the Pauline mission that it had 'turned the world upside down,'
Acts xvii. 6, xxiv. 5.

[4] Cf. 1 Thess. i. 8 with 2 Thess. i. 4.

[5] Similarly a heathen epitaph (now in Braunsberg) of an otherwise
unknown Egyptian lady, Seratus, and her relations, speaks of their
modesty as 'known in all the world' (Archiv für Papyrusforschung, 5,
p. 169, ὧν καὶ ἡ σωφροσύνη κατὰ τὸν κόσμον λελάληται), or when a
Christian letter of later date says of a (Bishop) John that his fame
goes through 'the whole world' (Archiv für Papyrusforschung, 4,
p. 558).

[6] Acts xxvi. 26, οὐ γάρ ἐστιν ἐν γωνίᾳ πεπραγμένον τοῦτο.

satisfying expression does not contradict the statement
that the new cult and its leading personalities still remained as good as unknown to the world at large, and
that we may look in vain to find any reflection of the
man Paul either in contemporary literature or in the
art of that day.

What Paul himself says about his outer man must
therefore suffice for us :[1] he bore the image of Adam
who was formed from the earth ; after laying aside this
earthly likeness he would however bear the image of
the second, the heavenly Adam, of the Lord Jesus
Christ who had been transfigured to spiritual glory.

The countenance then of a man looks upon us, as
we stand before Paul, the countenance of Adam upon
which is written all that is involved in that contradict-
ory double fate of the sons of Adam : they are 'the
image of God,'[2] yet they have been subjected to sin
and death.[3]

Unfortunately it is not superfluous strongly to emphasise the genuine humanity of Paul. The traditional
conception has too often made him either a parchment
saint, unacquainted with the world or else has suffered
the man to disappear behind the system. It is one of
the most satisfactory advances in the study of Paul that
in the last decades so much more interest has been taken
in the man Paul, whereas even Ferdinand Christian Baur
in his book *Paul,*[4] which was a classic in its own day,
touched upon the 'characteristic features of the individuality' of the Apostle only in an appendix.[5]

[1] 1 Cor. xv. 49, καὶ καθὼς ἐφορέσαμεν τὴν εἰκόνα τοῦ χοϊκοῦ, φορέσωμεν
καὶ τὴν εἰκόνα τοῦ ἐπουρανίου.

[2] 1 Cor. xi. 7.   [3] Rom. v. 12 ff., 1 Cor. xv. 22.

[4] *Paulus, der Apostel Jesu Christi, sein Leben und Wirken, seine
Briefe und seine Lehre,* 2nd Ed. (edited by Eduard Zeller), Leipzig, 1866 f.

[5] Well worthy of note amid the enormous modern literature about
Paul are the psycho-analytical study of O. Pfister, *Die Entwicklung des*

The letters viewed as confidential non-literary
sources have much to tell us of Paul the man. Each
letter of Paul is, as we saw, a picture of Paul ; yes, in
several of his letters there is a quick change of one
picture after another ; and in all these pictures unconsciously left by himself, he gives us a glimpse not only
of the frowns and smiles on his face but also of his very
soul.

In spite of such excellent witness to himself we
cannot entirely reconstruct him. Apart from the fragmentary character of the letters, this lies in the nature
of historical investigation, which in so far as it is concerned with exceptional men, always must stop at a
certain point, because there begins a mystery, which
even the most refined and sensitive psychological art
cannot altogether unveil.

For all that a large and essential part of the man
Paul is accessible to us. And the result of even a rapid
study of the personal confessions in his letters is one
deep impression : the man who wrote these fragments
is a great man, an unusual man of unusual gifts.

A remark that applies purely to a point of style
would make that clear, even to those who in studying
human greatness prefer to let considerations of form
predominate. The brilliant power of giving plastic
form to his thought which Paul possesses in a similar
degree to Heraclitus,[1] and which he uses without effort,

Apostels Paulus, Imago 6 (1920), p. 243-290, and the investigation of
Otto Schmitz, *Das Lebensgefühl des Paulus*, München, 1922, which
endeavour to approach the inner structure of the soul of Paul the
religious man, each by means of its own special method. Both these
very original pieces of work are as such with their independent points
of view yet another proof of the inexhaustible depths of Paul's
personality.

[1] I once read Heraclitus under the guidance of Hermann Diels,
who has since passed away, in the memorable evening sittings of the

is proof of the spontaneous freshness of his creative nature.

The letter killeth, the spirit giveth life,[1]—

the man who had only written this monumental line would have been for its sake immortal.

The Jews ask for signs, the Greeks seek after wisdom.[2]
The kingdom of God is not in word, but in power.[3]
Knowledge (Gnosis) puffeth up, but love edifieth.[4]
We know in part.[5]
The spirit searcheth all things, yea, the deep things of God.[6]

Such flashes and sparks come a hundred times in the letters, which were not intended for the applause of literary salons but came quietly and unassumingly to unknown people to help them in their need through power from above. We have everywhere not the meditated artificiality of the rhetorician counting the rhythm of his phrases, but the natural blazing out of hidden greatness. Supposing for a moment that all these brilliant phrases had not come down to us in their context in the letters, but in fragments scattered over the ancient literature of a thousand years—like the sayings of Heraclitus, the Obscure of Ephesus—the editor who for the first time brought them together would be showing us fragments of a hero.

The immense contrasts in Paul's nature, however, reveal even more of his human greatness. Paul had

Berliner Græca, and have made the above comparison deliberately. Hans Leisegang, *Der Apostel Paulus als Denker*, Leipzig, 1923, p. 39, similarly draws a parallel between the expression of thought by Heraclitus and by the Apostle.

[1] 2 Cor. iii. 6, τὸ γὰρ γράμμα ἀποκτέννει, τὸ δὲ πνεῦμα ζωοποιεῖ.
[2] 1 Cor. i. 22, Ἰουδαῖοι σημεῖα αἰτοῦσιν καὶ Ἕλληνες σοφίαν ζητοῦσιν.
[3] 1 Cor. iv. 20, οὐ γὰρ ἐν λόγῳ ἡ βασιλεία τοῦ θεοῦ, ἀλλ᾽ ἐν δυνάμει.
[4] 1 Cor. viii. 1, ἡ γνῶσις φυσιοῖ, ἡ δὲ ἀγάπη οἰκοδομεῖ.
[5] 1 Cor. xiii. 9, ἐκ μέρους γὰρ γινώσκομεν.
[6] 1 Cor. ii. 10, τὸ γὰρ πνεῦμα πάντα ἐραυνᾷ, καὶ τὰ βάθη τοῦ θεοῦ.

room in his personality for contradictions which would
have hopelessly shattered a small man, and which over-
burden the small-minded students of Paul with such a
mass of problems, that they have to get air for themselves by propounding their theses, 'not genuine' and
'interpolated.' But these contradictions did not shatter
Paul; they gave his inner life that tremendous tension
which expressed itself in the energy put forth in his
life-work.

The clearest case of these contrasts is that between
his ailing body and his physical powers of work. His
poor body was weak and ill, a fragile 'earthen vessel'
he calls it himself,[1] and the tentmaker compares it to
the light tent-dwelling which has no permanency.[2] He
speaks in Galatians of a severe attack of illness and it
appears to have been an illness whose symptoms aroused
disgust.[3] Most moving of all is his reference to a
severe chronic ailment with occasional attacks that
were very painful: he calls this illness

> a thorn in the flesh,
> a messenger of Satan to buffet me.[4]

and we cannot determine to what special disease these
symptoms point. Various conjectures have often been
attempted, but none are adequately convincing; the
sparing intimations of Paul himself warn us to be
cautious.[5] All we know is the thrice-repeated prayer
of the Apostle in his despair to the Saviour for healing,[6]

[1] 2 Cor. iv. 7, ἐν ὀστρακίνοις σκεύεσιν.
[2] 2 Cor. v. 1.   [3] Gal. iv. 13, 14.
[4] 2 Cor. xii. 7, σκόλοψ τῇ σαρκί, ἄγγελος Σατανᾶ, ἵνα με κολαφίζῃ.

[5] A small library could be gathered together all dealing with Paul's
illness. It must, however, on the whole be said that so far as the
writers come to definite statement they depend upon inadmissible
diagnosis from a distance which every honourable physican would
refuse to credit.
[6] 2 Cor. xii. 8.

cries for help, which, apparently unanswered, yet received a nothing less than divine answer :[1]

> My grace is sufficient for thee:
> For my strength is made perfect in weakness.

Strength in weakness! That is Paul's own description of the contrast we are studying. The enfeebled body is covered with the scars of frequent ill-treatment; he had endured a stoning,[2] five times he had received thirty-nine stripes,[3] thrice had he been beaten with rods.[4] What that means may be gathered from prison officials who have been present at the disciplinary punishment of refractory criminals.[5] Even after the fifth stroke blood often begins to spirt out, after twenty the back has been slashed into a bloody mass. In the tractate *Makkoth* of the Mishna we possess the instructions for the synagogue attendant, whose duty it was to carry out the scourging 'with all his strength,' while the judge read words from the Bible. By no means every delinquent had the physical strength to bear the thirty-nine stripes, many a one died under the executioner's hand; therefore delinquents were 'assessed' beforehand, e.g. to be able to endure only eighteen

---

[1] 2 Cor. xii. 9, ἀρκεῖ σοι ἡ χάρις μου · ἡ γὰρ δύναμις ἐν ἀσθενείᾳ τελεῖται.

[2] 2 Cor. xi. 25, cf. Acts xiv. 19.

[3] 2 Cor. xi. 24 : *The forty save one* is the punishment inflicted by the Jewish spiritual court of law. The note is of great importance; it illuminates as with a flash of lightning an almost forgotten piece of Paul's biography: his experiences with the officials of the Synagogue (mostly in the diaspora). He never formally separated himself from Judaism and to the end remained under the discipline of the Synagogue. The misdemeanours which were punished with scourging were amongst others breach of commandments regarding food and other ritual enactments.

[4] 2 Cor. xi. 25 : Punishment by officials of the state, cf. Acts xvi. 22.

[5] Compare the fragment *The Execution* in Tolstoi's *Resurrection*, Book I., chap. xlvi. [In the English translation by Louise Maude, this account is relegated to an appendix.—W.E.W.]

lashes. The paragraphs of this tractate [1] are a terrific commentary on that simple line in second Corinthians. In addition to the physical torment of this violently executed Jewish punishment there was also the agony of soul which Paul must have experienced as over and over again during the lashes of the attendant the mechanical reading of prescribed lines from the law [2] by the officiating scribe wounded his inner being as with corroding scorn :

> If thou will not observe
> To do all the words of this law,
> That are written in this book,
> That thou mayest fear
> This glorious and fearful name,
> Jahwe thy God . . .
>
> Then will Jahwe make thy plagues wonderful
> And the plagues of thy seed,
> Even great plagues and of long continuance,
> And sore sicknesses and of long continuance.

To all this must be added privations of hunger and frost, of thirst, heat and shipwreck [3] and the martyrdom of frequent arrest. [4] And Paul may often have experienced in his own person, what he had observed in his companion, Timothy : [5] that the drink of water found at last by the parched traveller, had the seeds of evil disease

[1] Easiest for reference in the small editions by Hermann L. Strack, Leipzig, 1910, and Gustav Hölscher, Tübingen, 1910.

[2] The tractate *Makkoth*, § 14, prescribes the terrible words, Deut. xxviii. 58 f., which in their content are closely allied to the words quoted by Paul in Gal. iii. 10, from Deut. xxvii. 26. It may be imagined with what feelings one who had been scourged would afterwards himself read and cite these words.

[3] 2 Cor. xi. 25-27.

[4] So Paul himself says, 2 Cor. xi. 23 and vi. 5. Long before he was arrested in Jerusalem, he had often been in prison. That is the starting-point of the Ephesian hypothesis (see above, p. 17 note).

[5] 1 Tim. v. 23.

hidden in it. If Paul could on occasion declare with a smile :

> in everything and in all things I have learned the secret, both to be filled and to be hungry,[1]

the list of his sufferings in second Corinthians (only apparently monotonous) speaks clearly enough.[2] It reflects the difficulties of climate to which the ailing man was exposed, but also the whole cruelty of fanaticism, which like a consuming fire rages through the religious history of the East, from the slaughter of the Priests of Baal to the stoning of Stephen, and from the Alexandrian Jewish pogroms under Caligula to the Armenian massacres of Adana, Tarsus and Antioch in 1909 ; not to mention all the cruelties of the World-war, far outstripping all ancient statistics of murder.

And now we see that this man, ailing, illtreated, weakened by hunger and perhaps by fever, completed such a life-work that, as a mere physical performance, challenges our admiration. Just measure out the mileage which Paul travelled by water and land, and yourself try to follow the course of his journeys. You sit, with your viséd pass and diplomatic recommendations in your pocket, in a comfortable modern carriage on the Anatolian railway, and travel in the evening twilight easily towards your destination on the permanent way which has been forced through rocks and over streams by engineering skill and dymanite. While, having already booked your rooms by telegraph, you are carried rapidly and without effort over the pass, you see in the fading light of evening, deep below you, the ancient road, narrow and stony, that climbs the pass, and upon that road a few people on foot and riding

---

[1] Phil. iv. 12, ἐν παντὶ καὶ ἐν πᾶσιν μεμύημαι, καὶ χορτάζεσθαι καὶ πεινᾶν.
[2] 2 Cor. xi. 23 ff. Cf. also i. 8 ff. ; iv. 7 ff. ; vi. 4 ff. ; xii. 10 ; 1 Cor. iv. 9-13 ; xv. 31 f. ; Rom. viii. 35 f.

donkeys, or in exceptional cases perhaps on horseback, are hurrying along towards the crowded, dirty inn. They are bound to reach it before darkness finally settles in, for the night is no friend to man ; the wild dogs of the inhospitable shepherds set themselves raging in the way, robbers are ready to take money, clothes, and beasts, and the demons of fever threaten the overheated and weary in the cold night wind, which is already blowing down from the side valleys.

Or exchange for once the modern Levant hotel with its lift and French cookery for the wretched kahn at the summit of the pass of the Syrian Gates on the way to Antioch and camp for a single night on the hard wood of the dirty plank-bed tormented by impure air, cold and vermin. Or if you travel from the east to Italy on a great Mediterranean steamer from Bremen, you may say to yourself : the storm that tosses us about in the gloomy night and gives us a taste of sea-sickness, but for all that cannot turn this immense ship aside from its course, at the same time dashes the little sailing ship, which without stars or compass is at the mercy of the billows, upon a reef or sandbank, and the few who manage to save themselves on scraps of wreckage are driven about for days starving on the waves.

It is Paul we have seen on that darkening road up the pass ; it is the wearied Paul who seeks repose on the hard wood ; and it was Paul who was tossed about on a broken ship's plank for a day and a night,[1] Paul, the man who suffered so much, hungry and thirsty. I had the great good fortune in 1906 and 1909 on my two journeys to travel over almost all Paul's routes. One of the most lasting impressions of these journeys, made for the most part with all modern conveniences for travel, is inexpressible astonishment at the purely

---

[1] 2 Cor. xi. 25, νυχθήμερον ἐν τῷ βυθῷ πεποίηκα.

physical achievement of Paul the traveller, who could
truly say, not without ground, that he buffeted his body
and brought it into subjection like a slave.[1] Strength
in weakness !

Another of the great contradictions of his nature is
this : Paul is of great humility yet he is also capable
of uttering words of the most majestic self-confidence.
Especially characteristic here is the confession of first
Corinthians :[2]

> I am the least of the apostles . . . But by the grace of God
> I am what I am . . . I laboured more abundantly than they all ;
> yet not I, but the grace of God which was in me.

Those are no mere phrases, but genuine confessions ;
with an almost Greek horror of arrogance [3] there is combined a virile sense of power : before God a worm,
before men an eagle.

Dependent upon his bodily weakness, but no doubt
also bound up with his whole structure of soul, is the
alternation of times of deep inner depression with
wonderful moments of complete freedom and an intoxicated sense of victory in having overcome the
world. Out of his own experience he speaks of 'the
earnest expectation of the creation' [4] and no less of
being cast down, of being straitened, of distresses,
anxieties, of heavy cares ; [5] longing for death thrills
through his soul, [6] and yet the dissolution of this earthly
tent is to him a horrible thought.[7] Out of his own

[1] 1 Cor. ix. 27, ὑπωπιάζω μου τὸ σῶμα καὶ δουλαγωγῶ.
[2] 1 Cor. xv. 9 f., ἐγὼ γάρ εἰμι ὁ ἐλάχιστος τῶν ἀποστόλων . . .
χάριτι δὲ θεοῦ εἰμὶ ὅ εἰμι . . . περισσότερον αὐτῶν πάντων ἐκοπίασα, οὐκ
ἐγὼ δὲ ἀλλὰ ἡ χάρις τοῦ θεοῦ σὺν ἐμοί.
[3] Compare the frequent warnings in Paul's letters against boasting.
[4] Rom. viii. 19 ff., ἡ ἀποκαραδοκία τῆς κτίσεως.
[5] 2 Cor. iv. 8 ff. ; vi. 4 ff. ; 1 Cor. iv. 9 ff. and other places.
[6] Phil. i. 23.   [7] 2 Cor. v. 2 ff.

personal experiences he has discovered the simplest and
most powerful chord expressive of all human suffering
in the *de profundis* of Romans : [1]

O wretched man that I am !

And the same man yet again glories in being completely
raised above all the troubles and perplexities of this
life. [2] It is bad psychology to refer the words of depression entirely to Paul's pre-Christian days, and to make
Paul the Christian speak only in words from the
heights. Even as a Christian Paul was still swallowed
up by the deep, just as surely as no doubt while still a
pious Jew he had seen the mountains from which his
help came.

Closely connected with this great contradiction of
his nature is another. Paul is by nature tender. He
weeps and he even speaks with antique simplicity of
his weeping. [3] He enters a new place of his missionary
work with timidity, with 'fear and trembling.' [4] He is
capable of the deepest feeling, calls the mother of a
friend in a popular good-humoured way his own mother, [5]
writes as a father, [6] can even feel like a mother, [7] emotion
and love flow from his lips. The intimate letter to the
Philippians and the gentle letter to Philemon are
monuments of this tenderness. The great thirteenth
chapter of first Corinthians, too, the song of songs of
brotherly love, welled forth from the depths of this
sensitive soul.

At times, however, this tender, gently smiling Paul,

---

[1] Rom. vii. 24, ταλαίπωρος ἐγὼ ἄνθρωπος.
[2] To the highest degree in Rom. viii. 35 ff.
[3] 2 Cor. ii. 4 ; Phil. iii. 18 ; cf. Acts xx. 19, 31.
[4] 2 Cor. ii. 3, ἐν ἀσθενείᾳ καὶ ἐν φόβῳ καὶ ἐν τρόμῳ πολλῷ.
[5] Rom. xvi. 13.
[6] 1 Thess. ii. 11 ; 1 Cor. iv. 14 f., etc.
[7] Gal. iv. 19 ; cf. 1 Thess. ii. 7.

who can sometimes be so tolerant of others,[1] is hard ;
he writes like a jailer, he is angry and his words of
wrath strike the offender like lightning.[2] The effect of
such words upon those for whom they are intended is
crushing, and his opponents scornfully object[3] that one
' whose bodily presence ' is so ' weak,' should when
absent write such ' weighty and powerful letters.' Even
more characteristic is what Paul himself experienced of
the effect upon the Corinthians[4] of a letter (no longer
in existence) written in deep depression.[5] The letter's
first effect was to give the church great pain ; perhaps
the Corinthians tore it up in the first blaze of anger, or
later purposely destroyed it, because there was in it so
much that hurt them—that would be the easiest explanation of the disappearance of this no doubt magnificent
letter.

In particular he is boundlessly severe towards
his opponents ; not shrinking from the bitterest tone,
he coins polemical phrases of an absolutely fanatical
coarseness,[6] whose death-dealing sharpness is scarcely
to be felt, when excited aftercomers, who are not worthy
to unloose the latchet of his sandals, presume to take
his sword in hand at the present day. He sometimes
even doubts the genuineness of his opponents' convictions, thus showing a classical instance of intolerance.[7]

One observation is here especially typical : Paul is
full of irony, of inexorable, biting irony.[8] Only so are
many of his words to be understood ; they vibrate like

[1] Cf. especially his attitude towards the ' weak ' brethren in 1 Cor.
viii. and Rom. xiv. 1—xv. 13.
[2] Compare the beginning of Galatians and many other places.
[3] 2 Cor. x. 10.
[4] 2 Cor. vii. 8 ff.
[5] 2 Cor. ii. 4 ; cf. above p. 14.
[6] Gal. v. 12 ; Phil. iii. 2, 18 ; 2 Cor. xi. 13 ff., 20 ; Rom. xvi. 18.
[7] Gal. i. 7 ; ii. 4 ; iv. 17 ; vi. 12.
[8] Cf. as a specially typical example 2 Cor. xi.

the ring of a dagger, when they are understood as ironical words used in conflict.

This mixture of mildness and severity in Paul reminds us, as does much else, of Luther; compare, for instance, the reformer's delightful letter to his son Hänsichen and his deadly words of controversy against the Pope.

It is understandable that a personality containing such violent contrasts has made very varied impressions on people. There has probably seldom been anyone at the same time hated with such fiery hatred and loved with such strong passion as Paul.

He sometimes quotes things his opponents said against him, which while they are no doubt caricatures, are most instructive. He is, they say, humble when present, but when absent full of courage;[1] he can write great and powerful letters, but his bodily presence is weak and his speech of no account;[2] he wants to talk people over to his side;[3] he does not write what he really thinks;[4] he is beside himself.[5] They do not even shrink from accusing him behind his back of deceit, uncleanness and guile,[6] and to whisper of dishonest dealings which he has been guilty of in money matters.[7] In light of this the meticulous care which Paul gave to the subject of collections is understandable. These humble people of his churches whose means of livelihood was reckoned in obols and denarii, these envious people, who themselves, as Paul once confessed with a sigh,[8] 'eat and devour one another,' and who by taking their miserable quarrels about matters of no account to be settled by heathen judges, exposed the brotherhood

[1] 2 Cor. x. 1, 2.   [2] 2 Cor. x. 10.   [3] Gal. i. 10.
[4] 2 Cor. i. 13.   [5] 2 Cor. v. 13.
[6] 1 Thess. ii. 3 f.   [7] 2 Cor. xii. 16.
[8] Gal. v. 15, ἀλλήλους δάκνετε καὶ κατεσθίετε.

to mockery,[1] these people (and this is the reverse side
of the social structure of early Christianity) were ready
to listen to common calumnies and good-for-nothing
gossip against a great man. According to the Apostle's
own testimony at any rate there were not lacking in the
Corinthian church people who formerly had been none
too scrupulous as to *meum* and *tuum*—'thieves' and
'extortioners,' says Paul bluntly.[2] Certain though it is
that Paul's persecutors with all this gossip did him
bitter injustice, there yet remained in other accusations
perhaps a little grain of truth, though made use of in
an untruthful way. This can be seen particularly
clearly in one case : Paul's impulsiveness, shown on one
occasion in sudden alteration of plans of travel, was
used by his opponents to put him in an unfavourable
light : they accused him of frivolously saying yes, yes
and no, no in the same breath.[3]

There is however no lack of evidence for an
absolutely enthusiastic devotion to him (a devotion
genuinely Oriental and southern in its naïve fire). Paul
reminds the Galatians of the time of their first love,
when they received him 'as an angel of God, even as
Christ Jesus' Himself, and would have counted themselves happy if they could have 'plucked out their own
eyes' for him.[4] The saints in Philippi loved him more
deeply because with greater constancy, as the letter
addressed to them shows.

From all this we may draw conclusions about Paul's
personality : being himself both tender and severe he
had made the people with whom he came into contact
friends or opponents. He did not know the comfortable quietness of the ordinary man. His way in life
lay through the fires and tempests of love and hate.

---

[1] 1 Cor. vi. 1-11.

[2] κλέπται . . . ἅρπαγες, 1 Cor. vi. 11, compare with 10. Cf. Eph.
iv. 28.

[3] 2 Cor. i. 17.   [4] Gal. iv. 13 ff.

That the man Paul, who has up to now been our study, was a man of the ancient world, goes without saying. But as a warning against every attempt at modernisation it is well to formulate the sentence expressly. Nevertheless it certainly ought not to be forgotten that in the great movements of the soul of man the difference between the so-called modern man and the man of antiquity is not so very great. But the differences which are really present are recognised by the eye sharpened by historical research.

The world of Paul is that ancient world, which we attempted to sketch in outline, and the ancient simple cosmogony with its above and below is the background of his religious certainties. Genuinely ancient is his belief in demons, which is to be discerned in a number of places in his letters. Just as innumerable men of antiquity, whose leaden tablets inscribed with bann and curse are still preserved, 'delivered'[1] their opponents over to the gods of the underworld, so he 'delivers'[2] the blasphemers Hymenæus and Alexander the coppersmith to Satan. Similarly he advises the Corinthians solemnly to 'deliver' an evil-doer to Satan.[3] The parting scene at Miletus[4] may be taken as the counterpart to this, at which Paul says to the elders of the Ephesian church :—

> And now brethren I commend you to God and to the word of His grace.

He has much to say of the wiles of Satan,[5] but he is confident that God will shortly crush the evil one under the feet of the saints.[6]

We see Paul as a man of the ancient world also in

[1] Cf. *Licht vom Osten*, p. 256 f.　　[2] 1 Tim. i. 20.
[3] 1 Cor. v. 3-5.　　[4] Acts xx. 32.
[5] 1 Thess. ii. 18 ; 2 Thess. ii. 9 ; 1 Cor. vii. 5 ; 2 Cor. ii. 11 ; iv. 4 ; xi. 14 ; xii. 7 ; Eph. vi. 11 f. ; 1 Tim. v. 15 ; 2 Tim. ii. 26.
[6] Rom. xvi. 20.

every case where the civilisation of the ancient great
city appears as the background of his mission. His
figurative language, very different from that of Jesus,
the Galilean, which, fresh as the dew and gay with
colour, is full of country life, reflects the life of the
great cities of antiquity ; we see in it the games of the
stadium,[1] military affairs,[2] slavery,[3] legal practice and
the law courts,[4] then the theatre,[5] home and family
life,[6] building,[7] handicrafts,[8] commerce,[9] sea voyaging.[10]
Probably it was military and legal affairs [11] which had
most interest for him. Illustrations taken from country
life are, on the other hand, but few and mostly more
conventional than the others.

From single passages in the letters, if we have learnt
how to look at fragments, we can reconstruct scenes

[1] 1 Cor. ix. 24 ; Phil. iii. 14 ; 2 Tim. iv. 7 f. (this passage is written
just in the style of an inscription recording a contest for a wager,
Licht vom Osten, 4th Ed., p. 262), etc.

[2] 1 Thess. v. 8 ; Eph. vi. 10 ff. ; Philemon 2 ; 1 Cor. ix. 7 ; xiv. 8 ;
2 Cor. x. 3 ff. ; Phil. ii. 25 ; 2 Tim. ii. 3. The illustration of the
triumphal procession is especially characteristic, 2 Cor. ii. 14 ;
Col. ii. 15.

[3] Numerous passages.

[4] Numerous places, especially the usage of the ideas κατακρίνειν,
condemn, and δικαιοῦν, *justify* (= *acquit*). When Paul (Rom. iii. 24)
especially emphasises the fact that God acquits us for nothing (without our paying him anything, δωρεάν) there may be behind this picture
the thought of some earthly judge who wished to be bribed. (Cf.
Acts xxiv. 26, see above, p. 45 f.)

[5] 1 Cor. iv. 9 ; Rom. i. 32.　　　　[6] Many places.

[7] 1 Cor. iii. 10 ff., cf. particularly the important illustration of the
building.

[8] Rom. ix. 21.

[9] Eph. i. 14 ; 2 Cor. i. 22 ; v. 5 ; ii. 17.

[10] 1 Tim. i. 19.

[11] This sphere has always received great interest ; cf. the collection
of references, *Licht vom Osten*, 4th Ed., p. 270 f. It may be worked
out to-day in a more plastic way, as the researches of Otto Eger
indicate.

from the life of the people in the great cities of antiquity.[1] We can imagine the bustle in the *macellum* at Corinth, the *bazar* of the butchers, where the various sorts of meat offered for sale occasioned serious scruples of conscience to timid Christians.[2] Afterwards, if the meat, which had perhaps been offered to idols, was roasted and served at table in the house of a heathen, it might make grave difficulties for any Christians who may chance to have been invited to the dinner-party.[3] The Gnosis-Christian, who boasted his enlightenment and feasted freely with the heathen even in the heathen temple, was a stumbling-block to the ascetically timid 'weak' brother,[4] who as he watched him with venomous glances, was indeed 'weak in faith,'[5] but strong in 'judging'[6] and in malicious 'evil-speaking.'[7] Or we almost hear the clink of tribute and custom money in the office of the collectors,[8] amongst whom there were, as Paul hints with a smile, some coarse worthies who did not merely require one to pay but also to tremble.[9] Like summer lightning Paul's sharp irony plays over the learned class: the heathen orators with their 'wisdom' and artificial rhetoric[10] and the Jewish scribes, who will only do business when you offer them miracles.[11]

We have already spoken of the quarrels of those who rush to the magistrate about some pitiably small

---

[1] On this point the words of Jesus are certainly very much richer; they are nothing else than classical documents for information about the people of Palestine.

[2] 1 Cor. x. 25.   [3] 1 Cor. viii. 10.   [4] 1 Cor. x. 27 ff.
[5] Rom. xiv. 1.   [6] 1 Cor. x. 29.
[7] 1 Cor. x. 30.   [8] Rom. xiii. 7 (a).

[9] Rom. xiii. 7 (b). In the original there is a pretty play upon words between φόρος, *tribute*, and φόβος, *fear*: τῷ τὸν φόρον τὸν φόρον . . . τῷ τὸν φόβον τὸν φόβον.

[10] 1 Cor. i. 19 ff.; ii. 4, 13.

[11] 1 Cor. i. 20, 22.

matter,[1] and of the dark picture of the moral corruption
of the great city.[2] Sharp instantaneous pictures pass
before us in the catalogue of domestic virtues in the
letters to the Colossians [3] and Laodiceans (Ephesians) [4]
and also in the warnings of the pastoral letters which
suggest such a wide experience of life. They allow us
in particular an inner view of family life. The apostolic
ethos is connected with the civilisation of the world in
general by a broad basis of moral convictions common
to the whole of antiquity.[5]

Paul as a man of the ancient world stands out
wonderfully clearly as we read his letters amid the
ruins of the cities he evangelised, which in our day have
been cleared of rubbish and again brought to light.
We may, for example, sit in the theatre at Ephesus,
which witnessed that tumult of Acts xix., oppressed with
the sultry loneliness of the Ephesian countryside and
read in a letter written at Ephesus of the Apostle's
many Ephesian opponents.[6] Or on the heights of the
Acro-Corinthus, with the sea to the right of us that
bears the sailing-ships to Ephesus and Palestine, and
to the left the Gulf of Corinth pointing towards Rome,
we may open the Epistle to the Romans, the letter in
which there below in Old Corinth Paul surveyed his
field of work from Jerusalem to Rome and to Spain.[7]
Then the Paul of ancient times, the subject of the
Emperor Nero, the contemporary of Seneca, stands out
a living man.

The contemporary of Seneca! The Christian of a
later generation who manufactured a correspondence

[1] 1 Cor. vi. 1 ff.   [2] Rom. i. 24 ff. ; Gal. v. 19 ff., etc.
[3] Col. iii. 12—iv. 1.   [4] Eph. v. 15—vi. 9.
[5] Cf. *Licht vom Osten.*, 4th Ed., p. 262 ff., the hints about ancient
popular ethics in the New Testament. The theme would repay a
more exact study.
[6] 1 Cor. xvi. 9.   [7] Rom. xv. 19, 23 f.

between Paul and Seneca, placed the Apostle in direct relations with the literary man. But as a matter of fact the two men had no contact with one another. Paul did once stand, an accused man, before Seneca's brother, Gallio, the Proconsul of Achaia.[1] The theme 'Paul and Seneca,'[2] which would be more interesting to a later age, may have arisen out of this occurrence at Corinth. But Paul is not to be classed with the philosopher. Seneca belongs to the select upper class, Paul belongs to the great mass of the weary and heavy-laden. To the aristocratic men of letters of his day, if they ever thought of him at all, he would have been nothing more than the *homo novus*. But—and here we must further develop a point of view already suggested[3] —he was not particularly striking to his own age. Not a single contemporary historian mentions him. This '*silentium sæculi*,' which has occasionally been used by the bodyless doctrinaire theorists of our day as evidence against the genuineness of Paul's epistles, is the perfectly natural consequence of the actual position of Paul in the world of his day. He was indeed no man of letters, whose works aroused interest, no man of learning, with impressive theories of culture. The appearance of this one religious travelling preacher amongst the many apostles of other cults in the great cities surrounding the Mediterranean would in those days gain no more attention than would in our day the activities of an American Adventist in Hamburg or Berlin. The word of his opponents, that he was 'unknown,'[4] which no doubt meant that he was not

[1] Acts xviii. 12 ff. Cf. below in Appendix.

[2] Cf. lately Rudolf v. Delius, *Zur Psychologie der röm. Kaiserzeit*, München and Leipzig (1913), p. 1-20 (with several mistaken inferences), and Ernst v. Dobschütz, *Begegnungen und Briefwechsel in Geschichte und Legende*, in Geschichtliche Studien, presented to Albert Hauck, Leipzig, 1916, p. 3.

[3] Cf. above, p. 56.   [4] 2 Cor. vi. 9.

recognised in the circle of the genuine apostles of Jesus, contains a profound truth when applied to the position of Paul in the world.

In this Paul's position is utterly different from that of Luther. From 1517 onwards Luther had a position of great publicity, as a man of letters, reformer, politician and organiser. Paul remained in obscurity. It was only long after his death that he became a person of historical importance.

Just as Paul described in glowing words in first Corinthians[1] the distance that separated the overwhelming majority of his converts from the upper-class with its culture, power and noble birth, so too in his own person he was sensible of this distance and expresses it when he speaks of himself as 'rude in speech,'[2] deals ironically with 'the wisdom of the world,'[3] and, in contrast with the wise, the scribes and the disputers, characterises himself as the messenger of divine 'foolishness,'[4] or when he regards the wise just as much as the unlearned as objects of his mission work.[5] This sense of contrast with the great world also is expressed in the bitterness of that passionate confession that God has set forth the Apostles 'last,' as 'filth' and 'offscouring' of humanity, fit to serve as a 'spectacle' to the world, to angels and to men (like the beasts and the criminals in the circus).[6]

If it be objected that Paul's letters, which supply us to-day with so many difficulties in exegesis, must have been too 'high' for simple people, and that therefore Paul must have had an eye to a circle of readers drawn from the educated public, it must be answered that the difficulty of interpretation proves nothing against our contention. There are contemporary papyrus letters which are

[1] 1 Cor. i. 26 ff.   [2] 2 Cor. xi. 6.
[3] 1 Cor. ii. 1 ff., 6-10; iii. 19 ff., etc.
[4] 1 Cor. i. 18-20.   [5] Rom. i. 14.   [6] 1 Cor. iv. 9-13.

certainly products of the lower classes; no doubt they were understood by their recipients, and in spite of that (or ought I to say—because of that?) are incredibly difficult for us to understand. In addition to this, numerous difficulties have been artificially introduced by the dogmatic misuse of Paul's letters. 'Some things hard to be understood' naturally remain: it was not Mark Rutherford who first correctly noticed that,[1] but a much older reader.[2] But nevertheless those six unknown people,[3] Speratus, Nartzalus, Cittinus, Donata, Secunda, and Vestia, the martyrs of Scilli, who on the 17th of July, 180, were obliged to state in evidence, before the Proconsul, what was in their box, certainly did not speak of unintelligible hieroglyphics but of the treasure of their souls, when they answered:[4]

> the books used by us, and besides these the letters of the holy man Paul.

Even to-day there are numbers of Christians, unlearned indeed, but knowing their Bibles and experienced in life, who in the main understand Paul's letters well. Lutheran peasants, Methodist tradesmen, Anglican colonists, Moravian women, Stundists of Michel Hahn, Presbyterian miners join with the simple confessors of Scilli in no small numbers. That Paul himself had the consciousness that he was writing for simple people,

[1] *Letters to Three Friends* (cf. The British Weekly, No. 1963, June, 1924, p. 232): 'Saint Paul, I confess, is hard, and I never read him without feeling that I have to stretch myself mightily in order to accommodate myself to him. In fact the last time I tried the Epistle to the Romans I had to give it up.'

[2] 2 Pet. iii. 16, δυσνόητά τινα.

[3] 'Plainly all plebians,' says Harnack, *Die Mission und Ausbreitung des Christentums in den ersten drei Jahrhunderten*, ii., 2nd Ed., Leipzig, 1906, p. 238. English Translation: *The Mission and Expansion of Christianity*, vol. ii., p. 278, note 2.

[4] *Akten der Scillitanischen Märtyrer* (Greek text edited by Usener), αἱ καθ' ἡμᾶς βίβλοι καὶ αἱ προσεπιτούτοις ἐπιστολαὶ Παύλου τοῦ ὁσίου ἀνδρός.

'babes' and the 'weak' is shown by occasional expressions of his own.[1]

Does Paul lose anything, when as a *homo novus* he is contrasted with the leading classes of his day? Yes, he loses something : the stilts he has been given. And he is set upon his own feet, upon the value of his own personality. We measure him no more by what he received, or ought to have received from without, but by what he was originally. Through the inexhaustible springs of the power of personality that was in him, this *homo novus*, Paul, standing in his own place, amongst the common people of the ancient world, rises high above the mass that surrounded him. Yes, his figure rises, too, above his famous contemporaries who sprang from the upper class. There is no single person of Nero's days who has left such permanent marks on the souls of men as Paul the *homo novus*.

The cosmopolitan trait that this unknown man here and there exhibits is the single silent prophecy of his future influence on the history of the world. Paul of Tarsus was not confined by the walls of his workshop or by the narrow, gloomy courts of his Ghetto. He was a citizen of the world ; to the Jews a Jew, to the Hellenists a Hellenist.[2] His attitude was friendly towards the Roman state of which he was a citizen ;[3] he on occasion even threw out the tremendous thought, that the government of the state is something divine, and that power is of the essence of that government.[4] What fruit have these few words in the tentmaker's letter borne later in the ecclesiastical and civil theories of the state ! Moreover, his great soul without learned training had absorbed much from the cosmopolitan civilisation

---

[1] 1 Cor. iii. 1 ff. ; Rom. vi. 19. [2] 1 Cor. ix. 20 f.
[3] Acts xxii. 25 ff. [4] Rom. xiii. 1-7.

of the east and west which was roaring around him,
and not least that common stock of ethics.[1] What
might be called his secular education was not drilled
into him, but breathed in. Some things he had picked
up from the rhetoricians, he was acquainted with pithy
sayings of the poets and lines that live in the mouths
of the people ;[2] he had no knowledge of the rhythm-
beating of the Asiatic prose-writers, which shows his
good sense.[3] He had his own ideas about heathenism,
gained from personal observation. He used indeed the
current controversial methods of the Jews against worship of idols and immorality,[4] but unlike the small-
minded dogmatic zealot he did not hold that the
heathen world as such was God-forsaken :

> Is He the God of the Jews only ?
> Is He not also of the Gentiles ?
> Yes, of the Gentiles also.[5]

He finds amongst the heathen the unwritten law of
conscience ;[6] he attributes moral sense to them,[7] and he
read upon the altars of heathenism a dedicatory inscription which he interpreted as a longing cry after the
One God.[8]

That he did not interpret such an inscription like
a modern student of inscriptions goes without saying.
Paul looked at everything from the religious standpoint.

[1] Cf. above, p. 73.

[2] 1 Cor. xv. 33 ; Acts xvii. 28 ; Tit. i. 12.

[3] Compare my thorough criticism of the hypothesis of Friedrich
Blass, Theol. Literaturzeitung, 31 (1906), col. 231 ff.

[4] Rom. i. 18-32 ; Gal. ii. 15.

[5] Rom. iii. 29, ἢ Ἰουδαίων ὁ θεὸς μόνον; οὐχὶ καὶ ἐθνῶν; ναὶ καὶ ἐθνῶν.

[6] Rom. ii. 14 f.   [7] 1 Cor. v. 1.

[8] Acts xvii. 23. A dedication probably similar to the inscription
at Athens has been found in Pergamum ; see below in Appendix. In
spite of Eduard Norden's famous investigation, I maintain that Luke's
reference to the Athenian inscription is to be accepted.

With this we come to the last clear characteristic
in Paul's character, to the characteristic which from
historical point of view was his real driving force.
The thing that made this significant man what he
became was his religious endowment.

Paul must be classed with the few people regarding
whom that much misused phrase ' religious genius ' can
rightly and fittingly be used. His was a mystical-
prophetical nature, and compared with this characteristic the theological almost entirely disappears. His
mysticism is not acting mysticism, but reacting
mysticism, not a mysticism which strives after ab-
sorption in the Deity but a mysticism which receives
communion with God as a gift of grace.[1] He was
mystical-prophetical also in the exceptional sense that
he was capable of ecstatic experiences. True, he
shuddered at the wild riot of unbridled wholesale
ecstacies whether heathen[2] or Christian,[3] and in
Corinth, where it once happened that some one in
ecstasy cursed Jesus,[4] he waged war against speaking
with tongues, although he recognised it in theory.[5] He
himself indeed had the gift of tongues,[6] and could tell
of datable[7] ecstasies and special revelations of his own.
Caught up into the third heaven, he had heard ' unspeakable words ' ' which it is not lawful for a man to
utter.'[8] In hours when he was unable to pray the
Spirit had suddenly taken possession and had prayed
for him in his stead ' with groanings which cannot be
uttered.'[9] In grace it was granted to him to hear the

[1] More is to be found on this question in Chapter VI.
[2] 1 Cor. xii. 2.   [3] 1 Cor. xiv. 23.
[4] 1 Cor. xii. 3.
[5] 1 Cor. xiv.   [6] 1 Cor. xiv. 18.
[7] 2 Cor. xii. 2 ; Gal. ii. 1. For dating of ecstasies cf. Isaiah vi. 1 :
' In the year that King Uzziah died . . .'
[8] 2 Cor. xii. 2-4.   [9] Rom. viii. 26 f.

voices from on high in words he could understand,[1] and
dreams became to him divine signs.[2]

The enlightened Philistine feels superior to the
delusions of the enthusiast, the dogmatic theologian
with his love of order mistrusts the mystical or refers
it to the faculty of philosophy or medicine. But the
historical student of religion knows that, puzzling as
they may be to him, the experiences of the great
enthusiasts are the sources of power in the history
of religion.[3] Whoever takes away the mystical element from Paul, the man of antiquity, sins against the
Pauline word :[4]

> Quench not the Spirit.

Some have quenched the Spirit in putting a spirited
Paulinism in place of the spirit-filled Paul,[5] and what

---

[1] 2 Cor. xii. 9; Acts xxii. 17 ff.; ix. 4 ff., etc.; xx. 23; xvi. 6, 7.

[2] Acts xvi. 9; xxvii. 23 f.

[3] Even Emil Brunner could know this and perhaps sometime will
know it. Now (*Die Mystik und das Wort,* Tübingen, 1924) contrasting mysticism and 'word' (or even mysticism and faith), he only
allows value to the 'word' (or to 'faith'), and overlooks the fact that
the 'word' is the precipitate of the mystical experience of certain
solitary souls who have been granted God's grace, and that 'faith' in
Paul's use is only another expression for the living communion with
God 'in' Christ. To contrast mysticism and the word is just as
erroneous as for instance to contrast creative genius in music with
musical score, or a charitable disposition with almsgiving. Compare
the apposite remark of Paul Tillich, *Rechtfertigung und Zweifel,*
Giessen, 1924 (Vorträge der theologischen Konferenz zu Giessen,
39th Series), p. 27. 'The "word" which Brunner opposes to
mysticism is only heard by the *homo mysticus,* that is he who is not
a mystic in the actual practising sense, but who has received and
continues to receive the fundamental revelation.' Here also there is a
valuable distinction between the 'practising' mystic and the 'revela-
tion-mystic'; compare my discussion of 'acting' and 'reacting'
mysticism, below, Chapter VI.

[4] 1 Thess. v. 19, τὸ πνεῦμα μὴ σβέννυτε.

[5] [I have tried to preserve the play upon words. The German is
' wenn er geistreichen Paulinismus an Stelle des Geistträgers Paulus

blazed and gleamed, like the tongues of fire on the heads of the Apostles at Pentecost, then chills us like the garish frozen light of an electrically illuminated Altar, with its hollow marble candles. For our part we will let the sacred fire burn, whose glow we trace in these letters. Paul is in the deepest sense of the word by the grace of God a *homo religiosus.*

And this soul predestinated to the unspeakable mysteries of the most blessed communion with God was born into a human communion in which the tremendous experiences of heroic saints of bygone days, although hardened into text and letter, still made itself felt, a communion in which religion was everything. Paul, the religious man, was born and grew up a Jew.

setzte,' which is more literally 'putting a clever Paulinism in place of the Spirit-carrier Paul.'—W.E.W.]

PAUL THE JEW

CHAPTER IV

PAUL THE JEW [1]

ANYONE going through the streets of a great Hellenistic city on the Mediterranean sea-board in the days of the Emperors Augustus and Tiberius, after he had admired the splendid marble temples of the ancient gods and of the dieties more recently arrived from abroad, would also perhaps notice in one of the less pretentious quarters of the city a plainly-built place of worship without an altar. At best it had for ornament a frieze of vine-leaves or olive-branches, but otherwise it was without outward decoration, and within the walls were bare and there was no image of a god. As the visitor entered his eye fell on a chest containing parchment rolls, and if the attendant approached to unroll them for the stranger, he saw that they were written in Greek uncials. A reading desk and benches, candle-sticks and lamps completed the scanty furnishing of the room.

In the cosmopolitan city of Alexandria, where the congregations which assembled round those parchment rolls had thousands of members, and had upon their lists high officials, rich merchants and well-known literary men, it may all have looked richer and more imposing. But in other cities that place of worship would not be better built or furnished than are the

[1] For this whole chapter see the highly interesting remarks of Ludwig Blau in his comprehensive review of the first edition of my *Paul* in Magyar-Zsidó Szemle (Budapest), April, 1912, p. 123-139. I am indebted to Herrn Pfarrer L. Musnai of Teaca (Siebenbürgen) for a translation into German.

majority of the synagogues of the Oriental Jews to-day.[1]
An inscribed stone,[2] discovered some decades ago, which
in the imperial period stood over the entrance of a
Corinthian Synagogue, bears the now mutilated words
"Synagogue of the Hebrews" in the same extremely
poor-looking rude script that is familiar to us in other
Jewish inscriptions of the period.

These unpretentious Jewish synagogues in the
heathen world were a quiet, yet the history of religion
tells us, a very effective protest against the worship of
images in polytheistic heathenism. In the Mediterranean basin, within the zone of the olive-tree, more
than one hundred and fifty Jewish congregations of the
imperial period are now known to us.[3] Their actual
number was certainly much greater.[4] In their Greek
rolls of parchment around which Sabbath by Sabbath
the congregation assembled to pray and to listen, they
possessed a centre of religious power, to which great
numbers of heathen were also attracted. The holy
scriptures of the Old Testament in the Greek translation
made by the Seventy brought the pious Jew of the dispersion who outwardly had become a Hellenist, and

[1] Such as I have myself visited, for example, in Constantinople,
Chalkis and Tiberias.

[2] Copy and text in *Licht vom Osten*, 4th Ed., p. 13.

[3] The Jews of Mesopotamia, Middle and Upper Egypt, and others,
are not reckoned in this calculation.

[4] The map which accompanied the first edition of this book
marked about 143 places outside Palestine where there were Jewish
settlements; but in several places there were various Jewish congregations; in Rome, for example, we know the names of nine synagogues.
The list given by Emil Schürer (*Geschichte des Jüdischen Volkes*, iii.,
4th Ed., Leipzig, 1909, p. 1 ff; English translation, *A History of the
Jewish People in the time of Christ*, Division II., vol. ii., p. 220 ff.)
and Johannes Oehler (Monatsschrift für Geschichte und Wissenschaft
des Judentums, N.F.\53 [1909], pp. 292 ff., 443 ff., 525 ff.), can be con-
siderably increased through discoveries, e.g. from Malta, Sicily,
Sardinia and Egypt.

generally was no longer able to understand the Semitic original, into ever-renewed contact, not merely with the traditions which told of the fortunes of his fathers and the divine guidance they experienced, but also with the religious experiences and hopes of the prophetic men who had arisen as gigantic figures in the religious history of the Mediterranean world during the thousand years before Christ.

The religion of the saints of old which was preserved alive in the Semitic Old Testament had not been mummified in the Bible of the Seventy, yet it was not offered without some interposition of Hellenistic culture. The Septuagint translation represents not only a formal, but also a material Hellenisation of Jewish Monotheism. On some chief points this amounted to a considerable alteration. This Greek Bible, in the light of universal history a book of both east and west, is an accommodation of the faith of the east to the western world,[1] and it made possible an extraordinarily effective propaganda for the One God of the Jews amongst heathen who had become weary and doubtful under polytheism.

Though apparently estranged by his Hellenistic Bible from his Semitic home, the cosmopolitan Jew had for all that not lost his close connection with the centre of the Jewish religion, the temple in Jerusalem. Everyone of full age paid his tax of two drachmæ annually for Jerusalem, and whoever was in the least able to do so made a pilgrimage to the holy city. Just as to this very day in the weeks before the spring fullmoon Jerusalem is the goal of many thousands of Jews, Christians, and Mohammedans, and just as the whole

---

[1] Further on this point in my article dealing with the subject, *Die Hellenisierung des semitischen Monotheismus*, Leipzig, 1903 (Reprinted from the Neue Jahrbücher für das klassische Altertum, etc., 1903).

world of Islam from Constantinople to the Sunda
Islands, and from the African colonies to China and
Japan, vibrates with a continual movement towards
Mecca, so also in those days, according to the words of
a contemporary writer,[1] many thousands out of many
' thousands ' of cities streamed up to Jerusalem to be
present at the temple at each feast.   Luke[2] in the
Pentecost narrative gives an international list of those
who had been pilgrims to Jerusalem and were now
settled down to live in the holy city.

And there in the city of the temple the Jew felt
himself, in spite of the foreign rule of Rome, proud as
one specially favoured with great privileges.   Warnings
in Greek and other languages inscribed in stone (one
of these is preserved to this day)[3] forbade on pain of
death any non-Jew from entering the holy enclosure of
the temple.[4]   At this abode of grace, where the sacred
fire of the burnt-offerings was never extinguished, the
longing of the pilgrims was satisfied.   Here they heard
the choirs of the singers and the sound of the harps ;
here sat the far-famed teachers of the law and gave of
their best ; here it was possible, if one was present in
the sanctuary on the great day of Atonement, to par-
ticipate, if it were but faintly, in the most solemn ritual
service of the whole year.   And here everyone breathed
the sultry atmosphere of the most fervently nationalistic
Messianic expectation.

Strangely differing types of Jew met one another at
the Temple Court, and to-day one has but to shut one's
eyes for a moment there in the broad open place before
the Dome of the Rock in Jerusalem, to see those
ancient figures as of old ; the rich Babylonian merchant,
who we can scarcely think of as having undergone the

---

[1] Philo, *De Monarchia* ii. 1.   [2] Acts ii. 9 ff.
[3] Text and copy *Licht vom Osten*, 4th Ed., p. 62 f.
[4] Cf. also Acts xxi. 28, 31 ; xxii. 22.

weariness of the long caravan journey, fills the hand of
the poor pilgrim from Rome, who begs to get together
the money for his return journey ; the Cilician artisan
and the Alexandrian scholar talk together shudderingly
of the Galilean pilgrims whose 'blood Pilate mingled
with their sacrifices.'[1]

Not a few of the strangers who came as pilgrims to
the feast stayed on permanently or remained for a considerable time in the holy city, as the list of the day of
Pentecost teaches us.[2] So there arose in Jerusalem
itself synagogues whose congregations were formed of
foreign Jews, in which fellow-countrymen were grouped
together. Just as to-day in the east the Sephardim
Jews and the Ashkenazim Jews, the Bochara Jews and
the Yemenites generally, have their separate synagogues,
and a similar arrangement is found in New York.[3] The
Book of Acts bears witness to the existence of a congregation formed of Jews from Africa and also of one
made up of those from Cilicia and other parts of Asia
Minor.[4]

This synagogue of the Cilicians and those from Asia
Minor in Jerusalem is probably the one to which the
young Cilician Jew, *Saul who is surnamed Paul*,[5] whose
family probably originally came from Galilee,[6] was
attached while for a considerable time in his youthful
years he stayed in Jerusalem. Here he will have found
personal connections for those future journeys, of which
he had then never dreamed, and in daily conversation
with widely-travelled men he will have learned all about
the geographical distribution of the Jewish dispersion
along with the travel-routes. When Acts relates that

---

[1] Luke xiii. 1.   [2] Acts ii. 9 ff.

[3] Cf. Ludwig Blau, *Papyri und Talmud in gegenseitiger Beleuchtung*,
Leipzig, 1913, p. 10.

[4] Acts vi. 9, ἐκ τῆς συναγωγῆς . . . τῶν ἀπὸ Κιλικίας καὶ 'Ασίας.

[5] Acts xiii. 9, Σαῦλος δὲ ὁ καὶ Παῦλος.

[6] Cf. below, p. 90 note 5.

the Jew born in Tarsus[1] was 'brought up' in Jerusalem,[2] it might at first sight be interpreted to mean that Paul came as a small child to Jerusalem.[3] But judging from the general impression that Paul makes upon us as we know him, it is on the whole probable that the son of Tarsus spent his boyhood in the city of his birth. Paul appears so very much as the Septuagint-Jew, and alongside the Aramaic[4] he has such sovereign command of the Hellenistic *lingua franca*, that we are bound to assume a strong influence of the Septuagint and the Hellenistic world about him as a child.

But though Palestine was his homeland, to him it was not only as the land of Israel, the land of his fathers in the sense it was to Jews in general, but according to an as yet unbroken family tradition it had been their real home: His family appears to have emigrated to Tarsus from Gishala in Galilee.[5]

[1] Acts xxii. 3; ix. 11; xxi. 39.

[2] Acts xxii. 3, ἀνατεθραμμένος δὲ ἐν τῇ πόλει ταύτῃ. But see below, p. 93 note 9.

[3] Later Paul had relations in Jerusalem. After his arrest his sister's son had put forth efforts on his behalf (Acts xxiii. 16 ff.). Did Paul's sister live with her son in Jerusalem? Or was the nephew merely passing through the Holy City as a pilgrim to the feast?

[4] Acts xxi. 40.

[5] The tradition found in Jerome (*In Philem.* 23 and *De viris inlustribus*, 5) which indicates the Galilean Gishala as Paul's home, is so remarkable (because not to be in any way derived from a combination of New Testament passages), that it cannot well be explained as a fiction. It probably is derived from the tradition of the family which traced back its origin to Gishala (cf. Theodor Mommsen, Zeitschrift für die neutestamentliche Wissenschaft, 2 [1901], p. 83). If Paul was born in Tarsus it is probable that his family was Galilean. It is strong evidence for this that he calls himself—with pride—' a Hebrew of the Hebrews' (Ἑβραῖος ἐξ Ἑβραίων, Phil. iii. 5, cf. 2 Cor. xi. 22). By 'Hebrews' in the Imperial period we are to understand Jews who spoke Aramaic. Cf. my remarks in Nikolaus Müller's *Die Inschriften der jüdischen Katakombe am Monteverde zu Rom*, published by Nikos A. Bees (Βέης), Leipzig, 1919, p. 24 (also pp. 58, 72, 98, 106 f., 112, 173).

Jesus and Paul—were they actually fellow-country-men? Are the nations indebted to 'Galilee of the Gentiles'[1] not only for the Great Light, but also for the light-bearer?

Peter and Paul—had the Aramaic of the Apostle of the Gentiles, when he spoke it in Jerusalem or Antioch,[2] still a Galilean accent, a Peter-accent?[3] There is nothing against the assumption, that the two protagonist-antagonists were also fellow-countrymen.

About the childhood of Paul we can with a high degree of probability deduce some information from what he himself tells us. In his early days it must have impressed him, that he belonged to the tribe of Benjamin,[4] that by birth he also possessed the Roman citizenship,[5] and that he, a Jew in the world, bore two names of different kinds,[6] the old Jewish famous name *Saul* (in Greek *Saulos*), and a worldly name, which sounded similar, was Latin in origin, and was also used in the Greek form *Paulos*.

Even in middle life an experience of his inner life in childhood remained clear in his mind, and in Romans [7]

---

[1] Cf. Matt. iv. 15 f.

[2] It is probable that in the famous Paul-Peter scene at Antioch (Gal. ii. 11 ff.) Paul spoke Aramaic. For Peter was not very able in Greek; he required a dragoman when he travelled in the Jewish dispersion (cf. the well-known words of Papias on Mark).

[3] Matt. xxvi. 73.   [4] Phil. iii. 5; Rom. xi. 1.

[5] Acts xxii. 28.

[6] As even to-day is the case with pious Jews: cf. the information by Salomon Frankfurter in my work *Die Urgeschichte des Christentums im Lichte der Sprachforschung*, Tübingen, 1910, p. 16. The important essay of Hermann Dessau, *Der Name des Apostels Paulus* (Hermes, 45 [1910], p. 347 ff.) has not convinced me. There was no change of names after the experience in Cyprus (Acts xiii.), however popular that idea may have become.

[7] Rom. vii. 9-11, ἐγὼ δὲ ἔζων χωρὶς νόμου ποτέ. ἐλθούσης δὲ τῆς ἐντολῆς ἡ ἁμαρτία ἀνέζησεν, ἐγὼ δὲ ἀπέθανον. καὶ εὑρέθη μοι ἡ ἐντολὴ ἡ

he gives moving expression of it. We might speak of it as his fall:

> For I was alive without the law once: but when the commandment came, sin revived and I died. And the commandment which was ordained to life, I found to be unto death. For sin taking occasion by the commandment, deceived me and by it slew me.

Paul is thinking here in the first place of his earliest years of childhood, which in another place [1] he speaks of as the time of childish irresponsibility; then the feeling of guilt was unknown to him along with the idea of 'sin.' But there came a sorrowful day never to be forgotten: the Law, the dumb parchment rolls of which he had seen from far as a child in the synagogue with awe and curiosity as they lay in their embroidered coverings [2]—that law itself entered for the first time peremptorily into his conscience, with its 'thou shalt' no doubt conveyed through the mouth of a parent. But the law's 'thou shalt' was closely followed by the child's 'I will not' and transgression. Paul does not say what the occasion was. But he indicates that this first conscious sin wrought terrible havoc in his sensitive young soul; he felt himself deceived, it was as though he had tasted death:

> I died.

We do not know when this tragedy took place in the soul of the young Paul. Many of us know from our own experience what agony the sense of guilt can produce even in childhood. Jewish teachers,[3] at least in later times, have, it is true, assumed that up to its ninth

---

εἰς ζωὴν αὕτη εἰς θάνατον. ἡ γὰρ ἁμαρτία ἀφορμὴν λαβοῦσα διὰ τῆς ἐντολῆς ἐξηπάτησέν με καὶ δι' αὐτῆς ἀπέκτεινεν. This passage has suffered much at the hands of doctrinaire exegesis through misinterpreting the 'I'.

[1] Cor. xiii. 11.   [2] 2 Cor. iii. 14.

[3] *Tanchuma* (a late commentary on the Pentateuch) on Gen. iii. 22.

year the child knows nothing of sin; but then with the awakening of the 'evil instinct' sin begins.

More important than the explanation in detail of that experience is the fact which can pretty certainly be inferred from it, that Paul, who had experienced this fall, cannot have had a sunny, cheerful youth. Law, Sin and Death already in early life cast their gloomy shadows in the soul of the gifted boy. Yes, even following his own suggestions, slavish terror[1] might be indicated as the prevailing tone in the mind of one who 'from a child had known the Scriptures'[2] and was being matured more and more into a conscious Jew. Terror, not only the fear of God in the old Biblical sense,[3] but the desperate anxiety of one 'born under the law'[4] about his soul's salvation:

O wretched man that I am!
Who shall deliver me from the body of this death?

Even after Paul became a Christian such a cry was still possible to him,[5] when the old struggle awoke again in him.

The terror of this struggle drove Paul into the sternest tendency of Judaism. Paul became a Pharisee.[6] Perhaps this was even in Tarsus; we know that the Pharisee propaganda extended over sea and land,[7] and his parents appear to have been Pharisees before him.[8] But in Jerusalem, whither he had emigrated and stayed for a considerable time in order to make a thorough study of the law,[9] at the feet of the famous Rabban

---

[1] Rom. viii. 15.　　　　　　　　[2] 2 Tim. iii. 15.
[3] 2 Cor. vii. 1; Rom. iii. 18.　　[4] Gal. iv. 4.
[5] Rom. vii. 24, Ταλαίπωρος ἐγὼ ἄνθρωπος· τίς με ῥύσεται ἐκ τοῦ σώματος τοῦ θανάτου τούτου;
[6] Phil. iii. 5; Acts xxvi. 5; xxiii. 6.　　[7] Matt. xxiii. 15.
[8] Acts xxiii. 6 must be so interpreted.
[9] This is probably the best interpretation of 'brought up,' Acts xxii. 3. The greatest teachers are the 'fathers.'

Gamaliel,[1] he clearly was a supporter not only of Pharisæan pietism, but, within that extraordinarily active and precise body, of the most fanatical enthusiasts. Comparing himself with those of his own age who used to sit beside him in the class-room memorising the Rabbinic traditions, he could justifiably speak of himself as being 'more exceedingly zealous for the traditions of my fathers.'[2] He had in those days shared to the full in the Puritanical exultation of the scribe who knew the law :

> A guide of the blind,
> A light of them which are in darkness,
> An instructor of the foolish,
> A teacher of babes.

these words of the letter to the Romans[3] written decades afterwards still shine with the reflected splendour of his own proud self-consciousness.

On the other hand, his clear and sincere eye was not blind to the contrast, which while constantly showing itself in his own life in the opposition between willing and doing,[4] was present, as everywhere in the world, in his surroundings, as a contradiction between external piety and inner depravity. He had detected one zealot in theft,[5] another in immorality,[6] and he seems once to have caught one of his co-religionists, no doubt a Jew of the dispersion, a man who used to speak with scorn of heathen idols, enriching himself through these idols by acting as receiver of goods stolen from a temple.[7]

---

[1] Acts xxii. 3.   [2] Gal. i. 14, cf. Acts xxii. 3.

[3] Rom. ii. 19 f., ὁδηγὸν τυφλῶν, φῶς τῶν ἐν σκότει, παιδευτὴν ἀφρόνων, διδάσκαλον νηπίων.

[4] Rom. vii. 15 ff.   [5] Rom. ii. 21.

[6] Rom. ii. 22 (a).

[7] So I try to explain this obscure passage (Rom. ii. 22b). In the remarkable sentence 'thou that abhorrest idols, dost thou rob temples?' there is probably contained a definite recollection of Paul.

Such observations certainly, even in his Jewish period, led Paul, the Pharisee, deep into the understanding of that great thought of the prophet of old,[1] 'the circumcision of the heart,'[2] in contrast to the merely outward circumcision in which many a Jew openly gloried,[3] while others, no doubt in fear of heathen ridicule, endeavoured to hide the Jewish sign when in the bath or stadium.[4]

The knowledge that beside the 'secret,'[5] that is the genuine Jews, there were also many merely 'outward'[6] ordinary Jews, who were judged to be sinners by the pious heathen,[7] and the deeply humiliating experiences of his own often vain strivings after 'righteousness' by personal achievement,[8] may well have caused thoughts from time to time to flash out in the glowing soul of Paul the Pharisee of the extraordinary and pre-eminent achievements of religious sacrifice. At times the ideal of the Maccabæan martyrs was alluring to him, it appeared the highest degree of piety to 'give his body to be burned'[9] for God's sake. He would have been

---

[1] Deut. x. 16 ; xxx. 6 ; Jer. iv. 4.

[2] Rom. ii. 29, περιτομὴ καρδίας.

[3] Rom. ii. 28. [4] 1 Cor. vii. 18.

[5] Rom. ii. 29, ὁ ἐν τῷ κρυπτῷ Ἰουδαῖος.

[6] Rom. ii. 28, ὁ ἐν τῷ φανερῷ Ἰουδαῖος.

[7] Rom. ii. 26 ff. [8] Rom. vii. 14 ff.

[9] 1 Cor. xiii. 3, ἐὰν παραδῶ τὸ σῶμά μου ἵνα καυθήσομαι. In spite of the thorough defence of the various reading καυχήσομαι by Adolf Harnack (Sitzungsberichte der Kgl. Preuss. Akademie der Wissenschaften, 1911, p. 139 ff.) I regard καυθήσομαι (or καυθήσωμαι, the subjunctive of the future, also is found in the papyri) as original. I cannot agree that martyrdom by fire had not occurred within Paul's horizon (p. 181 below). Even more important than the significant passage Dan. iii 28 is 2 Macc. which in vii. 3 ff. exactly describes a martyrdom by fire and especially 4 Macc., in Paul's time quite a modern book, which simply revels in martyrdom by fire and its details (v. 32; vi. 24 ff. ; vii. 4, 12; viii. 13; ix. 17, 19 ff. ; x. 14; xi. 18 ff; xii. 1, 10-20; xiii. 5, 9; xiv. 9 f. ; xv. 14 f., 20, 22; xvii. 1; xviii. 20. Cf. on this point my notes in Kautzsch's *Apokryphen und Pseudepigraphen*, ii., p. 149-177). That victory in martyrdom by fire was

capable of doing so, too, just as in after days as a
Christian he would gladly have sacrificed himself for
his people.[1]

Even when a Christian Paul preserved the most
genuine features of his Jewish nature. Therefore the
theme 'Paul the Jew' is not to be interpreted as if
Paul had been a Jew up to his conversion, but after
that was a Jew no longer. Paul remained a Jew while
also a Christian in spite of his passionate controversy
against the law. This is not intended in a merely
ethnological sense (naturally he did not divest himself
of his race when he was baptised), but also in a religious sense and as a sentiment. Far from mechanically
separating the Jew and Christian in Paul we may confidently call him the greatest Jewish Christian of primitive times. He had inherited his worship of God 'from
his fathers.'[2] We may surely assume that in his own
family there had been a similar continuity of earnest
piety generation after generation, as that which he
praises in Timothy's mother Eunice, and his grand-
mother Lois : their 'unfeigned faith' had been inherited
by their son and grandson.[3] And it may especially be
taken for granted that a thorough appreciation of the
outer expression of religion ran in his blood as an inheritance from his fathers. Only a religious man whose
feelings were rooted in religious observances could in
later times so passionately feel the problem of the law,

regarded as the highest evidence of faith, is shown by Heb. xi. 34 (cf.
4 Macc. xvi. 21 ff.; xviii. 12-14). But even Paul's own time had
known public burnings of Jews in the Jewish massacres at Alexandria
under Caligula (Schürer, i., 3rd Ed., p. 498, English Ed., Div. I., vol.
ii., p. 93 f.). And these Alexandrian sacrifices by fire were martyrs in
the true sense, because their cause was refusal of emperor-worship.
The variant from καυθήσομαι may have arisen through the reflexion
that Paul's own martyrdom was not a martyrdom by fire.

[1] Rom. ix. 3.   [2] 2 Tim. i. 3.   [3] 2 Tim. i. 5.

which was essentially a problem of religious observances, and fight it through as he did.

Paul never departed from the national and religious communion of his people;[1] he retained with pride the name 'Hebrew'[2] and the even more significant names 'Israelite'[3] and 'seed of Abraham,'[4] just as he also certainly reckoned himself one of the 'Israel of God.'[5] He speaks of Jews in the wilderness as the 'Fathers'[6] and 'forefathers,'[7] and to boast of 'father' Abraham[8] and 'father' Isaac[9] comes natural to him. He calls even the unbelieving Jews 'brethren, kinsmen according to the flesh' and for them he would willingly himself have received the curse if thereby he could have saved them.[10] He boasts, too, his descent from the tribe of Benjamin,[11] which he shared with King Saul,[12] and his circumcision on the eighth day.[13] And if anyone had denied that he was a Jew, the scars left by his frequent bloody scourgings at the hands of the synagogue Jurisdiction[14] would have been painful proof of his membership. His thinking is Jewish. So also in neutral things; for example he reckons the dates of journeys by the Jewish calendar of feasts.[15] Though standing himself above the letter of the law, he yet as an apostle continued to observe the hallowed customs

---

[1] With what follows cf. also Gustav Hoennicke, *Paulus als Patriot*, Deutsch-Evangelisch, 6 (1915), p. 61 ff., and the chapter 'The Patriot' by R. H. Strachan, *The Individuality of St. Paul*, 2nd Ed., London, undated (but Preface dated 1916). Both studies are amongst the few good fruits of theological war inspiration.

[2] Phil. iii. 5 ; 2 Cor. xi. 22, cf. above, pp. 90 n. 5, 91.

[3] 2 Cor. xi. 22; Rom. xi. 1. [4] *Ibid.*

[5] Gal. vi. 16. [6] 1 Cor. x. 1. [7] Rom. iv. 1.

[8] Rom. iv. 16. [9] Rom. ix. 10. [10] Rom. ix. 3.

[11] Phil. iii. 5 ; Rom. xi. 1. [12] Acts xiii. 21.

[13] Phil. iii. 5, περιτομῇ ὀκταήμερος.

[14] 2 Cor. xi. 24, cf. above, p. 61 ff.

[15] 1 Cor. xvi. 8; Acts xxvii. 9.

of his people : the references that point to this in Acts[1]
are not later touches by some one with a Jewish bias,
but indications of the actual carrying out by Paul of the
principle enunciated by himself, his becoming 'to the
Jews a Jew.'[2]

Also the feeling of contrast which the Jews
experienced towards 'sinners of the Gentiles'[3] was
not unknown to him, and just as he, with a sense of
his Hellenism, occasionally emphasises the separation of
'Greek' and 'Barbarian,'[4] so feeling as a Jew he
frequently employs the old Jewish contemptuous
expression 'heathen'[5] ('Gentile') for the non-Jews.
The Roman applied the same word also no doubt
contemptuously to the provincials. Here too belongs
that metaphor which makes the Jews the cultivated
olive-tree and the Gentiles the wild olive.[6]

How greatly Paul loved the people of his own race
is shown in the fiery confessions of Romans.[7] There it
is no theoretical question that torments him, but grief
over his people who have turned away from Jesus the
Messiah : the question, has God perhaps after all cast
aside his people, presses upon his mind.[8] And though
Paul was never able to discover an intellectual solution
of that problem, nevertheless in the enthusiasm of his
faith and through the love he bore to his people he was
in the end able to put the painful question aside.

The observation that Paul after his conversion
exhibits none of the renegade's hatred undoubtedly
points to a sympathetic trait in his general portrait.

---

[1] Acts xvi. 3 ; xviii. 18 ; xxi. 26.

[2] 1 Cor. ix. 20, καὶ ἐγενόμην τοῖς Ἰουδαίοις ὡς Ἰουδαῖος.

[3] Gal. ii. 15.   [4] Col. iii. 11 ; Rom. i. 14.

[5] For ἔθνη = provincials, cf. for example A. von Domaszewski in
the Strena Helbigiana, Lipsiae, 1899, p. 53 ; and David Magie, De
Romanorum juris publici sacrique vocabulis . . . , Lipsiae, 1905,
p. 58.

[6] Rom. xi. 17 ff.   [7] Rom. ix.-xi.   [8] Rom. xi. 1.

The harsh expressions against the Law, which he occasionally uses, are outweighed by other passages, in which he strives to do justice to the Law. Indeed he not infrequently continued to use the Law as authority quite in the manner of his fathers.[1]

Here we come to the most characteristic trait of Paul, the Jew. To the end Paul remained a pious Bible-Jew, a Septuagint Jew. What separated him on this question from other Jews of the Dispersion was the recognition, that in Christ the Law had lost its binding force and the promises had received their fulfilment. But the general religious and ethical contents of the Septuagint are for him the self-evident presupposition even of his Christian piety.

Paul, the Christian, never withdrew from the divine world of the Hellenistic Old Testament. To understand the whole Paul from the point of view of the history of religion one must know the spirit of the Septuagint. The historical presupposition of Paul's religious life is not the Hebrew Old Testament, and not necessarily what we should call 'Old Testament Theology,' but the faith contained in the Greek Old Testament. The task of reconstructing the Jewish background of Paul's Christianity on the basis of the Septuagint conceived as a complete and uniform Bible has scarcely been recognised by scholars, let alone solved. It resolves itself into a number of separate problems of which only a few can be mentioned : the certainties about God in the Septuagint ; the Spirit and Christ in the Septuagint ; faith and righteousness in the Septuagint and many others.

On some points of course the results of such separate investigations will be closely similar to the results of Old Testament theology as worked out on the basis of

[1] Cf. e.g., 1 Cor. ix. 9 ; Gal. iii. 13, etc.

the Hebrew Bible, but on many points this will not be so. Old Testament theology regards the Old Testament as the historical document of a complex of facts in the history of religion developing gradually over a stretch of many centuries in a number of separate phases. The student of the Septuagint, on the other hand, regards the Greek Old Testament essentially as Paul regarded it, and as a pious layman to-day regards the Old Testament—as something relatively uniform. The Greek translation has indeed almost completely removed the many lines by means of which in the original Hebrew text the stages of gradual stratification and development are noticed by the historical student. Bible statements from Genesis, from the Prophets and from quite late Psalms, documents of several hundred years apart, which perhaps in the original text cannot be combined at all, are in the Septuagint Bible united without difficulty, because the reader whose religious life is nourished on the Septuagint in his effortless simplicity hears the same unalterable Spirit speaking the same revelation in every roll of his Holy Scriptures.[1]

The great place held by Septuagint piety in the religious *psyche* of Paul is at once evident in the vast number of quotations from the Greek Bible which we find in his letters. It is not improbable that Paul made use of a text of the Septuagint which had already undergone a Jewish revision.[2]

Paul's connection with the Septuagint shows itself even more strikingly in his whole religious and ethical vocabulary. But it becomes clearest to us when pos-

[1] Compare my work mentioned, p. 87 note 1.

[2] Further on this question in my work, *Die Septuaginta-Papyri und andere altchristliche Texte der Heidelberger Papyrus-Sammlung*, Heidelberg, 1905, p. 69 f. What Alfred Rahlfs has to say on the matter, Z.N.T.W., 20 (1921), p. 182 ff., has not altered my opinion.

sessing an accurate knowledge of Paul's letters we read
the Septuagint itself, not merely a few lines quoted by
Paul, but the whole book, as the Hellenistic Bible.
Unfortunately there is still a great lack amongst us of
methodical reading of the Septuagint and even of what
should come before that, exegesis of the Septuagint.
But for the student of Paul there is scarcely anything
more interesting and instructive.[1]

The exegesis also, which Paul bestows upon the
Greek Bible, clearly indicates to us Paul, the Jew. It
is the exegesis of a completely authoritative document.
Although Paul indeed regarded one part of this document, the Law, as abolished in Christ, yet, as already
mentioned, he occasionally quotes passages from the
Law with the significant words ' it is written.' In the
Hellenistic world at that time ' it is written ' was the
formula used when people referred to the terms of an
unalterable agreement.[2] That is exactly how Paul uses
it. What is written cannot be disputed ; therefore
every quotation from Scripture is a proof from Scripture.
God Himself speaks in Scripture, Scripture was even
itself personified,[3] and the principle is laid down :[4]

> not to go beyond the things that are written.

With such an attitude to the letter of the Bible Paul,
as an exegete, appears slavishly bound from the outset.

[1] In preparation of my first piece of work on the formula ' in
Christ Jesus ' I read rapidly through the whole Septuagint in order to
establish the use in construction of the preposition ' ἐν.' (The English
Concordance [Hatch and Redpath] fortunately had not then reached ε).
I am indebted to this reading for great and continuous stimulus. For
some years now there have been lectures and classes on the exegesis of
the Septuagint held in the Theological Faculty at Berlin.

[2] For proofs of this juridical γέγραπται, see *Bibelstudien*, p. 109 f.
[English, *Bible Studies*, p. 112 f.] ; *Neue Bibelstudien*, p. 77 f. [English,
Bible Studies, p. 249 f.].

[3] E.g. Gal. iii. 8, 22.   [4] 1 Cor. iv. 6, μὴ ὑπὲρ ἃ γέγραπται.

But we know that means had long ago been discovered, in spite of the tyranny of the letter, to get beyond the letter. This means, which Paul is fond of using, is allegorical exegesis. It was not invented by Jews : they certainly took it over from Hellenism, which interpreted the poets allegorically, in order to get rid of their religious coarseness for those who through culture had become prudish.

The Jews, however, were very glad to borrow it, because they needed it. It would be unjust to the allegorical exegesis of Judaism and early Christianity to regard it as the abortion of a wholly irrational theosophical fanaticism. The mere observation that so great a mind as Philo Judæus made extensive use of it, should make us more cautious. As a matter of fact, in an age when inspiration was construed on a legal basis with mechanical literalism, allegorical exegesis was the only means open to prophetic and creative minds of escaping the grip of the letter ;[1] and with Philo, as also with Paul, allegorical exegesis, however paradoxical this may sound, was more a sign of freedom than of bondage, though it led both of them to great violence of interpretation.

Instances of such violence are, for example in Paul's letter to the Galatians,[2] the interpretation of the word ' the seed '[3] as singular, although the idea is actually intended to have a plural sense, and elsewhere is interpreted by Paul as plural.[4] Or the subtle explanation of the story of the fall favourably to the man.[5] Or the application of the words about the ox, which was not to be muzzled while threshing,[6] to the Apostles.[7] Paul,

---

[1] G. Klein also regards allegorical exegesis similarly (*Der älteste christliche Katechismus und die jüdische Propaganda-Literatur*, Berlin, 1909, p. 42 f.).

[2] Gal. iii. 16.   [3] Gen. xiii. 15.

[4] Rom. iv. 18 ; ix. 8.   [5] 1 Tim. ii. 13 f.

[6] Deut. xxv. 4.   [7] 1 Cor. ix. 9 f., cf. 1 Tim. v. 18.

moreover, when in the course of this interpretation he suggests that God does not care about oxen, speaks in these strangely unpractical and feeble words as a man from the city, who does not regard animals in a simple way because he has never lived with them ; and we notice how far he is from the splendid and powerful realism of the faith of Jesus, who from childhood onward had grown up in constant contact with animals and plants. Jesus cannot think that a sparrow falls to the ground without God's will,[1] and sees the flowers of the Galilean spring clothed by God Himself in their garments of more than royal splendour.[2]

On the other hand, Paul, the allegorical exegete, does succeed by means of this method in producing splendid religious ideas : the parallel between Sarah and Hagar and the two Covenants ;[3] the identification of the rock that gave water in the wilderness with the Spiritual Christ.[4] These, viewed in their ancient setting, are revelations of a great mind, and they cannot be diminished by modern objections. Here the Jewish allegorical method, which elsewhere lends crutches to the small masters of theology, gives the religious genius wings to rise up like the eagle.

In several other details the use of Scripture by Paul, the Jew, is dependent on his rabbinic tradition, especially on the peculiarities of the edifying legend, the so-called *Haggada*. From this source comes the theory mentioned in Galatians,[5] and noticed in other places,[6] that the Law was not given directly by God Himself but by the angels ; from this source comes the number 430, also in Galatians,[7] and that popularly

[1] Matt. x. 29 ; Lk. xii. 6, cf. Matt. vi. 26 ; Lk. xii. 24.
[2] Matt. vi. 28 f. ; Lk. xii. 27.
[3] Gal. iv. 22 f.   [4] 1 Cor. x. 4.
[5] Gal. iii. 19 (cf. also Col. ii. 16 combined with ii. 18).
[6] Acts vii. 53 ; Heb. ii. 2.   [7] Gal. iii. 17.

familiar touch[1] that the rock that gave water to the
fathers had followed them in their journeyings in the
wilderness.

The influence of his Jewish teachers is also to be
seen in what is generally called Paul's dialectic, and
particularly the influence of the methods of teaching
and proof used in oral discussions in the house of
instruction.   Paul's letters also as we must bear in
mind were mostly dictated orally : and the methods of
oral proof are quite fitting.   Apart from the proof of
all proofs the proof from Scripture, the proof from
analogy is a favourite ; for example, analogies from
Nature are used to illustrate the relationship between
the earthly and the heavenly body ;[2] similarly analogies
from agricultural and military life illustrate the right
of Apostles to support.[3]   Analogies from legal practice
are especial favourites, for that was of great interest
to Paul, the citizen of a great city :[4] another person
cannot add a clause to a testament :[5] the heir while a
minor is under guardians and stewards for as long as
the father has appointed.[6]   We find further the argument from less to greater[7] ('simple and complex,' the
Rabbis called it), or also the argument from the greater
to the less.[8]   The magnificent parallel drawn between
Adam and Christ in 1 Corinthians and Romans is also
typically Rabbinic.[9]
On the whole, however, in my opinion, too much has
been made of Paul's use of Rabbinic dialectic as of his
dialectic in general.   Logical proof in the strict sense
of the word, and progress in a direct line of argument,

---

[1] 1 Cor. x. 4.   [2] 1 Cor. xv. 35 ff.   [3] 1 Cor. ix. 7.
[4] Cf. above, p. 71 note 4.   [5] Gal. iii. 15.
[6] Gal. iv. 1, 2.   [7] E.g. Rom. xi. 12, 24.
[8] E.g. 1 Cor. vi. 1 ff. ; Rom. xi. 21.
[9] 1 Cor. xv. 22 ff. ; Rom. v. 12 ff.

are not Paul's strong points. Exegetes have treated
him far too exactingly in this connection, and their
many attempts to ' restore the true order of thought ' in
Paul's letters merely result in turning the free creations
of genius into something repulsively stiff and wooden.
Hoping to arrive with him at the end of a straight
road, you often find yourself brought back to the
starting-point of a circle. In controversy, for instance,
Paul is of much too impulsive a nature to be a great
dialectician. Rather than refute his opponents at
length, he disposes of them with a flash of his irony or
with an angry look, and in dealing with religious
problems he is more successful generally on the in-
tuitive and contemplative side than on the purely
speculative.

How far this intuitive-contemplative endowment of
Paul is a Jewish trait, I do not venture to say. In the
sphere of mysticism there are not a few analogies,
especially amongst the classical mystics of the middle
ages. In any case the idea of contemplation seems
better to characterise the distinctive feature of Paul's
religious contribution (as also that of the Evangelist
John) than the idea of theological speculation.[1]

In speaking of Pauline contemplation I do not
mean an action of the man [2] who, following a method
for the training of the soul which he has learnt, climbs
up the ladder to heaven rung by rung until he reaches
union with the Deity. Pauline contemplation is a
reaction to a divine visitation ; the strings within

[1] Compare with this also Ernst Troeltsch, *Die Soziallehren der
christlichen Kirchen und Gruppen*, Tübingen, 1912, p. 29. The lines
that stand there in quotation marks are taken from my sketch in the
Jahrbuch des Freien Deutschen Hochstifts (Frankfurt A/M), 1905,
p. 86.

[2] See above, p. 79 f. and Chapter VI.

vibrate at the touch of God's fingers; the trembling
soul reacts to revelation, whither it comes in the form
of deep sorrow or in the ecstatic rejoicing of the
Psalmist. 'Pass onward ye believing thoughts to the
broad field of Eternity!' Contemplation consists both
in the believer steeping himself, being submerged, in
the revealed 'deep things of God,'[1] and in a struggle
with practical problems which are not interesting from
the theological scientific point of view but are felt as
the torturing problems of religion. What can I say
further to describe it? In one of the greatest of his
confessions Paul himself described with inimitable
expertness the nature of this contemplative thought
process, the outcome of an endowment of the Spirit, of
inspiration.[2]

> But unto us God revealed them
> Through the Spirit.
> For the Spirit searcheth all things,
> Yea the deep things of God.

The results of contemplation cannot be put into
hard and rigid sentences, they are something tender,
living, working inwardly like a fervent. They do not
fly like a whizzing arrow straight to their mark but they
circle[3] around their booty in noiseless flight like an
eagle. There is often also in contemplation something
that causes the mind to stop and to brood; it guides
those who enter its school not so much into well considered progress in thought, as into a deepening of

---

[1] 1 Cor. ii. 10, τὰ βάθη τοῦ θεοῦ.

[2] *Ibid.*, ἡμῖν δὲ ἀπεκάλυψεν ὁ θεὸς διὰ τοῦ πνεύματος. τὸ γὰρ
πνεῦμα πάντα ἐραυνᾷ, καὶ τὰ βάθη τοῦ θεοῦ. The whole passage, 1 Cor.
ii. 6-16, must be the starting-point for an understanding of Paul on the
great scale. Richard Reitzenstein has grasped this better than many
in theological circles.

[3] Hans Leisegang, in *Der Apostel Paulus als Denker*, p. 9, on this
account speaks of 'a circle of thought in the literal sense of the
word.' On other points also this delicate study has much of value.

thought. It cannot be formed into a unified system
because it is the tumultuous movement of a deeply
stirred soul.

The well-known discussion in Romans of God's ways
with Israel is typical of this contemplative tumult of
the agitated soul.[1] It is here a problem of thought
indeed, but much more an agonising religious uncertainty that disturbs Paul, the Jew. No theoretical
solution is discovered ;[2] in spite of several attempts to
free himself, every time Paul becomes again entangled
in the net of the problem, and the answers he gives
are not solutions by means of speculative thought but
rendings of the net by the irresistible momentum of his
religious intuition.

The results of Paul's contemplation flow in the clearest
stream in the letter to the Colossians and the nearly
akin letter to the Laodiceans (Ephesians so-called).
There were no special problems of church life which
had to be discussed in these two letters ; and so Paul
could here express himself more in solemn hymn-like
utterances, which even in their style strike one with
their tone of priestly earnestness.   Here comtemplation
is reinforced by the inspiration of united worship and
streams forth in foaming rhythms, in psalmody—and
may I say it, in dynamically pre-existent cantatas ![3]

It must, however, again be emphasised that it is not
certain whether in the strongly contemplative trait of
Paul's character we are in touch with the specifically
Jewish side of his nature. It might be said that his
contemplation is Jewish in its want of system and in its
lack of balance on the theoretical side, that its constructive aids, and especially the proofs from Scripture

[1] Rom. ix-xi.   [2] Cf. above, p. 98.
[3] I cannot claim deep knowledge of Bach, but I can claim that I
have received much from him. When I open the chapel door of
the Epistle to the Colossians it is to me as if Johann Sebastian himself sat at the organ.

are Jewish. Or are we to call it all 'Semitic,' are we to call it simply 'Oriental'? Not much depends on a name.[1] Perhaps what is essential in this case cannot be traced back further at all, but must be regarded as a personal endowment of Paul which attained its full development after Damascus.

Be that as it may, Paul, the Jew, stands before us clearly, with all the strength that Judaism carried with it, and also with a part of the limitations that surrounded Judaism.

But the characteristic features of Paul, the Jew, come out even more clearly when we set him beside the Jew who had world-wide fame in the Hellenistic age as the Jew,[2] who in fact became a sort of Father of the Church, Philo of Alexandria.

These two, Philo the Jew and Paul the Jew, were contemporaries. Both came out of the Dispersion, were men of great cities and had a strongly cosmopolitan character. Both lived and moved in the Septuagint. Both were capable of ecstatic-mystical experiences and had many points of contact in details.

And yet there is a very sharp contrast between them, a contrast that reminds one of the antithesis between Seneca[3] and Paul, and in some of its main features is repeated in the contrast between Erasmus and Luther.

Philo was a writer, Paul a speaker (even his letters

---

[1] Nor does it depend much on in what chapter of a book on Paul we consider this peculiarity of the Apostle. It might be dealt with just as well in Chapter III. or Chapter VI.

[2] Charles Johnston—The Constructive Quarterly, 1 (1913), p. 810 : *Paul and Philo*—writes from another point of view. He discusses the possible influence of Philo and Paul. The comparison, on a basis of the History of Religion, by Gustav Hoennicke of Paul and Josephus, is very interesting (Neue Kirchliche Zeitschrift, 20 (1909), p. 650 ff.).

[3] See above, p. 74.

were spoken). The name of Philo probably reached
Paul, but Philo can scarcely have heard of Paul. Philo
was a professional author ; Paul was not. Philo left
behind him literary works, Paul unliterary letters.
Philo was an Atticist, was careful about the dual, the
optative, and the use of hiatus. Paul wrote as he
spoke and what he spoke was the living Greek of the
Hellenistic world. Philo was a philosopher. Paul
the fool, poured out the vials of his irony upon the
wisdom of the world.

Philo belongs to the upper-class, Paul to the middle
and lower classes ; Philo represents high literary
culture, Paul the strength that wells up from the
people. Philo is a Pharos, Paul a volcano. Philo is a
student and theologian, Paul a prophet and herald.
Philo worked at his desk for the great literary public,
Paul hurried from the workshop to the market-place
and the synagogue, to see his hearers face to face.
The nephew of Philo, Tiberius Julius Alexander, was
Procurator of Palestine and Præfect of Egypt and his
name is not only immortalised by Josephus, Tacitus and
Suetonius, but he has also a monument in stone on the
wall of the propylon of a temple in the Great Oasis—
one of the most famous inscriptions of the early imperial
period.[1] Paul's nephew, trembling for the safety of his
uncle, as he was questioned by Roman officers in
Jerusalem,[2] appeared an unknown man out of the
great crowd of the nameless and then at once dis-
appeared. Philo travelled as an ambassador to Rome
and was received by the emperor, Paul only had connections with the imperial slaves[3] and was transported
to Rome as a prisoner.

The whole mass of contrasts between the man of

[1] Dittenberger, *Orientis Graeci Inscriptiones Selectae*, No. 669.
Copy in *Licht vom Osten*, 4th Ed., p. 305.
[2] Acts xxiii. 16 ff.   [3] Phil. iv. 22.

Alexandria and the man of Tarsus may be summed up
thus : Philo is a Platonist, Paul will be what he will be
in Another ; Philo, the Jew, stands at the end of ancient
civilisation, Paul, the Jew, stands at the beginning of
the new world-religion.

It is true that before Paul, the Jew, takes his stand
upon the threshold of a new era, we see him as the
fanatical defender of the Pharisaic tradition, his face
turned backwards to the past. Paul, the Jew, first
comes upon the stage of history as the persecutor of the
new body of Christians.   In the passionate zeal therein
displayed he is also a genuine Jew.   The picture which
Acts[1] draws of the persecutor is no doubt in the main
correct ; in the chief features it is confirmed by the
painful, self-tormenting confessions of Paul's letters.[2]
And historically the explanation of this position of Paul
in his young days is simple enough.   The conflict in
which Jesus fell a victim was a conflict with the leading
party, the Pharisees.   Paul the persecutor is Paul the
Pharisee, who continued the war waged by his party
against Jesus by himself waging war against the group
of followers who reverenced the crucified.[3]

[1] Acts vi. 9; vii. 58; viii. 1 ff.; ix. 1 ff.; xxii. 3 ff.; xxvi. 4 ff.
[2] Gal. i. 13 f., 23 ; 1 Cor. xv. 9 ; Phil. iii. 6 ; 1 Tim. i. 13.
[3] [German, ' Kultgemeinde des Gekreuzigten.'   I know of no exact
equivalent to this in English.—W. E. W.].

PAUL THE CHRISTIAN

CHAPTER V

PAUL THE CHRISTIAN

THE NEW CULT. PRINCIPAL FACTS ABOUT THE NATURE, DISTINGUISH-
ING MARKS, AND ORIGIN OF THE CULT. THE PRIMITIVE APOSTOLIC
CULT OF JESUS (KYRIOSCULT). THE CONVERSION OF PAUL.

THE death of Jesus on the cross had as its immediate
result the dispersion of His little band of followers out
of Galilee and Jerusalem. In the great religious conflict
with the powerful Pharisees Jesus seemed to have been
finally defeated, although when foretelling his martyrdom [1] in prophetic words of foreboding He had also
spoken of His speedy return after the martyrdom.[2]

But very soon after the terrible experience of the
execution of Jesus, we find these fearful and despairing
followers again gathered together in the holy city. And
though before they had scarcely been united into an
organised church, now they appear bound together as a
religious cult holding fellowship by means of breaking
bread and prayers, while they look forward with longing
hope to the great final revelation of the Messiah. The
new cult had come into existence.

[1] The most important passages are Lk. xiii. 31 ff. ; Matt. ix. 15 ;
Lk. xii. 50 ; Matt. xxvi. 12 ; xxi. 37 ff. ; xx. 25-28, and with them the
words at the Last Supper, Mk. xiv. 22 ff. and its parallels ; to these
must be added the original of the words Mk. viii. 31 and its parallels
which have come down to us in a modified form due to their use in
the Church.

[2] Mk. viii. 31 and parallels (cf. note 1) and the words certainly
understood by the disciples as applying to Jesus, Matt. x. 23 ; xvi. 28 ;
xxiv. 34 ; xxvi. 64.

What is a cult and how does a cult arise ? [1]

Here it is first of all necessary to undertake an explanation of the meaning of the word.   The word *cult*
has both a narrower and a wider meaning, and in this
fact lies the cause of many misunderstandings in pro-
nouncements about cult-history and the methods of
studying cult-history.[2]   The case is in fact similar to
that of the use of the word mysticism.[3]

[1] I here wish in this new edition to draw attention, even if only in
passing, to the fundamental questions which in my view have to be
considered in dealing with Early Christianity from the point of view
of cult history.   In the first edition these were only touched on from
the methodological point of view in the preface, in contrast with Adolf
von Harnack's famous formula of the ' double gospel.'   The cult-history
method was itself carried out in the book.   I then meant and still mean
the term ' Religious History ' in the sub-title to be understood in the
sense of ' cult-history.'   That the cult-history method is a correct one
has since been recognised by many ; I mention (cf. Karl Ludwig
Schmidt, *Eschatologie und Mystik im Urchristentum*, Z.N.T.W., 21
(1922), p. 280 f.) Ernest Troeltsch, *Die Soziallehren der christlichen
Kirchen und Gruppen*, Tübingen, 1912, p. 58 ; Wilhelm Bousset, *Kyrios
Christos*, Göttingen, 1913, p. 107, 2nd Ed., 1921, p. 90 ; Reinhold
Seeberg, *Der Ursprung des Christusglaubens*, Leipzig, 1914, p. 17.
Bousset in the above-mentioned book has carried out the cult idea on
the great scale.

[2] The attitude taken by E. von Dobschütz in his comprehensive
review of my book *Licht vom Osten*, 4th Ed., in the Theologische
Studien und Kritiken, 1923-24, p. 328 f., is exceptionally instructive.
He opposes my technical word ' Christ-cult,' because he equates ' cult '
with ' cultus.'   Nevertheless he touches the real point when he says
emphatically ' Here clearly, as in the cases of mysticism, it depends
on the use of language : If you equate veneration with cult, then it is
not only possible, but obligatory, to speak of the primitive Christian
Christ-cult, just as you can speak of primitive Christian mysticism,
meaning thereby piety.   But in scientific study one's endeavour should
be to attain as far as possible an unambiguous terminology.'   That is
right, and for that reason I distinguish between *cult* and *cultus*.
Further, I cannot agree with von Dobschütz who, on his part, uses
cult in the (narrower) sense of cultus, when he denies the presence of
the cult idea (in the narrower sense of the cultus idea) in early
Christianity before the time of Clement of Rome.   He has even gone

[3] See below, Chapter VI.

Most people at the mention of the word *cult* only think of the *cultus*, of the solemnities practised in worship by an organised religious body and of the formal expression of these solemnities. That is the narrower idea for which in German the word *Kultus* is used and should be retained.

Cult in the wider meaning is what lies behind the cultus as its spiritual precondition : a practical dependence upon the deity, an attitude adopted towards the deity, a readiness for religious conduct, a readiness for religious dealing, religious dealing itself. The popular vocabulary [1] of many languages in its simplicity has grasped the fact that it is practical dependence upon the deity, that it is religious practice, which is the essential feature in the idea. And this has been

so far as further to narrow down his already narrow idea of cult by making temple, priest, and sacrifice the outward signs of the cultus and designates the purpose of cultus as 'exerting influence upon God.' To me this type is identical with the 'acting' cultus (cf. below, p. 117 ff.), but there is also a 'reacting' cultus. Such reacting cultus is to be seen in its powerful beginnings even in the earliest stages of the Christ-cult. Its traces in the New Testament are not even particularly infrequent. For further discussion of the subject, what von Dobschütz says on the cult question in Norsk teologisk Tidsskrift, 1922, must on no account be overlooked. Hegel long ago established a narrower and a wider conception of 'cultus,' cf. G. W. F. Hegel, *Begriff der Religion*, *Vorlesungen über Philosophie der Religion*, Erster Teil, neu herausg. von Georg Lasson, Leipzig, 1925, p. 229. 'Usually the expression "Cultus" is understood merely in the restricted meaning that brings to mind only the outward, public business [of religion] and does not much stress the inner business of the attitude of mind. But we shall understand cultus as the action embracing both the inner life and the outward phenomenon which above all endeavours to re-establish unity with the Absolute, and thereby is also essentially an inner conversion of the spirit and mind.'

[1] Cf. the at present indispensable article '*Kultus*' by Friedrich Pfister in *Pauly-Wissowa-Kroll Real-Enzyklopädie der klass. Altertums-Wissenschaft*, ii. (Stuttgart, 1922), col. 2106-2192 ; also Hermann Hering in *Hauck Real-Enzyklopädie*, 3rd Ed., 7, p. 7.

theoretically formulated by the experts.[1] What the languages call *abōdah* (*task, slave-service*), θεραπεία (*fostering care*, hence *worship*), θρησκεία (*concerning oneself, reverence*), λατρεία (*service*), ἐπιμέλεια (*watchful care*), λειτουργία (*liturgy, official service*), ἱερουργία (*sacred rites*), cultus (*cult, fostering care*), officium (*obligation*), servitium (*service*), Verehrung (*reverence, worship*), Gottesdienst (*divine service*), Dienst (*service*), *service, worship*, and so forth, that has been recognised by the clear eye of a Schleiermacher, a Hegel, a Richard Rothe, and many another, as something practical.[2]

Cult is a practical dependence upon, a practical attitude towards, the deity on the part of a single individual or of a community. It is a *modus colendi Deum*. It is not essential that it be a formal or collective attitude towards the deity; each stammering ejaculatory prayer of a single person is cult. But cult becomes historically influential (and generally only can be grasped at all historically) where it has developed into the foundation of a church or community. When that has occurred we make an objective word from the subjective *cult*, and 'a' cult is seen as a particular historical phenomenon, we set it alongside others similar or dissimilar, and thus form the plural *the cults*, distinguish the cults from one another and examine how they have arisen, how they have been developed, how the cults have each formed its own cultus.

Anyone who regards primitive Christianity as a phenomenon in cult-history will thereby raise a protest

[1] Even in cases where both usage and theory had perhaps only the narrower use of cultus in mind.

[2] These judgments (Schleiermacher uses the words 'Representative dealing'; Rothe has a similar expression; Hegel's phrase is, 'that the Cultus is the highest act of the human mind'), are well known. Cf. K. R. Hagenbach, *Encyklopädie und Methodologie der Theologischen Wissenschaften*, Leipzig, 1884, p. 444 f.

against the still wide-spread doctrinaire view that in
the Gospel (or in the two types of the 'double' Gospel)
we are concerned chiefly with doctrines of God and of
divine affairs, with theories which Jesus held, and
theories about Jesus, with 'Weltanschauung,' with a
chapter out of the History of Ancient Thought. This
protest does not overlook the fact that doctrine had an
important place even in the earliest times, but it does
not see in doctrine the main emphasis of the history.
It is indeed not entirely false, but it is a distortion or be-
fogging of the basal facts to deal with the inner history
of the beginnings of our religion in the two chapters
'The Teaching of Jesus' and 'The Teaching of the
Apostles.' The sacred history of those early days
actually had the source of its inner progress in the fact
that the Messianic movement released through the
Gospel of Jesus with its thoroughly practical attitude
towards the approaching end of the world and the
immediately expected Kingdom of God, in the end was
historically consolidated into a cult, a cult of Jesus as
Lord. To put it in other words; the Gospel became
transformed into Christianity.

The dividing line, which goes through the whole of
the history of Religion by means of which we are able
to differentiate in particular the separate types of
contemplation [1] and mysticism,[2] of course also goes
through the history of the cults. Cults are either
'acting' cults or 're-acting' cults. In both cases
an action takes place. But in the first type the
action is a spontaneous performance of the individual
or of the community, intended to produce in response
to it a performance on the part of the deity, effective
through its own execution, effective as *actio acta*,

[1] Cf. above, p. 105.
[2] Cf. above p., 79 f., and below, Chapter VI.

as *opus operatum*. In the second, the reacting type, on the other hand, the action of the man is an action in response, a reaction. Here it is God Himself who is really the *Leitourgos*, the *Theourgos* in the highest sense ; the individual or the community only says the amen.

These two types of cult behind which the battle of shadowy giants, champions in the hoary strife between works and faith, between man's will and God's Grace, is fought out, were grasped with admirable clearness in the Augsburg Confession when it contrasted the cult of Law and the cult of the Gospel and perceived the cult of the Gospel to be a reaction.

'The evangelical cult and service is acceptance, an acceptance of good things from God. On the other hand, the legal cult is an offer : we offer and present our good things to God. But it is utterly impossible for us to offer anything to God unless we have already been reconciled and born again.' [1] But Paul, the protagonist, himself long ago distinguished the two types by inimitably sharp contrasting formulæ, in denying *self-made cult* [2] and commending the *spiritual cult*. [3] He even reached the summit of cult intuition when he testified of a prayer that it was no human performance, but the gracious gift of the Spirit, [4] a prayer that Paul did not pray, but the Spirit.

I can only here touch upon the alluring questions that open out of this, concerning the mingling of the

---

[1] Article III. (R. 126, I. T. Müller, p. 140), " Ita cultus et λατρεία evangelii est accipere bona a Deo ; econtra cultus legis est bona nostra Deo offerre et exhibere. Nihil autem possumus Deo offerre nisi autea reconciliati et renati.' Luther's influence is clear here (cf. the passages given in *Praktische Theologie* of E. Chr. Achelis, Freiburg i. B. and Leipzìg, 1893, p. 217).

[2] Col. ii. 23, ἐθελοθρησκεία. [3] Rom. xii. 1, λογικὴ λατρεία.

[4] Rom. viii. 26 f., cf. above, p. 79.

two types of cult which are observable in the history of
religion, when I say that almost all cults arose as re-
actions ; afterwards when they became established they
were accepted and practically worked as acting cults.
This was the case in Christianity, of course.   The means
by which it was sought to keep Christianity free from
the danger of disfigurement from this source are
amongst the greatest achievements of both Catholic and
Protestant theology.   The Catholic method (coarser,
plainer and more adapted to the mass of men) was the
idea of the Church.   The Protestant method (simpler
and more profound) was the idea of Scripture and even
more the idea of revelation, especially when revelation
was not supposed to be contained within certain chronological boundaries.   Within this precinct, however it
were named, it was possible to tend the holy flame
ignited from God's own volcano, and there over and
over again as the lava became cool to re-melt it in the
fiery flood of the original heat.   But alas when Church
and Scripture themselves became chilled to black stone !
The whole history of Christian religious life can be
understood from this point of view as the struggle of
the reacting against the acting cult, and this struggle
has its eternal exemplar in the conflict between Law
and Faith which Paul lived through and wrestled
through.

What is the origin of a cult ?   This question ought
not to be raised without some knowledge of the difficulty
of the problem which lies behind the idea of *origin*.
The difficulty lies, at least as regards the greater number
of cults, in the extraordinary scantiness of the sources.
And this being so, *origin* can be thought of in the sense
of new creation as little as in the case of most other
spiritual movements of history.[1]   Even where, in the

---

[1] Johannes Weiss, *Das Problem der Entstehung des Christentums*,
Archiv für Religionswissenschaft, 16 (1913), p. 426 f., says perfectly

case of the artificially manufactured cult, like the cult of Antinous, we can observe the process fairly clearly, or where humbug-cults and business-cults scream their litanies, we have not to deal with a *creatio ex nihilo*: environment supplies both the disposition to form a cult and the customary usages of a cult, and these even in such cults are the pre-conditions.

Thus the question of the origin of a particular cult cannot be isolated any more than a newly formed volcano can be examined as an isolated phenomenon of Nature. Cults originate from the upward thrust of energies already present. Anyone who is interested in the origin of a cult, and especially in one of the great cults of mankind, finds himself at once placed in the midst of great world-wide contacts with primeval facts of the soul's life. In these his special problem is rooted and out of them no quick and easy answer is to be obtained.

Almost always the investigator, as he feels back towards the limits of knowledge, will come to the twilight or the darkness of a mystery. This is not only because his sources are insufficient, but above all it arises from the fact that the experienced mystery of a

correctly: ' What is " origin " in the life of history altogether? The question must be only raised in order to gain the answer that an " origin " in the sense of an entirely new creation never occurs— whether in History or in Nature—the " new " is always in the broad sense a re-grouping of older elements according to a new principle, based upon stronger forces and unique experience of actuality. Every life-phenomenon, even the strongest, at its entrance into history lies under the necessity of at first using means of expressing itself already in existence ; only gradually and in very modest degree can it proceed to widen the conditions of tradition by new forms of expression. This law prevails nowhere more definitely than in the history of religion.' Eduard Meyer, *Ursprung und Geschichte der Mormonen. Mit Exkursen über die Anfänge des Islâms und des Christentums*, Halle, 1912, is instructive from a methodological point of view with regard to this problem.

miracle is usually at the foundation of a cult.[1] Even the artificially manufactured cults, the products of 'action' alone, require a miraculous starting-point, though it be fictitious, and this is true even of those serving political and business ends. The reacting cults originate, according to their own testimony, practically always from miracle ; according to the testimony of history, which speaks another language, out of the exceptionally moving religious experiences of exceptional people.

Seeing that in the investigation of the origins of a cult there is as a rule something that has to remain unexplained, it might be asked whether this vacuum does not tend to bring the cult itself into question. I answer, No. For its vital influence the cult itself does not stand in need of a foundation mediated through history or indeed historically certain and complete. It is rather a dependence of the soul upon the presence of the Deity, and it has in itself the power continually to transform what we in the academic classroom call 'historical' into present fact. The cult, therefore, hands down the tradition of its own beginnings in the form of a Myth, or a 'Story of Salvation' and pushes them back into the super-historical sphere, that is to say, it makes them eternally present. It recognises no vacuum. It has no historical reading to offer; it opens the picture-book of legends. Genuine cult is never retrospective in the trivial sense of the chronicler of governmental documents and the registrar of archives. The memory of the cult even is not truly retrospective ; it also thinks of the past as present : a thousand years

----

[1] This thesis can be seen particularly richly illustrated in the case of those cults which according to statistics are the immense majority, the Filial-cults ; cf. my sketch *Panagia Kapuli* Die Christliche Welt, 20 (1906), p. 873 ff.

of the sacred past is for it a divinely hallowed to-day : for it the works of God are God working, the story of salvation is salvation now taking place.

Many amongst us have become cult-blind through a modern cult, the cult of the historical. And accordingly they try with historical means either to give Christianity a sure foundation, or to explode it into the air as a troublesome ruin. But Christianity, if it is reacting Christ-cult, cannot be exploded, and requires no historical justification. Its foundations are good. It stands to-day on the same basis upon which it stood originally, that is, it reveals the ever present God through the ever present Saviour.

Thus it is true that for science and for Christian people the question of the origin of Christianity is an inexpressibly important and interesting matter, but for the cult itself it is not fundamental. As cult Christianity lives till to-day by the manifestly great and divinely blessed secret that was revealed to a Galilean fisherman. Not that fisherman, Simon Barjona, but his secret, nay rather his revelation,[1] is the rock upon which the church is built.[2]

It was the Easter experiences of Simon Peter and the others[3] which formed the origin of the Jesus-

[1] Matt. xvi. 17.

[2] That is the transparent profundity of this passage in Matt. xvi. 17 ff., which as it now stands has been much transformed by cult influences.

[3] The most important sources are the monumental sentences, 1 Cor. xv. 1 ff. ; on which compare the penetrating investigations of Karl Holl, *Der Kirchenbegriff des Paulus in seinem Verhältnis zu dem der Urgemeinde*, Sitzungsberichte der Preuss Ak. d. W., 1921, p. 920 ff., and of Adolf von Harnack, *ibid.*, 1922, p. 62 ff. But also in passages such as Lk. xxiv. 34 and 1 Tim. iii. 16, the old formula of confession, ὤφθη, echoes, and in 1 Cor. ix. 1 and John xx. 18, cf. 25, the ἑώρακα (ἑωράκαμεν) is the primitive Easter formula of Confession, somewhat in the tone of the *Courage, ye Mystai !* To my mind it is

cult, exceptionally moving religious experiences of exceptional people. The content of these experiences, which can never be fully analysed by historical means, is described in the same way by men and women : Jesus, they said, appeared to them as one raised up by God from the dead in divine glory, with words of comfort and promise on his lips.

These apostolic experiences are the psychological starting-point of the first Jesus-cult in Palestine and the genuine pre-condition for the rise of the Christian cult-community which now began to organise itself. They transformed the Prophet of the Kingdom of God into the object of apostolic piety, by setting the seal upon His Messianic self-revelation. They even went so far as to cast the reflection of divinity upon the figure of the Messiah—Christ elevated to *Kyrios*, a miracle of grace made out of the tormenting problem of the cross, the Holy Scriptures of old time opened and confessors and prophets made to arise in a great resurrection. With all this the new cult is the classical embodiment of a re-acting cult.

For the understanding of primitive Christianity from the standpoint of the history of religion it is of the utmost importance that we learn to recognise these beginnings of the organised Christian Church, as the beginnings of a new *cult*, the Jesus-Christ-cult.

Jesus Himself established no new cult ; He foretold the new age. But even during His earthly life His person became the centre for His faithful followers : His immense consciousness of His own person had

certain that here we have very ancient primitive Apostolic cult-formulæ. Alfred Seeberg had a fine sense for such things. That Peter was the first to have the sight is unanimous tradition, but John xx. 3 ff. indicates that the competition between Ephesus and Rome (John xx. 4, ἔτρεχον δὲ οἱ δύο ὁμοῦ), between East and West, sought afterwards to weaken the uniqueness of this sight.

exerted a selective and combining influence upon men. So historically the consciousness of Jesus that He was the Christ and the Jesus-cult of the Apostles work into one another : nevertheless the cult itself first came to birth as a result of the mystery of the Apostles' Easter-experiences. And if we cannot penetrate the sacred morning twilight of this secret with light from the torch of exact scientific study and thus reduce the whole ancient mystery into modern obviousness, clear as day, we yet possess in the beginnings of the Jesus-cult an exemplar of the origin of a new cult probably unique in the whole history of ancient religions. And this, disregarding for the moment the real inner value of the apostolic piety, is what distinguishes this new cult from all others : the cult figure did not remain hidden in the cloudland of mythology, but was personally known [1] to most of the first members of the cult as a man of flesh and blood and was daily present to them in imperishable and incomparable words handed down in a living stream of tradition ; the possession of these words was at the same time the protection against the degeneration of the elements of phantasy in the cult into the phantastic.

Looking at the origin of Christianity from below (the right point of view for the historian) there is exposed to our view in that position a great cosmopolitan mixture of races.

The Gospel of Jesus connected the beginnings of our religion most closely with its mother-religion, Judaism. Then the apostolic Jesus-cult cast into the crucible, in the cult nature peculiar to it, an element essentially foreign to Judaism, at any rate on its official

[1] Right up to the fifties of the first century several hundred eyewitnesses were still alive (1 Cor. xv. 6), and blood relations of Jesus lived in Palestine down to an even later date.

side,[1] and thereby in the very moment of its origin received the prophecy of its future break with Judaism and of its world-wide expansion. Through the cult-nature the other group of forces providentially present as part of the *præparatio evangelica* came into creative action : the ancient world of the 'Gentiles.'

Long before that 'Hellenisation' of Christianity which worked itself out in the uplands of later dogmatic thought, and created new forms of expression for the completed cult, the adoption of the apostolic religion had been accomplished in Palestine[2] by means of ancient types of piety foreign to Judaism. The inheritance transmitted by this adoption is not so much the cult itself, with its great content, the Lord, the Kyrios Jesus Christ, but the predisposition of soul, the cult feeling and sentiment, and with that a valuable

[1] On this question I have had many a conversation both in Marburg and Berlin with my revered teacher Hermann Cohen, and have always received the impression that the stone of stumbling is even more the practice of the Christ-cult than the theory involved in it (the doctrine of the deity of Christ). Cohen in 1906 gave a passionate expression to this feeling of protest in an essay *Gedanken über Jugendlektüre* which is now printed in Hermann Cohen's Jüdische Schriften, vol. ii., Berlin, 1924, p. 126 ff. Compare p. 128, ' The cult of the Hero is contrary to our deepest nature,' and p. 129, ' Our religion opposes the deity of Christ.' There was present already in the popular Judaism of Palestine a tendency of thought making for a cult of saints, as the cult of the graves of saints at the time of Jesus shows (cf. e.g. Matt. xxiii. 29; Luke xi. 47 f.). Moreover, in 1909 I observed in Tiberias a cult of graves maintained by Jewish immigrants which had thoroughly ancient features, features which from the point of view of official Judaism were unjewish. Thus even Judaism (right up to to-day) has its sediment of primitive cult-religion.

[2] Bousset's thesis that the Kyrioscult arose in Syria is not illuminating to me. Compare against it also Ed. Meyer, *Ursprung und Anfänge des Christentums*, 3rd Ed., Stuttgart and Berlin, 1923, p. 218. We ought to think of Palestine far more than we have hitherto as penetrated not only with specially 'Hellenistic' influences but also with a general tendency towards cosmopolitan cult ideas.

treasure of forms by which ancient cults expressed themselves in language and ritual.

We can describe this great synthesis in religious history by transforming an illustration which Paul used in conscious paradox.[1] Primitive Christianity, already developed into a cult, was an olive-tree grown in the Holy Land into which the twig of an oleaster, wild yet abounding in strength, was grafted. The wild twig received by this means a part of the strength derived from the roots of the cultivated tree,[2] which on its side gained an accession of fresh life, stimulating new power of growth in its flow of sap.

The outer signs of the primitive apostolic Jesus-cult are recognisable clearly enough in Acts. That book being a pious book for popular reading naturally does not speak of the earliest Church in dry tones, such as would be used, for example, in the statistical tables of our ecclesiastical bureaucracy, but with that depth of religious feeling which one associates with annual meetings of Missionary Societies. The one who told this first missionary story for the community of the saints kindled the enthusiasm both of himself and his readers, and the whole is naturally to be seen in a transfiguring glory of light. But the historical lines are unmistakable. Those who shared cult membership in the living Jesus Christ had already made for themselves the beginnings of an organisation carried on by brother-hood, not by organised communism; possessed in Baptism and the Lord's Supper two sacramental cult-institutions, which can be called the two primitive

---

[1] Rom. xi. 17 ff., cf. above, pp. 38, 98 ; for the consciousness of the paradox compare xi. 24 (*against nature*, παρὰ φύσιν). On this question see Th. Daechsel, *Kulturgeschichtliche Streifzüge durch die Paulinischen Schriften*, Dresden, A, 1910, p. 53 f.

[2] Rom. xi. 17.

Christian Mysteries (using the words in the antique technical sense); and they had already early begun within their environment in Palestine and even as far as Phœnicia, Syria and Cyprus, to carry on propaganda for their cause, in order to gather together the community that would be worthy for the Kingdom of God, so soon expected with the coming of the Lord.

Historically the most remarkable document of this earliest Palestine Jesus-Christ-cult is an Aramaic hieroglyph, which later we find in a letter of Paul,[1] but which arose as a primitive Aramaic word in the Aramaic-speaking primitive Church.[2] It was the ejaculatory prayer sent up longingly to Christ by the believers, perhaps at the end of the celebration of the Lord's Supper :[3]

> Marana tha (Our Lord, Come !)

Thus the early Church sighed to its Lord for His Advent in divine glory at the final Epiphany of the Kingdom of God.

The self-sacrificing enthusiasm of the young community soon led it into the same conflict with those in power which had brought Jesus to His death. The first martyr blood was shed, and at the death of Stephen, the first witness to give his blood, we find the zealous Pharisee, Saul, who was also called Paul, sharing the moral guilt.[4] For the young man sprung from the sultry

---

[1] 1 Cor. xvi. 22, Μαρανα θα; cf. Revel. xx. 20, ἔρχου κύριε Ἰησοῦ! Come, Lord Jesus !

[2] I hold this is the correct view, contrary to Bousset, Kyrios Christos, pp. 103 and 107.

[3] Cf. with this the occurrence of the ejaculation in the earliest known prayer at the Lord's Supper, see Didache, x. 6, εἴ τις ἅγιός ἐστιν, ἐρχέσθω. εἴ τις οὐκ ἔστι μετανοείτω. Μαρανα θα. ἀμήν. He who is holy, let him come ! He who is not, let him repent ! Marana tha. Amen !

[4] Acts vii. 58; viii. 1.

atmosphere of the Cilician plain must have been inspired
with a fanatical hatred of the followers of Jesus of
Nazareth, whose tremendous proclamation of woe
against Pharisaic type of religion was not forgotten.[1]
Step by step the propaganda of the Gospel was followed
by a counter-propaganda of forcible suppression. It
was organised by Saul Paul. In the service of the
same disciplinary authority whose scourgings were later
to lacerate his own back, he hastened—already an
apostle in this—northwards to Damascus,[2] to extinguish
the fire of the new cult which was already glimmering
there.

It was upon this journey and close to the city of
Damascus itself[3] that there came to Paul an experience
which meant an entire transformation. It was his
conversion.

Concerning this event[4] which, though no heathen
historian has noticed, was yet of world-wide importance,
we have two sources : the Apostle's own references,
and three sketches in Acts,[5] not in all their details quite
in agreement with one another, which however—this is
in the very nature of the case—must be in some way
derived from accounts by Paul himself.

Here again, as in the Christophany seen by Peter

[1] Matt. xxiii. and other places.

[2] Gal. i. 13 ff.; Acts ix. 22, 26.

[3] This is derived by combination of Gal. i. 13 with i. 17 without
reference to Acts. For the chronology, which can now, on the basis
of the Gallio-inscription (see below Appendix I.), be reckoned earlier,
cf. Adolf Harnack in the Sitzungsberichte der Kgl. Preuss. Ak. d. W.,
1912, p. 673 ff. Here it is conjectured that the conversion took place
in autumn of the year 31.

[4] Julius Wellhausen, *Kritische Analyse der Apostelgeschichte*,
Berlin, 1914, p. 17 : ' The Christophany at Damascus is in itself an
unshakeable fact.'

[5] Acts ix. 1 ff. ; xxii. 3 ff. ; xxvi. 10 ff.

and by other members of the Easter community, we shall never reach the point of completely unravelling this experience psychologically, not even by the help of the numerous analogous accounts of conversion in the history of religion.[1] But we can decide with a high degree of certainty how Paul himself regarded the occurrence.

He described it once,[2] with the same words which he used of the Christophanies to the other Apostles,[3] words, be it noted, which were already technical words for a divine epiphany in the Septuagint :

> He appeared also to me.

He speaks of the living Christ, and hints that the appearance of Christ to him was the last in a series.

Another time[4] he says with even more of ancient vividness :

> I have seen Jesus our Lord,

or he confesses, using an inner mystical expression :[5]

> I was apprehended of Christ Jesus.

In a fourth case[6] he uses almost modern psychological terms of the experience, speaking of a revelation of God's Son produced by God 'within him'; in a fifth case[7] he says in a more general way that the Christ-mystery has been made known to him by revelation. In the memory of that hour at Damascus there was no doubt always the impression of a tremendous shining light, like the light of the first day of God's Creation

---

[1] On this point compare the valuable hints of Rudolf Otto, ' *Das Auferstehungserlebnis als pneumatische Erfahrung* ' in his *Aufsätze, das Numinose betreffend*, Stuttgart-Gotha, 1923, p. 159-170.

[2] 1 Cor. xv. 8, ὤφθη κἀμοί.   [3] 1 Cor. xv. 5, 6, 7, ὤφθη.

[4] 1 Cor. ix. 1, Ἰησοῦν τὸν κύριον ἡμῶν ἑώρακα.

[5] Phil. iii. 12, κατελήμφθην ὑπὸ Χριστοῦ Ἰησοῦ.

[6] Gal. i. 16, ἀποκαλύψαι τὸν υἱὸν αὐτοῦ ἐν ἐμοί.

[7] Eph. iii. 3, κατὰ ἀποκάλυψιν ἐγνωρίσθη μοι τὸ μυστήριον.

shining out of the darkness, as is hinted in second Corinthians.[1] So too the Book of Acts,[2] using the ordinary colours of antiquity, paints it all in that glorious blaze of light, in which the appearance of the Divine is always represented.

An experience, which Paul regarded as caused by God, which meant the revelation of the living Christ or Christ taking inner possession of him, and which included in itself both an inner transformation and the call to the Apostolate[3] of the before-time persecutor,— that was the occurrence in Damascus for Paul himself. And this characterisation of the conversion is amply sufficient for the historian.

Linking this single experience with the whole of Paul's later mystical experience of Christ, we can obtain one more important result, by combining together two confessions from Galatians. For the man who describes his position as a Christian with the phrase :[4]

Christ lives in me,

Damascus was the beginning of that indwelling of Christ :

God revealed His Son *in me*.[5]

What happened at Damascus ought not to be isolated, but it should be regarded as the basal mystical experience of the religious genius to whom also in later life extraordinary and even ecstatic experiences were vouchsafed.[6] All that can be called Paul's Christ-

[1] 2 Cor. iv. 6, ὁ θεὸς ὁ εἰπών · ἐκ σκότους φῶς λάμψει, ὃς ἔλαμψεν ἐν ταῖς καρδίαις ἡμῶν πρὸς φωτισμὸν τῆς γνώσεως τῆς δόξης τοῦ θεοῦ ἐν προσώπῳ Χριστοῦ.

[2] Acts ix. 3; xxii. 6, 9; xxvi. 13.

[3] Gal. i. 16, ἵνα εὐαγγελίζωμαι αὐτὸν ἐν τοῖς ἔθνεσιν.

[4] Gal. ii. 20, ζῇ δὲ ἐν ἐμοὶ Χριστός.

[5] Gal. i. 16 (see above, p. 129 note 6).

[6] Cf. p. 79 f. above. Rudolf Otto now also emphasises this, see *Aufsätze*, p. 161.

mysticism is the reaction to this initial experience. Damascus is perhaps the clearest example of an initial impulse to reacting mysticism,[1] a mystical initiation arising from a divine initiative.

The conversion of the persecutor into a follower and of the Pharisee Apostle into the Apostle of Christ was a sudden one. Yet it was no magic transformation, but had its psychological preparation both negative and positive.

Negative in the experiences through which the soul of the young Pharisee had gone in its passionate hunger for righteousness under the yoke of the law ; in the letters of the convert decades later we still hear the echo of his sighs at that time : the terrible discovery[2] had come to him as a curse, that even for the most earnest conscience, in fact especially for the most earnest conscience, it was impossible really to keep the whole law.

The positive preparation for the conversion came, on the one hand, through the prophetic inwardness of the Old Revelation which had influenced Paul even as a Jew ; on the other hand, through a relatively close touch with the genuine tradition of Jesus and with the effects wrought by Him in the characters of the confessors whom Paul persecuted. I do not regard it as probable that the young zealot ever was personally acquainted with the earthly Jesus, although weighty voices have again declared recently in favour of this hypothesis.[3] But it is most certainly probable that the Pharisee was acquainted with his opponent through

---

[1] Cf. on this point Chapter VI. below.

[2] Gal. iii. 10, and many sad words in Romans.

[3] The phrase in 2 Cor. v. 16 is to be understood otherwise; if 'we have known Christ after the flesh' (κατὰ σάρκα) refers to personal acquaintance with the earthly Jesus, then the conclusion ' now we know him so no more ' is a triviality.

His words and the influence He continued to exert on His disciples.

So the lightning of Damascus strikes no empty space but finds deep in the soul of the persecutor plenty of inflammable material. We see the flame blaze upwards and after a generation we can still feel that the glow then kindled has lost none of its power in the man grown old : Christ is in Paul, Paul in Christ.

PAUL THE CHRISTIAN (*Continued*)

CHAPTER VI

PAUL THE CHRISTIAN (*Continued*)

PAUL'S SPIRITUAL EXPERIENCE AS CHRIST-INTIMACY (CHRIST-MYSTICISM).
PAUL'S EXPERIENCES OF CHRIST. FUNDAMENTAL CONSIDERATIONS
ABOUT THE NATURE OF MYSTICISM AND ITS TYPES. THE PECULI-
ARITY OF THE PAULINE CHRIST-MYSTICISM.

WE have not merely recognised the secret of Paul's
spiritual life but also described it with sacred Pauline
formulæ when we use the two phrases :

Christ in Paul,[1] Paul in Christ.[2]

It is no doubt generally admitted that Paul's religious
experience was Christo-centric ; but how differently
people view that Christo-centric Christianity of Paul !
Often Christo-centric has been identified with Christological. But Paul's religion is Christo-centric in a much
deeper and more realistic sense. It is not first of all
the product of a number of convictions and elevated
doctrines about Christ ; it is ' fellowship ' with Christ,[3]
Christ-intimacy.[4] Paul lives ' in ' Christ, ' in ' the living

[1] Gal. ii. 20, etc.

[2] Numerous passages. Cf. p. 139 ff. below.

[3] 1 Cor. i. 9 ; x. 16 ; Phil. iii. 10. The inimitably vivid expression
is κοινωνία.

[4] [German, ' Christ-Innigkeit '—W.E.W.] With the coming of this
expression ' *Christ-Innigkeit* ' I hope to render a service to those who
in carrying on Christian work at the present day want to speak about
Paul's Christ-mysticism without using a word so productive of misunderstanding as ' *Christusmystik*.' In using this term ' *Christ-
Innigkeit* ' I am consciously linking on to the ancient usage of *innic*
and *innikeit* in the German mysticism of the Middle Ages (cf. Otto

(135)

and present spiritual Christ, who is about him on all sides, who fills him,[1] who speaks to him,[2] and speaks in and through him.[3] Christ is for Paul not a person of the past, with whom he can only come into contact by meditating on the words that have been handed from him, not a 'historical' personage, but a reality and power of the present, an 'energy,'[4] whose life-giving powers are daily expressing themselves in him,[5] and to whom, since that day at Damascus, he has felt a personal-cult dependence.

The difference between these two conceptions of Paul's Christo-centric religion can be well expressed in Greek by contrasting *Christologos* and *Christophoros*.[6] Certainly Paul was also a *Christological* thinker, but

Zirker, *Die Bereicherung des deutschen Wortschatzes durch die spätmittelalterliche Mystik*, Jena, 1923, pp. 66 f. and 12.) For me the bridge was our word Gott-Innigkeit. For Zirker's other references cf. p. 297 below.

[1] Gal. ii. 20.   [2] 2 Cor. xii. 9.   [3] 2 Cor. xiii. 3.
[4] Phil. iii. 21 ; Col. i. 29 ; Eph. i. 19.
[5] 2 Cor. xii. 9 ; Phil. iii. 10 ; 1 Cor. i. 24 ; v. 4. I have attempted more closely to describe the primitive realism of this Apostolic religion of power in the essay, *Tragende und stählende Kräfte des N.T.*, in the *Festgabe für D. Dr. Julius Kaftan*, Tübingen, 1920, pp. 44-55. French authors have seriously misunderstood my term 'Religion of Power,' cf. *Die Eiche*, 12 (1924), April issue, p. 240 f.

[6] Χριστολόγος and Χριστοφόρος. I have no ancient document to quote for the first word, but the second comes from the earliest ages of Christianity. Probably the first occurrence is Ignatius, Eph. ix. 2, where the Christians appear as '*procession of the God-bearers, and temple-bearers, of Christ-bearers and bearers of holy things*' (ἐστὲ οὖν καὶ σύνοδοι πάντες, θεοφόροι καὶ ναοφόροι, Χριστοφόροι, ἁγιοφόροι). Ancient Christendom used this beautiful word still in the fourth century as a technical term, for example of one specially gifted in prayer, like Paphnutius, a father lately become known to us through the discovery of the considerable remnants of his original writings. Cf. H. Idris Bell, *Jews and Christians in Egypt*, London, 1924, pp. 101 and 108 f. ; accordingly in my *Septuaginta-Papyri*, p. 96 f., in the letter of Justinus, χρηστοφόρ[ῳ] should be read. From the technical term, no doubt the proper name Christopher was quickly derived.

above all and in everything (even in his ' *Christology* ')
he was a *Christ-bearer*.[1]

We must first of all try to understand the Christ of
the Apostle. Usually the attempt is made under the
title ' The Christology of the Apostle Paul.' But it is
more accurate because more in accord with historical
sense to inquire about the 'Christophory' or 'Christolatry' of the Apostle, or, if that sounds too strange,
about his 'knowledge of Christ,' about his 'experiences
of Christ' or his 'revelations of Christ.' Any tendency
to petrify the original fellowship with Christ pulsating
with life into a doctrine about Christ is mischievous.

We ask what Christ did Paul know, experience, carry
with him into the world and bring into the depths of
the souls of his churches? The answer can only be:
it was the spiritual, living Christ.

This certainty of Christ, nevertheless, has different
tendencies. In each case indeed the living, risen Christ
stands at the centre, but two chief, opposing tendencies
can be distinguished.

On the one hand, Christ to the Apostle is the Son of
God 'highly exalted'[2] to the Father, who dwells in
Heaven above 'at the right hand'[3] of God in glory, and
'is coming' soon to the earth as Judge.[4]

This assurance about Christ which has strong Jewish tendencies, being especially influenced by Psalm cx.,
might be called in doctrinaire phrase the assurance of
the transcendence of Christ. In more Pauline phrase,
and therefore historically more correctly, it is called
the assurance of the 'highly exalted' Christ. That

[1] This name is furthermore well fitted to mark him out as a
communion-mystic and to distinguish him from the unity-mystic (on
this distinction cf. what is said below in this chapter).

[2] Phil. ii. 9, ὁ θεὸς αὐτὸν ὑπερύψωσεν.

[3] (Following Ps. cx. 1), Col. iii. 1; Eph. i. 20; Rom. viii. 34.

[4] Cf. the numerous references to the *Parousia* in Paul's letters.

word 'highly exalted'[1] is indeed especially Pauline, and
though in later days it gave very strong stimulus to
dogma, it was originally not a word artificially formed
for dogmatic use, but a simple popular expression of
the assurance about Christ that sprang out of the cult.

Even more characteristically Pauline is the other;
it exhibits more the Hellenistic-mystical tendency of the
experience of Christ : the living Christ is the Pneuma.
As Pneuma, as Spirit the living Christ is not far off,
above clouds and stars, but near, present on our poor
earth he dwells and rules in His own. Here again,
there is no lack of suggestion in this direction in the
Septuagint, and Paul himself created the significant
formulæ :

> The Lord is the Spirit,[2]
> The last Adam became a life-giving Spirit,[3]
> He that is joined to the Lord is one Spirit.[4]

and others like them. Perhaps even more important
than such symbolical phrases is the fact, that in a
number of places Paul makes precisely similar statements of Christ and of the Spirit. This is specially to
be noted in the parallel use of the mystical formulæ
'in Christ' and 'in the (Holy) Spirit.' The formula
'in the Spirit,' which occurs in Paul's writings only
nineteen times, is in almost all these places connected
with the same specifically Pauline fundamental ideas
which elsewhere he connects with the formula 'in

---

[1] Phil. ii. 9 (cf. John iii. 14 ; viii. 28 ; xii. 34).   Certainly Isaiah
xxxiii. 10 according to the LXX sounds like a programme of the Pauline-
Johannine 'Christology' : νῦν ἀναστήσομαι, λέγει κύριος, νῦν δοξασθήσομαι,
νῦν ὑψωθήσομαι' (' Now will I rise up saith the Lord, now will I be
glorified, now will I be exalted ').

[2] 2 Cor. iii. 17, ὁ δὲ κύριος τὸ πνεῦμά ἐστιν.   In the first place this
sentence is an exegetical note on the immediately preceding quotation
from the Septuagint ; but it is also regarded by itself typical for
Paul's view of Christ.

[3] 1 Cor. xv. 45, ἐγένετο . . . ὁ ἔσχατος Ἀδὰμ εἰς πνεῦμα ζωοποιοῦν.

[4] 1 Cor. vi. 17, ὁ δὲ κολλώμενος τῷ κυρίῳ ἕν πνεῦμά ἐστιν,

Christ': faith,[1] righteousness,[2] being justified,[3] being in,[4] standing,[5] rejoicing and joy,[6] free gift,[7] love,[8] peace,[9] sanctified,[10] sealed,[11] circumcised and circumcision,[12] testifying,[13] speaking,[14] being filled,[15] *one* body,[16] the temple of God,[17]—all this is seen and experienced by the Christian who is 'in Christ,' but also by him who is 'in the Spirit'; that means as a matter of fact 'in Christ who is the Spirit.' Therefore also the technical expressions 'fellowship of the Son of God' and 'fellowship of the Spirit' are parallel in Paul's use.[18] For it always refers to the same experience whether Paul says that Christ lives in him,[19] or that the Spirit dwells in us,[20] and whether he speaks of Christ making intercession for us with the Father,[21] or of the Spirit who helps us in prayer.[22]

This Christ-experience of the Apostle might be called in doctrinaire phrase the experience of the immanence of Christ; it is more Pauline and therefore also

[1] Gal. iii. 26, etc.; 1 Cor. xii. 9.

[2] 2 Cor. v. 21, etc.; Rom. xiv. 17.

[3] Gal. ii. 17; 1 Cor. vi. 11.   [4] 1 Cor. i. 30, etc.; Rom. viii. 9.

[5] Phil. iv. 1, etc.; Phil. i. 27.   [6] Phil. iii. 1, etc.; Rom. xiv. 17.

[7] Rom. vi. 23; 1 Cor. xii. 9.   [8] Rom. viii. 39, etc.; Col. i. 8.

[9] Phil. iv. 7; Rom. xiv. 17.

[10] 1 Cor. i. 2; Rom. xv. 16, etc.: cf. 1 Cor. vi. 11 where the two certainties are stressed together.

[11] Eph. i. 13, etc.; Eph. iv. 30.

[12] Col. ii. 11; Rom. ii. 29.   [13] Eph. iv. 17; Rom. ix. 1.

[14] 2 Cor. ii. 17, etc.; 1 Cor. xii. 3.

[15] Col. ii. 10; Eph. v. 18.   [16] Rom. xii. 5; 1 Cor. xii. 13.

[17] Eph. ii. 21; Eph. ii. 22.

[18] 1 Cor. i. 9; Phil. ii. 1; 2 Cor. xiii. 13.

[19] Gal. ii. 20; cf. 2 Cor. xiii. 5; Rom. viii. 10.

[20] Rom. viii. 9; 1 Cor. iii. 16; vi. 19.

[21] Rom. viii. 34 f.

[22] Rom. viii. 26 ff. In John, who calls the Spirit (John xiv. 16, 26; xv. 26; xvi. 7) and Jesus Christ (1 John ii. 1) 'advocate' παράκλητος this great Pauline conviction is still more clearly worked out than in Romans.

historically more correct to speak of the experience of the Spirit-Christ.

This certainty of the nearness of Christ occurs far more frequently in Paul's writings than the thought of the distant Christ 'highly exalted' in Heaven.

Christ in me

—that is indeed a confession poured forth from the depths of the soul, the confession of an assurance which illuminates and holds under its sway the remotest recesses of the ego. Corresponding to this assurance is the other :

I in Christ.

Christ is Spirit ; therefore He can live in Paul and Paul in Him. Just as the air of life, which we breathe, is 'in' us and fills us, and yet we at the same time live in this air and breathe it, so it is also with the Christ-intimacy of the Apostle Paul : Christ in him, he in Christ.

This primitive Pauline watch-word 'in Christ' is meant vividly and mystically, as is the corresponding phrase 'Christ in me.' The formula 'in Christ' (or 'in the Lord') occurs 164 times in Paul's writings : it is really the characteristic expression of his Christianity. Much misunderstood by exegetes, rationalised, applied to the 'historical' Jesus in isolation, and thereby weakened, often simply ignored, this formula—so closely connected in meaning with the phrase 'in the Spirit' — must be conceived as the peculiarly Pauline expression of the most intimate possible fellowship of the Christian with the living spiritual Christ.[1] That it is used by

[1] Compare here and with this whole chapter my essay: *Die neutestamentliche Formel ' in Christo Jesu,'* Marburg 1892. [Now published by J. C. B. Mohr (Paul Siebeck), Tübingen]. It has taken a comparatively speaking long time for the importance of this problem to gain general recognition. At the present time, however, the question is well to the front. I set down here, without any attempt at

Paul with differing shades of meaning is true ;[1] there
are, for example, places where it is already used in a

completeness, the most important contributions: E.
Schräder, *Die Bedeutung des lebendigen Christus für die
Rechtfertigung nach Paulus*, Gütersloh, 1893, pp. 36 ff.
and 52 ; Johannes Weiss, *Paulinische Probleme*, 2. *Die
Formel ἐν Χριστῷ Ἰησοῦ*—Theol. Studien und Kritiken,
1896 ; Wilhelm Karl, *Beiträge zum Verständnis der
soteriologischen Erfahrungen und Spekulationen des Apostels
Paulus*, Strassburg, 1896 ; Julius Boehmer, *Das biblische
'im Namen,'* Giessen, 1898 ; Lucien Delieutraz, *De
l'Importance de l'expression ' ἐν Χριστῷ Ἰησοῦ ' dans
Saint Paul* (Thèse), Geneva, 1899 ; Albrecht Dieterich, *Eine
Mithrasliturgie*, Leipzig, 1903, 2nd Ed., 1910; Wilhelm
Heitmüller, *Taufe und Abendmahl bei Paulus*, Göttingen,
1903 : Joh. Weiss, Monatsschrift für Pastoral theologie, 5
(1909), p. 314 f. ; Mönkemöller in *Lehre und Wehr* (St.
Louis), 1911 ; Bernhard Weiss, *Theol. Stud. u. Krit.*, 1911, p.
531 ff. ; W. Bousset, *Kyrios Christos* (1913), p. 142 ff. ;
Eduard Norden, *Agnostos Theos*, Leipzig, 1913, p. 19 ff. ;
Traugott Schmidt, *Christus in uns—Wir in Christus*
(Dissertation), Göttingen, 1913, cf. also his posthumous
book : *Der Leib Christi* (Σῶμα Χριστοῦ), Leipzig, 1919 ;
Hans Böhlig, *Ἐν κυρίῳ* in *Neutestamentl. Studien für
Georg Heinrici*, Leipzig, 1914, p. 170 ff. ; Joh. Weiss, *Das
Urchristentum*, Göttingen, 1914, p. 359 ff. ; Johannes
Lundberg, *Kristusmystiken hos Paulus*, in Uppsala
Universitets Årsskrift, 1916 ; W. Morgan, *The Religion and
Theology of Paul*, Edinburgh, 1917, Part II. ; Kurt Deissner,
Paulus und die Mystik seiner Zeit, Leipzig, 1918, 2nd. Ed.,
1921 ; H. A. A. Kennedy, *The Theology of the Epistles*,
London, 1919, Part I., Chap. VI. ; Hans Emil Weber, *Die
Formel ' in Christo Jesu' und die paulinische
Christusmystik*, Neue kirchliche Zeitschrift, 1920; J. P. Bang, *Var
Paulus Mystiker ?* Teologisk Tidsskrift, 1920 ; A. M. Brouwer,
Paulus Mysticus ? Utrecht, 1921 ; Rudolf Paulus, *Das
Christusproblem der Gegenwart*, Tübingen, 1922 ; José M. Bover, S.J., *La
Unión Mistica ' en Cristo Jesús' según el Apóstol San Pablo*, Barcelona,
1922 ; Lyder Brun, *Zur Formel ' in Christus Jesus' im Brief des
Paulus an die Philipper*, Symbolae Arctoae, fasc. I., Kristiania (Oslo),
1922, p. 19 ff. ; E. von Dobschütz, *Zeit und Raum im Denken des
Urchristentums*, Journal of Biblical Literature, 41 (1922) ; Otto Schmitz,
in the book referred to more fully below on the use of the genitive by
Paul (1924), p. 238 ff. ; Ernst Sommerlath, *Der Ursprung des neuen
Lebens nach Paulus*, Leipzig, 1923, p. 65 ff. ; Wilhelm Mundle, *Das
religiöse Leben des Apostels Paulus*, Leipzig, 1923, p. 73 ; Wilhelm
Weber, *Christusmystik*, Leipzig, 1924, especially p. 51 ff.

[1] Johannes Weiss and others have rightly drawn attention to this
point.

really formal sense. And it may reasonably be assumed that the Christ-intimacy of the Apostle itself had also its differing degrees of elevation. After the mountain peak of Damascus there followed the normal life in Christ moving upon a less exalted plane of personal experience, then in the rare times of trouble and consecration it rose again to a passionately intensified communion of prayer with the Saviour.[1]

Related to this, if not identical with it, is the similarly misunderstood formula ' through Christ,' which also in far the greater number of cases is to be referred to the spiritual Christ.[2]

It may now be asked What was Paul's conception of the spiritual Christ ? The answer depends upon the way in which the Spirit, as Paul uses the term, is defined. Here it seems best to start with the sharp contrast always made between *pneuma*, spirit, and *sarx*, flesh. *Pneuma*, at any rate, is something not *sarkic*,[3] not earthly,[4] not material. True, the Spirit-Christ has a *soma*, a body, but a spiritual body,[5] that is a heavenly body,[6] a body consisting of divine effulgence.[7] Sharp, philosophically pointed definition of the concept of 'spiritual' is happily absent from Paul's writings. The Apostle remains popular, and in ancient style, vivid in his formulation. He probably thought of some light, ethereal form of existence, such as he doubtless attributed to God. But there is no binding definition. We have the greatest possible latitude if we desire to transplant the Apostle's ideas of Christ into our religious thinking. To Paul the Spirit, God, the living Christ is

[1] Cf. e.g., 2 Cor. xii. 8 f.

[2] Cf. Adolph Schettler, *Die paulinische Formel ' Durch Christus,'* Tübingen, 1907.

[3] The classical passage is 1 Cor. xv. 35 ff.

[4] 1 Cor. xv. 47 ff. [5] 1 Cor. xv. 45 f.

[6] 1 Cor. xv. 47 ff. [7] Phil. iii. 21.

a reality, the reality of all realities ; therefore he does not puzzle about definitions. The Spirit that is living in Paul searches all things, even the deep things of God [1] but it brings to light no definition of God. Religious definitions are always attempts at salvage, but Paul had not suffered shipwreck over the problem of Christ's person.

If Paul had attempted a definition, he would have defined like a man of the ancient world, in a manner more realistic, more massive, more concrete perhaps than a speculative thinker of our own times, but certainly not in ordinary materialistic terms. The Spirit has nothing of the fleshly, nothing of the earthly ; it is divine, heavenly, eternal, holy, living, and life-giving— these are all predicates which Paul applies to it or could apply, and they can all also be applied to the spiritual Christ.

But here there is a point that must not be overlooked.[2] The Spirit-Christ of Paul is no feeble, indistinct image set up by the phantasy-producing power of religious imagination, which evaporates into a boundless, empty cloudland ; on the contrary, He has his hold on concrete reality at the cross. He is, and remains, the crucified.[3] That is to say, mystical communion with the Spirit-Christ transforms all that we call the 'historical' Christ, all that found its climax on Golgotha, all that had been entrusted to the Apostle as tradition about Jesus, into a present reality. It is here that the mystical dependence [4] of the cult religion shows itself particularly clearly. The basis of facts in the past, which, when regarded only as material for christological formulations, may easily become wooden and thus impossible to assimilate,—this, as it is made a present reality by the

[1] 1 Cor. ii. 10.   [2] Cf. below, Chapter VIII.
[3] ἐσταυρωμένος, Gal. iii. 1 ; 1 Cor. i. 23 ; ii. 2.
[4] See above, pp. 121, 122.

mystical power of the cult, receives again its flow of
sap. Thereby also the Christ-mystic is protected from
the danger that threatens him of becoming a 'reed
shaken by the wind' and 'a man clothed in soft raiment'
—the danger that the straying of 'believing thoughts
into the broad fields of eternity'[1] may lead to nothing
better than vague, stumbling wandering.

These great certainties, too, it must be confessed,
were not 'defined' by Paul. What he introduced into
Christ-mysticism was not definitions, but a rich treasure
of technical phrases, which express often in popular
pictorial language the spiritual communion between
Christ and His own. The not unimportant problem of
setting forth in order this technical vocabulary of Paul,
a few details of which we have sketched, has not yet
been solved in all its bearings, and can be mentioned
here only as an object of research.[2] He who desires
to solve it must be at home in the atmosphere and language of the mysticism both of the East and the West.

The question, What according to Paul brings about
the communion with Christ? is answered by the hints
which we have given about Paul's conversion. It is
God Who brings about the communion with Christ.[3]
He has the initiative at the mystic initiation. Not that
every Christian experiences anything like the occurrence
at Damascus, but everyone who possesses the living

[1] Cf. p. 106 above. The quotation is from the opening lines of the
well-known hymn of Johann Gottfried Hermann († 1791).

[2] Cf. the hints in my lectures, *The Religion of Jesus and The Faith
of Paul. The Selly Oak Lectures*, 1923, *on the Communion of Jesus
with God and the Communion of Paul with Christ*, London, 1923, p.
162 ff. (Exegetical Preliminaries).

[3] 1 Cor. i. 9, 30; 2 Cor. i. 21 f.; iv. 6. In this category we must
also place the passages in which Paul speaks of our being chosen and
called by God. They ought not to be isolated and made into a separate
piece of doctrine.

Christ, or the Spirit, has received Him from God, or
has been 'apprehended' by Christ Himself.[1] Those
passages are numerous in which God is celebrated as
giver of the Spirit.[2]

The assertion that according to Paul baptism is the
means of access to Christ, I hold to be incorrect. There
are passages which, taken in isolation, can be made to
prove it,[3] nevertheless it is, I think, more correct to say,
that baptism does not bring about communion with
Christ, but seals it.[4] In Paul's own case, at all events,
baptism was not the deciding factor, but the Christophany at Damascus, and not baptism but preaching the
gospel was in his view the purpose of his apostleship.[5]
Also the Lord's Supper is not for him the real cause of
communion with Christ, but an expression of that communion. It is a peculiarly intimate contact with the
Lord.[6] The Lord's Supper does not bring about the
communion, it only brings it into prominence. Neither
baptism nor the Lord's Supper is regarded as of magical
effect.[7] The decisive factor in each case is God's grace.
The Pauline Christian can say with Paul,[8]

> By the grace of God I am what I am.

Powerful and original as the spiritual experience of
Christ was with Paul, there were not lacking other
stimuli, which influenced him, derived most directly, I

---

[1] Phil. iii. 12.

[2] Gal. iv. 6 ; 1 Cor. vi. 19 ; ii. 12 ; Rom. v. 5 ; viii. 15.

[3] E.g. Gal. iii. 27.

[4] Just as in Rom. iv. 11, circumcision is the seal ($\sigma\phi\rho\alpha\gamma\iota\varsigma$) of the
righteous standing already possessed by Abraham.

[5] 1 Cor. i. 17.   [6] 1 Cor. x. 16.

[7] 1 Cor. x. 1-12. This passage is simply decisive that Paul did
not hold magical ideas. In this case also single passages about the
Lord's Supper must not be isolated, but interpreted along with all the
others.

[8] 1 Cor. xv. 10, $\chi\acute{a}\rho\iota\tau\iota$ $\delta\grave{\epsilon}$ $\theta\epsilon o\hat{v}$ $\epsilon\grave{\iota}\mu\grave{\iota}$ $\ddot{o}$ $\epsilon\grave{\iota}\mu\iota$.

think, from the Septuagint religion. The Greek Old Testament has, and here we must recognise an important Hellenisation of the original, a great number of prominent passages in which the formulæ 'in God' or 'in the Lord' are used in a mystical sense. The words of the prophet :[1]

> Yet I will rejoice in the Lord

sounds like the prelude of the Pauline Jubilate :[2]

> Rejoice in the Lord.

The formula 'in God' which is especially frequent in the Septuagint Psalms is a great favourite with Paul[3] and is closely connected with the formula 'in Christ.'[4] The confession in the speech on Mar's Hill,[5]

> In Him (God) we live and move and have our being,

comes from the pre-Christian Jewish[6] mysticism of Paul which had been inspired by the Septuagint, but Paul did not understand this being-in-God in a neo-platonic sense such as is presented to us in the works of Dionysius the Areopagite. The watchword 'in Christ,' inspired by the Damascus experience, seems to be a more vivid substitute for the sacred formula 'in God.' But it only seems to be so. In reality the wider mystic circle 'in Christ' lies like a concentric circle containing the older circle, as though protecting it and inviting to that holy of holies 'in God,' which from now onwards

[1] LXX., Hab. iii. 18, ἐγὼ δὲ ἐν τῷ κυρίῳ ἀγαλλιάσομαι.

[2] Phil. iii. 1 ; iv. 4, χαίρετε ἐν κυρίῳ.

[3] 1 Thess. ii. 2 ; Col. iii. 3 ; Eph. iii. 9 ; Rom. ii. 17.

[4] 1 Thess. i. 1 ; 2 Thess. i. 1.

[5] Acts xvii. 28, ἐν αὐτῷ γὰρ ζῶμεν καὶ κινούμεθα καὶ ἐσμέν.

[6] The question of Jewish mysticism before Paul's time is one that greatly needs to be solved. The Septuagint version of the Bible, which not infrequently softened the severities of the original in a mystical direction and then as the Greek Holy Scriptures had a further mystical influence, and Philo are the most important sources.

appears really accessible [1] 'through Christ' and 'in Christ.' [2]

To speak of Hellenistic influence is surely justifiable here, when we remember the importance in Greek mysticism of those inspired people who were filled with their God and given power by their God.[3] Placed in the great context of mysticism in general, Paul's religion gains the stamp which indicates its true place in the history of religion. It is Christ-mysticism.

My energetic advocacy of the classification of Paul's religion as mysticism has had all sorts of results for me : sharp aversion and discord, which sometimes expressed itself in explosions of extreme irritation, personal following, at best of a romantic sort (which was no misfortune), at other times tending towards fanaticism (which for many is the most painful thing that earth produces), ridicule, elaborate irony, friendly caution. Looking back upon these experiences, and upon thirty years of most fruitful discussion with my students and at theological conferences and lecture courses in Germany, Sweden and England it has become perfectly certain to me, that the explanation, which is certainly to be desired, is only possible, as also in the cult question,[4] by first of all coming to an understanding as to the idea conveyed by *mysticism*. I ought to have done this before. We talk at cross purposes and over one another's heads if we do not do it. And discussion

[1] Eph. ii. 18 ; iii. 12 ; Rom. v. 2 ($\pi\rho\sigma\alpha\gamma\omega\gamma\dot{\eta}$).

[2] Cf. the diagrams in the Appendix.

[3] Of great importance is R. Reitzenstein, *Die hellenistischen Mysterienreligionen*, Leipzig and Berlin, 1910 (2nd Ed., 1920), who rightly indicates that Paul was a mystic even before his conversion. Kurt Deissner, *Paulus und die Mystik seiner Zeit* (see above, p. 141 n.), gives a valuable piece of preparatory work in spite of some of his results which are not very illuminating.

[4] See above, p. 113 ff.

carried on internationally [1] adds further misunderstanding, as for example when we translate the English term *Mysticism* (which is used in a by no means bad sense) into German by *Mysticismus*, that word of evil associations.[2]

We must recognise that with us in the last few decades the idea of *Mystik* [3] has been employed by many in a perfectly definite narrow sense, that of the Neoplatonic type of deification mysticism, or to give it a more fitting name mystical oneness with the diety. Many even think of *Mystik* in even narrower ways, having in mind only well-known caricatures and imitations. But this narrowing of the idea is only a recent academic usage. Even at the time when the conflict over Albrecht Ritschl's attitude to mysticism was blazing, Köstlin [4] very justly protested against the narrowing of the idea of mysticism which was already clearly coming into fashion, and Reinhold Seeberg [5] also is on

[1] For our special problem the stimulating chapter 'Is Paul a Mystic' in Robert Harvey Strachan's *The Individuality of St. Paul* (2nd Ed., London, c. 1916) must not be overlooked. Paul Wernle has repeatedly expressed regret at the confused use of language [cf. e.g. Deutsche Lit. Zeitg., 33 (1912), col. 3016 ff., and Die Christliche Welt, 27 (1913), col. 1063 f.] and worked out the narrower and wider use : for his own part, however, he objects to the wider use.

[2] It ought to be emphasised, that according to my observation the numerous English words ending in *-ism* have not the doctrinaire stiffness of the German words in *-ismus*.

[3] Especially in lay circles this word plays a fatal rôle.

[4] *Religion nach dem N.T., mit besonderer Beziehung auf das Verhältnis des Sittlichen und Religiösen und auf das Mystische in der Religion*, Theol. Studien u. Kritiken, 61 (1888), p. 82.

[5] Cf. p. 150 n. 2. It is interesting that younger scholars who have grown up out of living academic contact with the older terminology, as Friedrich Heiler and Wilhelm Koepp, reject the wider usage as a peculiarity of the 'newer' Protestant theology (cf. Fr. Heiler, *Das Gebet*, 2nd Ed., München, 1920, p. 249). Similarly Deissner (2nd Ed., p. 134) calls the narrower usage the 'older' appealing to Heiler. One can see how easily, even in our well-documented world,

the right line when he speaks of the confiscation of the term '*Mystik*' for the Neo-platonic type. Thus I am no innovator, but seek rather to re-establish the old German usage, when I understand '*Mystik*' in the wider sense and give the name *Mystik* to every religious tendency that discovers the way to God direct through inner experience without the mediation of reasoning. The constitutive element in mysticism is immediacy of contact with the diety.

There is a double bifurcation of the types of mysticism according as they are judged by their origin or by their results, and this leads on to a great multitude of blendings and combinations in which widely differing forms are often found in union.

First, when we investigate the question of origins, we see that 'great dividing' line in the history of religion, which we noted in the case of the cult,[1] also drawn through the history of mysticism. The decisive matter is the initiative : who is it that gives (or gave in the first instance) the impulse to the mystical movement of the soul ? There is acting mysticism and re-acting

traditions can be broken. Much valuable material on this question and on the use of language is given by Georg Wobbermin, *Das Wesen der Religion*, Leipzig, 1921, pp. 147 ff., 265 ff., 291 ff., and 457 f.; by Rudolf Otto, *Das Heilige*, 11th Ed., Stuttgart, Gotha, 1923, pp. 21 ff., 99, and *Aufsätze*, p. 71 ff. [English translation of *Das Heilige*, from 9th German Ed., by J. W. Harvey, *The Idea of the Holy*, Oxford, 1923, pp. 21 ff., 88] ; Erich Schaeder, *Das Geistproblem der Theologie*, Leipzig, 1924, p. 18 ff. Wobbermin's concise but full notice in Theol. Lit. Zeitg., 49 (1924), p. 383 f., must also be considered. The therein-mentioned reference to the important British investigators of mysticism, Baron Friedrich von Hügel, William Ralph Inge, and Evelyn Underhill (Mrs. Stuart Moore), I would here emphasise and pass on. It is thanks to these contemporaries that in England an atmosphere peculiarly adapted for the understanding of mysticism has lately been produced.

[1] See above, p. 117 ff.

mysticism, *anabatic* and *catabatic* mysticism. Man approaches God, or God approaches man.[1] Mysticism of performance or mysticism of grace![2] Striving mysticism and mysticism of the divine gift.[3]

Secondly the aim of mysticism is either *unio* or *communio*; either oneness with God, or fellowship with God; either loss of the human personality in God or sanctification of the personality through the presence of

---

[1] 'The one asserts ability to control God, the other to be controlled by God, the one to compel God, the other to be compelled by God.' (G. Mehlis, *Formen der Mystik*, Logos II., p. 242 f., rightly quoted by H. E. Weber (Neue kirchliche Zeitschrift, 31 (1920), p. 234) as a good characterisation of the types.

[2] Reinhold Seeberg (*Christliche Dogmatik*, vol. i., p. 42 f., Leipzig, 1924), with a profound knowledge of the subject, makes a similar classification : ' The specific distinguishing characteristic of religious mysticism' consists in this ' that the human will feels itself moved by the divine will without any rational intervention being recognised.' Similarly (p. 63 f.) mystical experiences consist ' in a movement of life or will directly caused by the divine energy, and this forms an inspiration which powerfully sets in motion the whole inner life.' He goes on to describe the transformation of this ' voluntative mysticism of experience with its fresh and living religious life,' into the ' mysticism of knowledge ' (p. 64), in which the object ' is the increase of knowledge obtained by means of ecstatic gaze or contemplation guided by cult methods.' ' This form of mysticism, which through Neo-platonism has penetrated deeply into Christianity and for that reason has often in current usage appropriated the term mysticism for itself, is really to be regarded as a phenomenon of the senility of religion or of periods in the history of religion threatened with scepticism ' (p. 64). This is important also for the question as to the meaning of the term mysticism which was touched upon above. For the distinction between acting and re-acting mysticism, cf. the words of Tillich quoted in note 3 to page 80 above. My distinction between acting and re-acting mysticism (first made in *The Religion of Jesus and the Faith of Paul*, London, 1923, p. 196 ff.) is approved by A. E. Garvie, The Expository Times, Vol. 36, No. 6 (March, 1925), p. 250.

[3] [In the German the word ' charismatisch ' is used, which it seemed better to paraphrase, as in English ' charismatic ' is not in frequent use.—W.E.W.].

God ; either transformation into the deity, or conforma-
tion of the human towards the divine ; either participa-
tion in the deity or prostration before the deity.   In
fact ego-centric mysticism or Theo-centric mysticism !
Mysticism of æsthetic intoxication or mysticism of
ethical enthusiasm !   Mysticism that denies personality,
or mysticism that affirms personality ! [1]

I make no attempt to set forth in detail those
blendings and combinations of the different types, nor
to describe even for example the reaction mysticism
which has lost its original nature and become reduced
to the pure acting type, or the acting *unio*-mysticism, or
the peculiar form of *communio*-mysticism which develops

[1] The further development of the characterisation formulated
above has been the special work of Nathan Söderblom.   To his
writings already cited by F. Heiler in *Das Gebet* the following should
be added : *Ett bidrag till den kristna uppenbarelsetrons tolkning*
(Uppsala Universitets Årsskrift, 1911, Program 6) ; *Översikt av
allmänna religionshistorien*, 3rd Ed., Stockholm, 1919 ; *Baron Friedrich
von Hügels andliga självdeklaration* in *Studier tillägnade Magnus
Pfannenstill*, Lund, 1822, p. 168 f.   The Archbishop in a letter of
Sept. 26, 1924, referred me to his lectures at Munich on the difference
between practising mysticism and revelation-mysticism.   This last
formulation is related to my own (acting and re-acting mysticism).
Cf. also Adalbert Merx, *Idee und Grundlinien einer allgemeinen Geschichte
der Mystik* (Academical Address), Heidelberg, 1893, p. 10 :   'The aim
of the endeavours of such souls is to attain complete insight into the
Being of God ; and the progressive unity with Him that is derived
from that is thought of by some as losing oneself in Him, by others is
regarded as compatible with the retention of their own personality.'
Heiler's well-known division of personal religion into mysticism and
prophetic religion, is like a division of railway trains into passenger
trains and express trains.   But no doubt he had in mind the narrower
type of mysticism.   General-Superintendent Zoellner very correctly
formulates Christian *communio*-mysticism in the journal ' Das Evangelische Deutschland, 1 (1924), p. 12 :   'Even Christianity recognises
mysticism, even Christianity emphasises the irrational.   But it is the
mysticism of fellowship with the personal God, which does not
extinguish personality and self-consciousness but raises them to
perfection.'

into *unio*-mysticism.   Only I must obviously explain
one thing, namely how I classify Paul, the mystic.[1]

Paul is a reacting mystic and a *communio*-mystic.
He was even as a Jew a fellowship mystic, but an
acting mystic at any rate as regards his longings,[2] only
it would seem that through his action he did not reach
real communion with God.[3] He felt the fact that he
remained far off from God to be the bankruptcy of
'works,' the tragedy of this can still be felt as we read
the letters he wrote as a Christian.   It was Damascus
that transformed his acting mysticism into the reacting
mysticism and the soul shaken and thrown open to
creative energy by that impact from that time onwards
had its firm support 'in Christ' :   In communion with
Christ he found communion with God ;[4]   Christ-intimacy

---

[1] I have referred above (p. 114 n. 2) to E. von Dobschütz, who in his
great review of my *Licht vom Osten*, 4th Ed. (just the sample of what
a critique intended to encourage a colleague should be), in denying my
theory of a Christ-cult, founds his argument upon too narrow a conception of cult.   The same applies to his criticism of my view
of Paul as a mystic (in above-mentioned review, p. 326 ff.).   Here also
he works with an entirely too narrow conception, not without letting
it be seen later that a wider conception of mysticism is possible, but to
use it is to regard all piety as mystical (p. 327, cf. p. 329).   I would
not entirely deny the last.   But for the rest there is some misunderstanding, if von Dobschütz (p. 328) thinks I class mysticism with the
mysteries.   The mysteries are in most cases mysticism which has
developed into a cult, but everywhere where they have degenerated to
pure action they have been false to their origin and replace mysticism
by magic.   On the other hand, there are very numerous forms of
mysticism which are (and remain) free from the mysteries.

[2] He himself would probably have spoken of it as ἀποκαραδοκία,
Rom. viii. 19.

[3] This can be expressed with his words of Rom. xi. 7 (though they
referred to something else), ὁ ἐπιζητεῖ Ἰσραὴλ τοῦτο οὐκ ἐπέτυχεν, 'That
which Israel seeketh for, that he obtained not.'

[4] Here I think I touch H. Weber's more profound conception (*Die
Formel 'in Christo Jesu,'* p. 229 f.).

was experience and confirmation of God-intimacy.[1]
He was not deified nor was he transformed into spirit
by this communion, nor did he become Christ. He was
not like some who at a later day imagined themselves
Christ,[2] though they were only possessors of a second-
hand Christology and were further removed from Christ
than was Paul.[3] But he was transformed by God, he
became spiritual and he was one whom Christ possessed[4]
and a Christ-bearer.[5]

Paul himself was conscious of the difference between
acting and reacting mysticism. His conflict with the
' spirituals ' at Corinth[6] is the protest of reacting mysticism against the ecstatic chaos caused by the mysticism
of intoxicated enjoyment developing into unrestrained
action. But he had also conquered in the same battle

[1] Cf. the diagram below in the Appendix. For this whole
section see also the valuable attempt at a general statement made by
Wilhelm Weber (Mannheim) in *Christus-Mystik. Eine religions-
psychologische Darstellung der paulinischen Christusfrömmigkeit*, Leipzig, 1924 (in H. Windisch's *Untersuchungen zum Neuen Testament*,
Heft 10).

[2] Gal. ii. 20, cf. iv. 19 and other passages are not intended in this
sense.

[3] Cf. Harnack, *Lehrbuch der Dogmengeschichte*, i., p. 788 (4th Ed.,
1909).

[4] Gal. iii. 29; v. 24; 1 Cor. i. 12; iii. 23; xv. 23; 2 Cor. x. 7 (cf.
Licht vom Osten, 4th Ed., p. 322 f.).

[5] Cf. above, p. 136. Paul might also be called one who was ' through-
Christ ' if the vivid expression were not too unusual. I saw the word
durchchristen (although used in an un-Pauline acting sense) first in
Christian Morgenstern's *Wir fanden einen Pfad, Neue Gedichte*,
München, 1919, p. 18 :

> ' . . . doch wer's ganz vollbringet,
> siegt sich zum Stern,
> Schafft, sein selbst Durchchrister,
> Neugottesgrund—
> und ihn grüsst Geschwister
> Ewiger Bund.'

[6] 1 Cor. xii-xiv.

within his own breast, when the old mystical activism
had whispered to him its words of temptation, *eritis
sicut Deus*—' ye shall be as God.'   No doubt it was out
of such a struggle that that wonderful paradox was
born :

I—yet not I

which repeatedly flashes out of the lines of his letters.[1]

A generation ago, in my student days, a heavy hand
stretched out from the side of the dogmatists and
banished mysticism, which was forced into one narrow
pattern, from the German lecture-rooms.[2]   The study

---

[1] 1 Cor. xv. 10 (cf. also vii. 10) ; Gal. ii. 20.

[2] For criticism of Ritschl's position cf. Wilhelm Dilthey, *Das
Problem der Religion*, 1911, in Gesammelte Schriften, vol. vi., 2nd
half, Leipzig and Berlin, 1924, p. 300 f.   I would like to quote
Dilthey's most interesting words : ' If Ritschl and his school thought
more historically, if frankly in Ritschl's historical intuition the course
of historical process was more profoundly grasped in the concrete
example of Christian piety, if he endeavoured to understand the value
of the religious structure through a study of its actuality in history,
if he made a freer pathway for theology, by discarding with neo-
Kantianism every rational, metaphysical system, and so making a
freer broader space for the irrational character of religion, yet this
remarkable mind was at the same time so closely confined, that thereby
everyone of his fundamental conceptions were, in spite of their deriva-
tion from history, not true to history.   The outlook on universal
history [typical of Schleiermacher's] Reden, in which lay the germ
of the coming general science of religion, was given up by him.
Schleiermacher's recognition of the importance of mysticism in religion
was pushed on one side owing to an unhistorical hatred of the mystical
element in religion.   The importance of religious experiences in the
history of what religion has produced were beyond the comprehension
of this dry-as-dust mind.   Thus also in concentrating his studies upon
Christianity alone he failed to give true value to the experience which
lies at the basis of Christianity.   For the experience of Jesus of God's
action in Him, can only be thought of as a mystical experience, that
is as immediate perception.   And just as he did not understand the
importance of mysticism in the experience of Christ Himself so like
the experience of Paul in visions, the ecstacies of the solitaries become

of Paul suffered, along with other things, from this anathema. The few scholars who then emphasised the mystical element in Paul could have appealed to teachers greater than Albrecht Ritschl. Luther[1] and Calvin had a sympathetic understanding of the Apostle's Christ-mysticism, and going further back we find the real Paul alive in the ancient Church, especially in the Greek Fathers.[2] But the greatest monument of the most genuine understanding of Paul's mysticism is the gospel and epistles of John. Their Logos-Christ is the Spirit-Christ, once more made incarnate for the congregation of the saints in a time of fierce conflict, by the evangelist who was inspired in equal degree by the earthly Jesus, by Paul and by the Spirit-Christ.

This also supplies the answer to the question, How did Paul influence later thought? The witty saying that in the second century only *one* man understood Paul (Marcion) and he misunderstood him, only has truth in it, if the enquiry as to Paul's influence is confined to his ' doctrine,' perhaps indeed to the ' doctrine of Justification.' But if enquiry be made about Christ-mysticism, the traces of the Apostle's influence are clear, and shine through from the most ancient times down to our own day, being seen not least clearly in the two Catholic Churches.

There can be no doubt that Paul became influential

confused with the neo-platonic aceticism, vision and ecstacy. In pantheistic mystic, in the religious life of the sects and in pietism he only saw counterfeits of Christianity.'

[1] Hans Emil Weber has rightly drawn our attention to the pressing need of a clear light on the Christ-mysticism of Luther (*Das Geisteserbe der Gegenwart und die Theologie*, Leipzig and Erlangen, 1925, p. 86).

[2] It is an indication of good understanding that even in the fourteenth century Nikolaos Kabasilas entitled his book on Mysticism ' Life in Christ ' ($\pi\epsilon\rho\grave{\iota}$ $\tau\hat{\eta}\varsigma$ $\dot{\epsilon}\nu$ $X\rho\iota\sigma\tau\hat{\varphi}$ $\zeta\omega\hat{\eta}\varsigma$). Cf. *Die Mystik des Nikolaus Cabasilas*, edited and explained by W. Gass, Greifswald, 1849.

in the world's history precisely through his Christ-mysticism.[1] The spiritual Christ was able to do what a dogmatic Messiah could not have done. The dogmatic Messiah of the Jews is fettered to the country of his origin. The spiritual Christ could move from place to place. Coming from the East, He could become at home in the West, and in defiance of changing centuries He could spread out His arms over every generation.

> The Spirit bloweth where it listeth.[2]

Paul would certainly not have had this influence on the great scale, if the fires of the mystical elements in him had consumed the ethical. On the contrary, the ethos in his case stood the test of fire. The Pauline Christ-intimacy is no magic transformation, and it is no intoxication of ecstatic enthusiasts who are left as yawning sluggards when the transport is over. Paul himself subordinated ecstasy to ethos.[3] Thus we may rightly and fittingly apply to him the conception of ' voluntary ' mysticism, which has lately come into vogue, understanding thereby ' the inner coming of the spiritual life-energy which directs us in the depths of our own being.'[4] Christ-mysticism is in him rather a glowing fire than a flickering flame. He who was ' apprehended ' by Christ speaks with deep humility :[5]

> Not that I have already obtained [Him].

But he also makes the heroic confession :[6]

> I can do all things in Him that strengtheneth me.

---

[1] Cf. with this also Max Meinertz, *Mystik und Mission*, Zeitschrift für Missionswissenschaft, 13 (1923).

[2] John iii. 8.   [3] 1 Cor. xiii. 1-3.

[4] R. Seeberg, *Die Lehre Luthers* (*Lehrbuch der Dogmengeschichte*, iv., 12/3), Leipzig, 1917, p. 310. Cf. above, p. 150 n. 1. For historical information on ' voluntary ' mysticism see Erich Seeberg, *Zur Frage der Mystik*, Leipzig and Erlangen, 1921, p. 30 ff.

[5] Phil. iii. 12 ff., οὐχ ὅτι ἤδη ἔλαβον . . .

[6] Phil. iv. 13, πάντα ἰσχύω ἐν τῷ ἐνδυναμοῦντί με.

Similarly, too, the gifts of the Spirit set the saints of Paul's churches mighty tasks : they who had ' put on Christ,'[1] were daily to put Him on anew,[2] and 'in' this Christ only that faith is of value whose energy is proved by love.[3]

Let us look back for a moment ! Christ the Living, exalted with the Father, but by God's Grace as Spirit in Paul and Paul in Him—that is the Apostle Paul's assurance of Christ and experience of Christ. According to the doctrinaire view 'Paulinism' contains at this point an 'antinomy' through the 'dualism' of the transcendence and immanence of Christ. But in fact we see here two moods of Paul's piety, which could exist side by side in his great soul. They no more represent an internal contradiction than do the mutually intertwined experiences of the transcendent and the immanent God which every believer knows. Rather it is the polar contrast of these two moods that gives the inner life of the Apostle its prophetic tension.

This tension finds its release in an abundance of detailed assurances, experiences, and confessions.

---

[1] Gal. iii. 27. [2] Rom. xiii. 14.
[3] Gal. v. 6, πίστις δι' ἀγάπης ἐνεργουμένη.

THE JOURNEYS OF ST. PAUL

The Biblical sources for the routes, which are numbered as they appear on the map, *The World as known to St. Paul.*

1. *Tarsus-Jerusalem* Acts 22_3.
2. *Jerusalem-Damascus* Acts 9_9.
3. *Damascus-Arabia* Gal 1_{17}.
4. *Arabia-Damascus* Gal 1_{17}.
5. *Damascus-Jerusalem* Gal 1_{18}.
6. *Jerusalem-Tarsus* Acts 9_{30} Gal 1_{21}.
7. *Tarsus-Antioch in Syria* Acts 9_{25} Gal 1_{21}.
8. *Antioch in Syria-Seleucia Pieria-Cyprus-Perga-Antioch in Pisidia-Iconium-Lystra-Derbe-Lystra-Iconium-Antioch in Pisidia-Pisidia-Pamphylia-Perga-Attalia-Seleucia Pieria-Antioch in Syria* Acts 13_{14} 2 Tim 3_{11}.
9. *Antioch in Syria-Jerusalem* Gal 2_1 Acts 15_3.
10. *Jerusalem-Antioch in Syria* Acts 15_{30} Gal 2_{11}.
11. *Antioch in Syria-Syria-Cilicia-Derbe-Lystra-Phrygia-Galatia-Alexandria Troas-Samothrace-Neapolis-Philippi-Amphipolis-Apollonia-Thessalonica-Beroea-Athens-Corinth-Cenchreae-Ephesus-Caesarea-Stratonis-Jerusalem-Antioch in Syria* Acts 15_{40}-18_{22} Gal 4_{13} ff 1 Thess 2_2 2_1 3_1 1 Cor 2_1 ff.
12. *Antioch in Syria-Galatia-Phrygia-Ephesus* Acts 18_{23}-19_1.
13. *Ephesus-Corinth-Asia (Miletus?),* by combining 1 and 2 Cor and 2 Tim 4_{20}.
14. *Asia (Miletus?)-Alexandria Troas-Macedonia-Illyricum-Nicopolis-Corinth* Acts 20_1 f 2 Cor 1_8 2_{12} 7_5 Rom 15_{19} Tit 3_{12}.
15. *Corinth-Macedonia-Alexandria Troas-Assos-Mitylene-Chios-Samos-Trogyllium-Miletus-Cos-Rhodes-Patara-Cyprus-Tyre-Ptolemais (Ace)-Caesarea Stratonis-Jerusalem* Acts 20_3-21_{17}.
16. *Jerusalem-Antipatris-Caesarea Stratonis* Acts 23_{31-33}.
17. *Caesar Stratonis-Sidon-Cyprus-Myra-Cnidus-Crete-Claudia-"Adria"-Melita-Syracuse-Rhegium-Puteoli-Appii Forum-*The Three Taverns-Rome Acts 27 28.

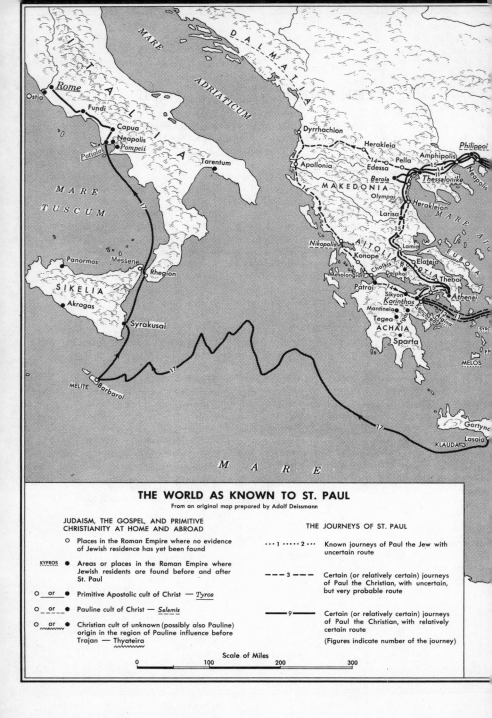

THE WORLD AS KNOWN TO ST. PAUL

From an original map prepared by Adolf Deissmann

JUDAISM, THE GOSPEL, AND PRIMITIVE CHRISTIANITY AT HOME AND ABROAD

○   Places in the Roman Empire where no evidence of Jewish residence has yet been found

KYPROS   ●   Areas or places in the Roman Empire where Jewish residents are found before and after St. Paul

○ or ●   Primitive Apostolic cult of Christ — *Tyros*

○ or ●   Pauline cult of Christ — *Salamis*

○ or ●   Christian cult of unknown (possibly also Pauline) origin in the region of Pauline influence before Trajan — *Thyateira*

THE JOURNEYS OF ST. PAUL

···1·····2···   Known journeys of Paul the Jew with uncertain route

——— 3 ———   Certain (or relatively certain) journeys of Paul the Christian, with uncertain, but very probable route

——— 9 ———   Certain (or relatively certain) journeys of Paul the Christian, with relatively certain route

(Figures indicate number of the journey)

Scale of Miles

0   100   200   300

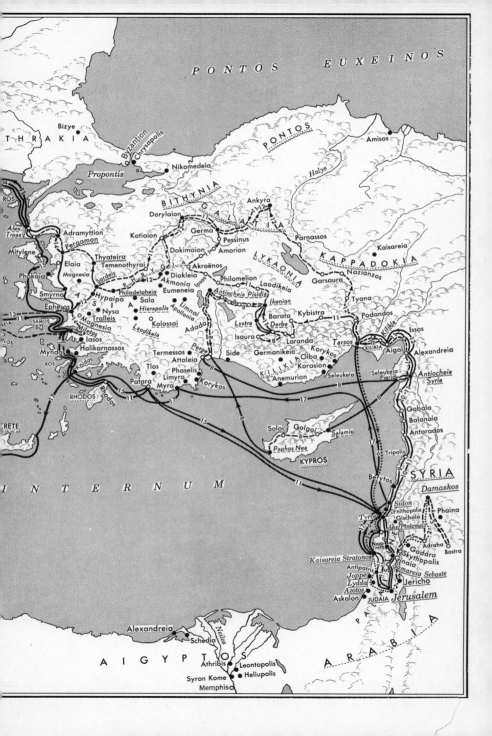

PAUL THE CHRISTIAN (*Continued*)

CHAPTER VII

PAUL THE CHRISTIAN (*Continued*)

'FAITH IN CHRIST' AS THE EXPERIENCE OF SALVATION. THE UNITY
OF THE EXPERIENCE OF SALVATION, AND THE VARIETY OF ITS
FORMS OF EXPRESSION.

WITH the assurance of Damascus 'Christ in me' and
the assurance of equal content 'I in Christ,' an inexhaustible religious 'energy'[1] was concentrated in the
deep, and to religious impulses extremely sensitive, soul
of the convert. In every direction Paul now radiated
the 'power of Christ'[2] that ruled in him, gave out the
'riches of Christ,'[3] the 'blessing of Christ,'[4] and the
'fulness of Christ'[5] which had come to him.

To designate this abundant 'power of Christ,' which
flowed through him and took effect from him, Paul used
a well-known technical religious word, the Greek term
pistis, which we are accustomed to translate 'faith.'

Though one of the most frequently considered Pauline
'conceptions,' the faith of the Apostle can perhaps be
more precisely formulated than it usually is. Generally
faith as used by Paul is defined as believing ' on ' Christ,
and thus the frequent genitival construction the 'faith of
Christ Jesus,'[6] and the prepositional constructions 'faith

[1] Cf. above, p. 136, notes 4 and 5.
[2] 2 Cor. xii. 9, ἡ δύναμις τοῦ Χριστοῦ ; cf. 1 Cor. v. 4.
[3] Eph. iii. 8, τὸ πλοῦτος τοῦ Χριστοῦ ; cf. ii. 7.
[4] Rom. xv. 29, εὐλογία Χριστοῦ.
[5] Eph. iv. 13, τὸ πλήρωμα τοῦ Χριστοῦ.
[6] πίστις Χριστοῦ Ἰησοῦ, Gal. ii. 16, 20 ; iii. 22 ; Eph. iii. 12 ; Phil.
iii. 9 ; Rom. iii. 22, 26.

in Christ Jesus,'[1] and 'to believe in Christ Jesus,'[2] are identified with belief 'on' Christ.

I believe that this proceeding obliterates a characteristic Pauline feature on one of the most important points. Faith is in Paul's usage faith 'in' Christ, that is to say, faith is something which is accomplished in union of life with the spiritual Christ. That is the meaning of those passages in which Paul connects the preposition 'in'[3] with the words 'faith,' 'believer,' 'believe,' and also of the passages in which the genitival construction appears.

It is not yet generally recognised[4] that Paul uses the genitive 'of Jesus Christ' in a wholly peculiar manner. We have numerous passages in Paul in which the usual rough classification of 'subjective genitive' or 'objective genitive' is insufficient. Later Greek (and Latin) has also in addition to these a genitival use, sometimes rather remarkable, which is to some extent the result of the survival of an older type.[5] So, too, in Paul, it

---

[1] πίστις ἐν Χριστῷ Ἰησοῦ, Gal. iii. 26; v. 6; Col. i. 4; ii. 5 (εἰς); Eph. i. 15; 1 Tim. i. 14; iii. 13; 2 Tim. i. 13; iii. 15.

[2] πιστεύειν εἰς Χριστὸν Ἰησοῦν, Gal. ii. 16; Phil. i. 29 (Eph. i. 13). Cf. 'the faithful in Christ' [lit. believers], πιστοὶ ἐν Χριστῷ Ἰησοῦ, Eph. i. 1; Col. i. 2.

[3] ἐν or εἰς, the distinction between the two prepositions is not great in popular Greek.

[4] Otto Schmitz, *Die Christus-Gemeinschaft des Paulus im Lichte seines Genetivgebrauchs*, Gütersloh, 1924, has now thoroughly investigated this problem. Here and there, perhaps, he sees genitival constructions with too indistinct lines between them, but he has raised for the exegesis of many Pauline passages new questionings and new suggestions by means of abundance of most original, detailed observations. Martin Dibelius (Theologische Blätter, 3 [1924], col. 282 ff.) agrees with the final outcome of Schmitz' work, but reduces the number of these genitives. His weighty hints on the Pauline final clauses ought also to be noted. He rightly regards them also as an example of grammatical phenomena used as expressions of a religious phenomenon.

[5] Cf. E. Nachmanson, *Syntakt. Inschriftenstudien*, Eranos, 9 (1909), p. 30 ff., and Einar Löfstedt, *Genetivus Causae im Latein*, Eranos, 9 (1909), p. 82 ff.

would be possible to establish the use of a special type of genitive, which might be called the 'genitive of fellowship' or the 'mystical genitive,'[1] because it indicates mystical fellowship with Christ. 'Of Jesus Christ' is here in the main identical with 'in Christ.'

'The faith of Christ Jesus' is 'faith in Christ,'[2] the faith which the Christian has in fellowship with Christ.

Numerous other religious root ideas are similarly bound up with the mystical genitive.[3] Alongside 'faith of Christ' we find in Paul the 'love of Christ,'[4] the 'hope of Christ,'[5] the 'peace of Christ,'[6] the 'meekness and gentleness of Christ,'[7] the 'tender mercies of Christ,'[8]

---

[1] The name of this genitive and the problem itself are both rejected by several of my critics with merry irony. There is nothing to prevent them making merry if they like, but I cannot give them the feeling for language which they lack. It is something one either has or has not. Anyone who concerns himself with Greek Syntax, a study, on the whole, unaccountably neglected by our generation, knows what an abundance of interesting new problems there are precisely connected with the use of cases. And original expressions cannot be classified by means of terms whose meaning has been worn away by technical use. Also Wilhelm Havers' 'Dativus Sympatheticus' (*Untersuchungen zur Kasussyntax der indogermanischen Sprachen*, Strassburg, 1911) will raise merriment amongst the critics whose feelings are dulled, but it has awakened 'sympathetic feelings amongst linguists and philologists' (cf. A. Debrunner, Deutsche Lit. Zeitg., 33 (1912), p. 291). Schmitz (p. 237) thinks that there is no need to have a separate name for the genitive considered above. That, of course, is a matter for discussion, but there is some advantage in indicating the problem with a vivid short designation.

[2] Cf. passages above, p. 161, note 2 ff.

[3] [At this point the author says 'this can best be imitated in German by a compound substantive' and writes Christ-faith, Christ-love, etc. Such forms are not really adapted to our English usage, so the genitival forms as they appear in our English Bible are used in translation.—L.R.M.S.].

[4] 2 Cor. v. 14; Eph. iii. 19; Rom. viii. 35, ἡ ἀγάπη τοῦ Χριστοῦ.

[5] 1 Thess. i. 3, ἡ ἐλπὶς τοῦ κυρίου ἡμῶν Ἰησοῦ Χριστοῦ.

[6] Col. iii. 15, ἡ εἰρήνη τοῦ Χριστοῦ.

[7] 2 Cor. x. 1, ἡ πραΰτης καὶ ἐπιείκεια τοῦ Χριστοῦ.

[8] Phil. i. 8, σπλάγχνα Χριστοῦ Ἰησοῦ.

the 'patience of Christ,'[1] the 'obedience of Christ,'[2] the 'truth of Christ,'[3] the 'fear of Christ,'[4] the 'circumcision of Christ,'[5] the 'sufferings of Christ,'[6] the 'afflictions of Christ,'[7] and other similar technical expressions.[8] Throughout it is understood that these special experiences or assurances of the soul in the Christian come about through the mystic-spiritual fellowship with Christ.

So too 'the faith of Christ' is faith which is alive in fellowship with the spiritual Christ, and it is faith 'on'[9] God, in its content identical with the faith which Abraham had in the sacred past, an unconditional reliance upon the living God in spite of all temptations to doubt. This faith of Abraham,[10] heroic by its 'nevertheless,' which afterwards was made impossible by the law,[11] has in Christ again become possible and real for us. 'Separated from Christ,' Paul says in one place,[12] we are 'without God in the world'; in union with Christ we have boldness to approach God.[13]

The faith of Paul is then the union with God which

---

[1] 2 Thess. iii. 5, ἡ ὑπομονὴ τοῦ Χριστοῦ.

[2] 2 Cor. x. 5, ἡ ὑπακοὴ τοῦ Χριστοῦ.

[3] 2 Cor. xi. 10, ἀλήθεια Χριστοῦ.

[4] Eph. v. 21, φόβος Χριστοῦ; cf. 2 Cor. v. 11.

[5] Col. ii. 11, ἡ περιτομὴ τοῦ Χριστοῦ.

[6] Phil. iii. 10; 2 Cor. i. 5, τὰ παθήματα τοῦ Χριστοῦ.

[7] Col. i. 24, αἱ θλίψεις τοῦ Χριστοῦ. On these two last expressions cf. Arnold Steubing, *Der paulinische Begriff 'Christusleiden,'* Diss. Heidelberg, Darmstadt, 1905.

[8] Cf. eg. the conceptions mentioned above, p. 161 f., 'the power of Christ,' 'the riches of Christ,' 'the blessing of Christ,' 'the fulness of Christ,' and the complete list given by Schmitz, p. 268.

[9] This 'on' (ἐπὶ) is by Paul joined with 'God,' Rom. iv. 5, 24 (ix. 33), x. 11; with 'Christ,' 1 Tim. i. 16.

[10] Rom. iv. 12, 16 πίστις Ἀβραάμ.   [11] Gal. iii. 12, 23.

[12] Eph. ii. 12, ἦτε . . . χωρὶς Χριστοῦ . . . ἄθεοι ἐν τῷ κόσμῳ.

[13] Eph. iii. 12, ἐν ᾧ ἔχομεν τὴν παρρησίαν καὶ προσαγωγὴν ἐν πεποιθήσει διὰ τῆς πίστεως αὐτοῦ; cf. also Eph. iii. 17.

is established in fellowship with Christ. It is, like that of Abraham, an unshakable confidence in the grace of God. God-intimacy in Christ Jesus, God-intimacy of those who are Christ-intimates,[1] that is Paul's faith.

The unshakableness, which often makes faith appear as something paradoxical, is just as important as the other characteristic, that faith as Paul uses the term is not a conviction reached by reason, but something practical, an inner personal dependence, an attitude of the personality, and inner bearing. Thus Paul's conception of faith is to be transferred out of the sphere of dogma into that of mysticism and cult religion. 'Faith or consciousness of faith and mysticism belong together.'[2]

And now we must try to recognise this 'faith of Christ' of the Apostle as the centre of energy, from which the many separate confessions concerning salvation in Christ radiate. We must seek to understand the rich variety of Pauline experience and testimony about salvation which finds expression in the confessions in Paul's letters as refractions of the one beam of light, 'faith of Christ.'

Here, in my opinion, lies the most important problem of the study of Paul, as far as that is concerned

---

[1] ἔνθεον εἶναι ἐν Χριστῷ 'Ιησοῦ—thus it could be even more clearly expressed in Greek. The phrase coined by Paul himself might also be applied, Col. iii. 3, ' hid with Christ in God ' if it could be divested of its narrower sense (eschatological) in the place where it occurs and applied in a more general sense.

[2] This profound sentence of Schaeder (*Geistproblem*, p. 118) can rightly be applied to Paul. The same may be said of the term ' Faith-mysticism ' used by E. Weber, *Die Formel ' in Christo Jesu*,' p. 235 ff. (also Th. Lit. Blatt., 45 [1924], col. 89), and Schaeder, p. 120 ff. The right suggestion already was made by M. Dibelius in Lietzmann's Handbuch, iii., 2nd Ed. (1912), p. 108. E. Brunner, in *Die Mystik und das Wort*, p. 122, 1st Ed., completely misapprehends the exegetical result. Further on ' Faith-mysticism ' cf. also Mundle, *Das relig. Leben des Ap. Paulus*, p. 71.

with Paul's inner self. The solution of the problem lies in the recognition that the Pauline testimonies concerning salvation are psychically synonymous.

In the older study of Paul it was generally the custom first to isolate the so-called 'concepts' of justification, redemption, reconciliation, forgiveness, and so forth, and then from these isolated and thereby theologically stiffened 'concepts' to reconstruct the 'system' of 'Paulinism.' Paulinism so constructed appeared according to one theologian as a triangle, according to another as a square or a hexagon, and occasionally it looked like the side view of a staircase—in any case it was very geometrical and conventional. In our conception of it also there are straight lines, but they do not form closed geometrical figures, rather like rays of light, unlimited and immeasurable, they stream in all directions from the central point, the light of the experience of Christ.[1]

It was the result of that dogmatic method with its isolation and imposed system, that 'Paulinism' appeared so hard and cold, so calculated and scholastic, so angular and complicated and so difficult to assimilate, and that on account of 'Paulinism' Paul seemed to many to be 'the evil genius of Christianity.'[2]

If however we may draw conclusions as to character from historical effects, then we may say : the message of Christ which the tentmaker of Tarsus preached to the simple people of the great Hellenistic cities in the age of the Cæsars, must have been simple—or at any rate understandable by the simple—transporting and

[1] Compare the diagram below in the Appendix.

[2] Adolf Friedrich Graf von Schack coined this expression (see above, p. 4) in 1849 in Jerusalem, as he drew a contrast between the teaching of the great Master, Jesus, and the fantastic ideas of Paul, the fanatic (cf. his Autobiography, *Ein halbes Jahrhundert*, ii., Stuttgart, 1889, p. 265 ff.).

inspiring to the common people. There is a way by
which we can recognise even to-day the popular
simplicity of the Pauline gospel. We must take
seriously the observation, which is also to be made in
the case of Luther,[1] Paul Gerhardt,[2] Herder[3] and most
other classical religious writers, that in the numberless
confessions about Christ which follow one another
without system in the letters of Paul the reference is
not to a diversity of many objects but to a diversity of
the psychological reflections of the one object of religion. To this one object the confessor bears witness
in a continually new variation of figurative words of
similar meaning and often with the parallelism of
prophetic emphasis. And it is our business to grasp
the figurativeness, the ancient popular pictorial character of these testimonies.

We will select only those of Paul's pictorial expressions for salvation in Christ, which have most
seriously suffered violence at the hands of Paulinism-
investigators. There are other synonyms,[4] but the
following five are the most important : justification,
reconciliation, forgiveness, redemption, adoption (Luther
uses the word ' sonship ').

These classical words have exerted such an enormous influence upon later dogma that they have themselves in the passage of centuries become covered with

[1] Cf. e.g. the so-called Autobiography of 1545 which M. Rade
translated ' Die Christliche Welt,' 29 (1915), col. 875 ff., especially
col. 901, where Luther gathers up ' the same sense in other words.'
G. Kawerau has here rightly indicated a great problem for investigation
(Theol. Lit. Zeitg., 41 (1916), col. 277).

[2] Eugen Aellen, *Quellen und Stil der Lieder Paul Gerhardts*, Bern,
1912.

[3] Elisabeth Hoffart, *Herders ' Gott*,' Halle, 1918, p. 7 f.

[4] It would be a valuable piece of work again to restore all of them
to their ancient pictorial meaning as I have endeavoured to do with
the five here mentioned.

so thick a coating of dogmatic verdegris, that for many
people it has become difficult to recognise their original
meaning. But to the pre-dogmatic simple person of
the ancient world the original meaning was clear
because he understood without difficulty that the
apostolic words were pictorial.

In each of these five picture-words man stands
before God—each time in a different guise before the
same God : first as an accused person, secondly as an
enemy, thirdly as a debtor, fourthly and fifthly as a
slave. He stands there before God, but he is separated
from God by a terrible barrier : by sin, the flesh, the
world, the law. Transferred into the position 'in
Christ' he experiences the setting aside of this barrier
and finds access to God. And in accordance with the
particular picture which Paul uses, this access to God
in Christ is called acquittal, or reconciliation, or remission, or redemption, or adoption. Paul, the architect,[1]
did not plan five or more doors side by side, or one after
the other into the royal palace of grace, but one single
open door. But he had many different sketches of the
janua vitæ—the doorway to life—in his mind.

As an accused person[2] man stands before God's
judgment seat as part of the mighty complex of religious
imagery which surrounds the fundamental word justification. This imagery has its psychological starting-
point in the old Jewish and old apostolic expectation of
judgment at the last day. In Christ this accused
person becomes unaccused ;[3] he is awarded not con-
demnation[4] but liberty.[5] 'Acquittal' is the meaning of

---

[1] 1 Cor. iii. 10, ὡς σοφὸς ἀρχιτέκτων.

[2] Rom. viii. 33, τίς ἐγκαλέσει κατὰ ἐκλεκτῶν θεοῦ.

[3] 1 Cor. i. 8 ; Col. i. 22, ἀνεγκλήτους.

[4] Rom. viii. 1, οὐδὲν ἄρα νῦν κατάκριμα τοῖς ἐν Χριστῷ Ἰησοῦ.

[5] ὁ γὰρ νόμος τοῦ πνεύματος τῆς ζωῆς ἐν Χριστῷ Ἰησοῦ ἠλευθέρωσέν σε
ἀπὸ τοῦ νόμου τῆς ἁμαρτίας καὶ τοῦ θανάτου.

the Pauline justification.[1] And the acquittal experienced 'in Christ' coincides with justification 'out of faith,'[2] 'through faith'[3] or 'by faith,'[4] because faith is indeed union with Christ,[5] and is only realised 'in Christ.'

Paul's justification 'out of' faith or 'through' faith or 'by' faith has often been misunderstood and to-day is still often misunderstood by uneducated Protestantism in something like this form: justification is reckoned as the reward given by God to man's achievement of faith. Paul himself perhaps gave occasion for this misunderstanding by his strong emphasis, especially in the fourth chapter of Romans, upon the phrase in the Septuagint[6] about Abraham's faith.[7]

In this quotation

His faith was reckoned

the word 'reckoned'[8] lends support to that mechanical interpretation.

But we must not isolate this passage, and we cannot look upon 'reckon' as the characteristic word to use in connection with justification. Paul employs (the thoroughly unpauline) word 'reckon' under compulsion of the terms of his quotation. When due regard is paid to the whole of his confessions about faith and righteousness, it must be said: faith, as he uses the term, is not action, but reaction, not human achievement before God, but divine influence upon man in Christ, and justification 'out of' faith or 'through' faith is really justification

[1] Gal. ii. 17; Phil. iii. 9; 2 Cor. v. 21; Rom. iii. 24; viii. 33.

[2] Gal. ii. 16; iii. 8, 24; v. 5; Rom. iii. 26, 30; v. 1; ix. 10; x. 6.

[3] Phil. iii. 9.   [4] Rom. iii. 22, 28, 30.

[5] Cf. above, p. 161 ff.

[6] LXX, Gen. xv. 6 (in the form in which Paul quotes), ἐπίστευσεν δὲ Ἀβραὰμ τῷ θεῷ καὶ ἐλογίσθη αὐτῷ εἰς δικαιοσύνην.

[7] Rom. iv. 3 f.; 9 f.; 22 ff. Cf. also Gal. iii. 6.

[8] ἐλογίσθη.

'in' faith,[1] justification 'in Christ,'[2] justification 'in the name of Jesus Christ,'[3] justification 'in the blood of Christ.'[4] Faith is not the pre-condition of justification, it is the experience of justification.

Being justified in Christ the believer possesses the 'righteousness of God' in Christ.[5] This frequent technical expression,[6] once replaced and explained by the phrase 'righteousness from God,'[7] is used by Paul of the normal condition conferred upon us in Christ by the grace of God. But that this is nothing in the nature of a magical transformation is shown by the passage[8] which speaks of a 'waiting for' the desired righteousness : Before all men lies the last judgment, which at length will bring definitive justification. The justified man is therefore not a completely righteous man : he still has a goal of righteousness before him.[9] In the apostle's thoughts on justification, as elsewhere, we see the peculiar dynamical tension between the consciousness of present possession and the expectation of future full possession.

As an enemy [10] man stands before God in the second group of metaphors, which surrounds the idea of

---

[1] The formula 'in faith' ($\dot{\epsilon}\nu$ [$\tau\hat{\eta}$] $\pi\acute{\iota}\sigma\tau\epsilon\iota$) is used frequently by Paul, Gal. ii. 20 ; 1 Cor. xvi. 13 ; Col. ii. 7 ; 2 Cor. xiii. 5, and even more frequently in the Pastoral Epistles. That it is not united with 'justification' in the Epistles is, so far as I can see, an accident. The contrasting formula 'in the law' ($\dot{\epsilon}\nu$ $\nu\acute{o}\mu\psi$) is so united in Gal. iii. 11 ; v. 4.

[2] Gal. iii. 17.   [3] 1 Cor. vi. 11.

[4] Rom. v. 9. (Cf. below, Chap. VIII.)

[5] 2 Cor. v. 21, $\delta\iota\kappa\alpha\iota\sigma\acute{v}\nu\eta$ $\theta\epsilon\sigma\hat{v}$ $\dot{\epsilon}\nu$ $\alpha\dot{v}\tau\hat{\psi}$.

[6] 2 Cor. v. 21 ; Rom. i. 17 (not iii. 5) ; iii. 21, 22, 25, 26 ; x. 3.

[7] Phil. iii. 9, $\tau\grave{\eta}\nu$ $\dot{\epsilon}\kappa$ $\theta\epsilon\sigma\hat{v}$ $\delta\iota\kappa\alpha\iota\sigma\acute{v}\nu\eta\nu$.

[8] Gal. v. 5, $\dot{\eta}\mu\epsilon\hat{\iota}s$ $\gamma\grave{\alpha}\rho$ $\pi\nu\epsilon\acute{v}\mu\alpha\tau\iota$ $\dot{\epsilon}\kappa$ $\pi\acute{\iota}\sigma\tau\epsilon\omega s$ $\dot{\epsilon}\lambda\pi\acute{\iota}\delta\alpha$ $\delta\iota\kappa\alpha\iota\sigma\acute{v}\nu\eta s$ $\dot{\epsilon}\pi\epsilon\kappa\delta\epsilon\chi\acute{o}$-$\mu\epsilon\theta\alpha$.

[9] Mysticism and eschatology in Paul !

[10] Col. i. 21 ; Rom. v. 10, $\dot{\epsilon}\chi\theta\rho\sigma\acute{\iota}$; cf. Rom. viii. 7, $\dot{\epsilon}\chi\theta\rho\alpha$ $\epsilon\dot{\iota}s$ $\theta\epsilon\acute{o}\nu$.

reconciliation. In the marriage problem, as treated by Paul, which contemplates the separation and reconciliation of husband and wife,[1] we have a human example to help us to understand this figure. As an enemy man is estranged from God and separated from Him.[2] Through Christ we are again reconciled to God.[3] It is not to be thought that God is reconciled, but it is God[4] who in Christ brings peace to us, transforming enemies into reconciled persons. Therefore we have 'through Christ peace and communion with God'[5] or 'in Christ the peace of God'[6] or summing up the whole matter :[7]

Christ is our peace.

It is quite clear that the 'concept' of reconciliation which has often been so strongly developed into dogma completely coincides in Paul's usage with the undogmatic thought of 'peace.'[8]

As a debtor[9] man stands before God in the third set of metaphors, in which the Apostle by use of the word *forgiveness* clearly links on to the original Gospel's[10] estimate of sin as a debt. In Christ the debtor experiences the remission of his debt.[11] For in His grace God presents us in Christ the amount of the debt

[1] 1 Cor. vii. 11.

[2] Col. i. 21, ἀπηλλοτριωμένους ; Eph. ii. 13, οἵ ποτε ὄντες μακράν.

[3] Cor. v. 18 ff. ; Rom. v. 10.

[4] Col. i. 20 ; 2 Cor. v. 18.

[5] Rom. v. 1, εἰρήνην ἔχομεν πρὸς τὸν θεὸν διὰ τοῦ κυρίου ἡμῶν Ἰησοῦ Χριστοῦ.

[6] Phil. iv. 7, ἡ εἰρήνη τοῦ θεοῦ . . . ἐν Χριστῷ; cf. John xvi. 33, 'in me . . . peace.'

[7] Eph. ii. 14, αὐτὸς γάρ ἐστιν ἡ εἰρήνη ἡμῶν.

[8] Cf. especially Rom. v. 1. compared with v. 11.

[9] Cf. Col. ii. 14, τὸ καθ' ἡμῶν χειρόγραφον.

[10] Matt. vi. 12 ; Lk. xi. 4.

[11] Col. i. 14, ἐν ᾧ ἔχομεν . . . τὴν ἄφεσιν τῶν ἁμαρτιῶν ; Eph. i. 7, ἐν ᾧ ἔχομεν . . . τὴν ἄφεσιν τῶν παραπτωμάτων.

incurred through our trespasses.[1] 'Remission,' that is
the meaning of the word 'forgiveness,' and I do not
believe that there is a great difference between the two
Greek words that Paul used here.[2] Anyone who has
seen one of the numerous records of debt on the papyri
that have been discovered, will realise that the metaphor, which Paul carries out so strikingly of the bond
nailed to the cross, after being first blotted out and so
cancelled,[3] was especially popular in its appeal.

And now comes the important series of metaphors,
obviously valued and loved above the others by the
Apostle, which gathers round the word 'redemption.'
Probably it is the most frequently misunderstood ; but
when it is looked at in its connection with the civilisation
of the surrounding world of Paul's day there is no
mistaking its comforting simplicity and force. While
for us this circle of metaphors is not immediately
understandable, to the Christians of ancient days,
amongst whom there were certainly many slaves, it
presented no difficulty because it was closely connected
with slavery, the common social institution of the ancient
world. Here man stands as slave before God, and
there are various powers who in Paul's thought figure
as the 'masters' of the unfree man : Sin,[4] the law,[5]
idols,[6] men,[7] death (corruption).[8] In Christ the slave
receives freedom.[9] This liberation of slaves in Christ[10]
is suggested in the word redemption.[11] Just as justifica-

---

[1] Col. ii. 13, χαρισάμενος ἡμῖν πάντα τὰ παραπτώματα.

[2] ἄφεσις, Col. i. 14 ; Eph. i. 7 ; and πάρεσις, Rom. iii. 25.

[3] Col. ii. 14. Cf. *Licht vom Osten*, 4th Ed., p. 282 f.

[4] Rom. vi. 6, 17, 19, 20 ; Tit. iii. 3.   [5] Gal. iv. 1-7 ; v. 1.

[6] Gal. iv. 8, 9.   [7] 1 Cor. vii. 23.   [8] Rom. viii. 21.

[9] Gal. ii. 4, τὴν ἐλευθερίαν ἡμῶν ἣν ἔχομεν ἐν Χριστῷ Ἰησοῦ ; cf. Gal.
v. 1 ; John viii. 36.

[10] Col. i. 14 ; Eph. i. 7 ; Rom. iii. 24.

[11] ἀπολύτρωσις, Col. i. 14 ; Eph. i. 7, 14 ; iv. 30 ; 1 Cor. i. 30 ; Rom.
iii. 24 ; viii. 23.

tion is the acquittal of the accused, so redemption is the emancipation of the slave. It is not improbable that Paul had in mind a saying of Jesus,[1] to which he also probably alludes elsewhere :[2]

> The Son of Man came not to be served, but to serve [as a slave] and to give His life a ransom for many [slaves].

The greatest impetus to the development of the circle of metaphors of redemption came from the custom of sacral manumission, widespread in the ancient world (and continued also amongst Hellenistic Jews and even amongst Christians), with which we have now again become acquainted, chiefly thanks to inscriptions.[3] Amongst the various legal forms under which in the time of Paul the manumission of a slave could be effected, we find the solemn ritual purchase of the slave by a deity. The owner comes with the slave to the temple, sells him there to the god, and receives from the temple treasury the purchase money which the slave has before paid in out of his savings. By this means the slave becomes the property of the god, but as against men he is free.

From this point of view the words which occur twice in first Corinthians :[4]

> Ye were bought with a price,

and the sentence in Galatians[5] about Christ redeeming them that were under the law, become vividly intelligible, especially when we see that Paul uses the regular

---

[1] Mark x. 45 = Matt. xx. 28, καὶ γὰρ ὁ υἱὸς τοῦ ἀνθρώπου οὐκ ἦλθεν διακονηθῆναι, ἀλλὰ διακονῆσαι καὶ δοῦναι τὴν ψυχὴν αὐτοῦ λύτρον ἀντὶ πολλῶν.

[2] Phil. ii. 7, μορφὴν δούλου λαβών, ' He took the form of a slave.'

[3] For full references see *Licht vom Osten*, 4th Ed., p. 271 f.

[4] 1 Cor. vi. 20; vii. 23, τιμῆς ἠγοράσθητε. Hans Lietzmann, *Handbuch zum N.T.*, 9, 2nd Ed. (Tübingen, 1923), p. 28, translates τιμῆς appropriately by ' *spot cash* ' [German ' bar '].

[5] Gal. iv. 5, ἵνα τοὺς ὑπὸ νόμον ἐξαγοράσῃ ; cf. iii. 13.

formula which occurs in inscriptions relating to manumissions, and that amongst the people to whom Paul wrote there were slaves who would naturally know all about that particular form of law. Freed through Christ (or 'in'[1] Christ, as 'in' the temple of the god) those who have hitherto been slaves of sin, slaves of the law, etc., are now slaves of Christ,[2] Christ's property,[3] the body of Christ,[4] but otherwise free men,[5] who must not again be made slaves.[6]

The same contrast between present possession and future full possession, which we found in the Apostle's assurance of justification,[7] can also be observed in his idea of redemption : those who are already redeemed still 'wait' for the 'redemption of the body,'[8] the 'day of redemption' still lies before them.[9]

Instead of slaves we become free men in Christ. How little Paul binds himself dogmatically with this metaphor is shown by the fact that he occasionally employs the figure of a slave in making another contrast; instead of slaves we become in Christ sons of God.[10] This contrast is carried out by Paul through the use of the ancient legal concept of *adoption*. Numerous inscriptions and also papyri have enabled us not only to illustrate the word Paul here uses,[11] but have also taught

[1] Gal ii. 4.   [2] Gal. i. 10; Eph. vi. 6, etc.

[3] Gal. iii. 29; v. 24; 1 Cor. i. 12; iii. 23; xv. 23; 2 Cor. x. 7.

[4] 1 Cor. xii. 27, etc., the words σῶμα has a double meaning and indicates both 'body' and 'slave.'

[5] Gal. v. 1, 13.   [6] Gal. ii. 4; v. 1; 1 Cor. vii. 23.

[7] Above, p. 170.

[8] Rom. viii. 23, ἡμεῖς καὶ αὐτοὶ ἐν ἑαυτοῖς στενάζομεν υἱοθεσίαν ἀπεκδεχόμενοι, τὴν ἀπολύτρωσιν τοῦ σώματος ἡμῶν.

[9] Eph. iv. 30, εἰς ἡμέραν ἀπολυτρώσεως.

[10] υἱοὶ θεοῦ, Gal. iv. 5 f.; iii. 26; Rom. viii. 14.

[11] υἱοθεσία = *adoption* (Luther uses *sonship*), Gal. iv. 5; Eph. i. 5 Rom. viii. 15, 23. Quotations from ancient sources in *Neue Bibelstudien*, p. 66 f. (*Bible Studies*, p. 239).

us how frequent adoption was in the Hellenistic world of those days, and how readily understood by the people the Apostle's metaphor must have been. This is especially true of a thought which is entitled to a place in this circle of metaphors, and which Paul found in the Septuagint [1] and in the words of Jesus,[2] that God has drawn up a 'testament'[3] in our favour, and that we therefore are to expect an 'inheritance':[4]

> And if children,
> Then heirs;
> Heirs of God,
> And joint-heirs with Christ.[5]

How clear and comforting must these words and others like them:[6]

> Thou art no longer a slave but a son;
> And if a son, then an heir through God,

have sounded in the heart of a man of antiquity, who, without explanation, understood that the adopted son was also the heir.[7]

But this whole series of ideas is not made dogmatically rigid: the adoption through God, which we have

---

[1] Very frequent.

[2] Cf. particularly the words at the Last Supper in the light of Lk. xxii. 29.

[3] διαθήκη, Gal. iii. 15 ff.; iv. 24; 1 Cor. xi. 25; 2 Cor. iii. 6.

[4] κληρονομία, Gal. iii. 18; iv. 1 ff.; Col. iii. 24; Eph. i. 14, 18; v. 5, etc.

[5] Rom. viii. 17, εἰ δὲ τέκνα, καὶ κληρονόμοι· κληρονόμοι μὲν θεοῦ, συγκληρονόμοι δὲ Χριστοῦ.

[6] Gal. iv. 7, ὥστε οὐκέτι εἶ δοῦλος, ἀλλὰ υἱός· εἰ δὲ υἱός, καὶ κληρονόμος διὰ θεοῦ.

[7] On adoption by testament with simultaneous appointment as heir cf. F. Schulin, Das griechische Testament verglichen mit dem römischen, a programme, Basel, 1882, especially p. 15 ff. and 52; Ernst Lohmeyer, Diatheke, Leipzig, 1913, p. 11 ff., especially 29, 142; for later times, Giannino Ferrari, Formulari Notarili inediti dell' Età Bizantina, Rome, 1912, p. 42.

experienced in Christ,[1] still remains the object of our 'expectation,'[2] and of our 'inheritance' we possess through the Holy Spirit at present only 'earnest money.'[3]

That all these 'concepts' of justification, reconciliation, forgiveness, redemption, adoption are not distinguishable from one another like the acts of a drama, but are synonymous forms of expression for one single thing, is proved by a peculiarity which occurs repeatedly in Paul's letters—a mark of the holy warmth of their enthusiasm. The Apostle is fond of adding one conception to another, so as to explain the one by the other : adoption stands side by side with redemption,[4] similarly justification[5] and forgiveness are explained by redemption,[6] or justification by forgiveness.[7] Illegitimate catachreses from the rhetorical point of view, these pilings up of mixed metaphors were no doubt, judged from the standpoint of the popular preacher, very effective. In any case Paul's churches did not dogmatically vivisect confessions like this sentence in first Corinthians[8] :

> But of Him are ye in Christ Jesus,
> Who was made unto us wisdom from God,
> And righteousness and sanctification and redemption—

but entered into the feeling expressed in them as into the exultation of a psalmist.

It is furthermore remarkable, that all five of the

---

[1] Rom. viii. 15 ff., ἐλάβετε πνεῦμα υἱοθεσίας, ἐν ᾧ κράζομεν· Ἀββᾶ ὁ πατήρ.

[2] Rom. viii. 23, υἱοθεσίαν ἀπεκδεχόμενοι.

[3] Eph. i. 14, ὅς ἐστιν ἀρραβὼν τῆς κληρονομίας.

[4] Gal. iv. 5 ; Rom. viii. 23. [5] Rom. iii. 24.

[6] Col. i. 14 ; Eph. i. 7. [7] Rom. iv. 6-8.

[8] 1 Cor. i. 30, ἐξ αὐτοῦ δὲ ὑμεῖς ἐστε ἐν Χριστῷ Ἰησοῦ, ὃς ἐγενήθη σοφία ἡμῖν ἀπὸ θεοῦ δικαιοσύνη τε καὶ ἁγιασμὸς καὶ ἀπολύτρωσις.

groups of metaphors just mentioned are taken from the practice of law. We have other proof that Paul was fond of legal metaphors[1] which would present itself especially easily to the city-dweller, and would be well understood by his churches.

We shall not comprehend Paul until we have heard all these various testimonies concerning salvation sounding together in harmony like the notes of a single full chord.[2] Once accused before God, an enemy of God, a debtor, a slave—now in Christ acquitted and redeemed, free from debt, the friend of God and the son of God—the man who makes this confession testifies that in Christ he is no longer 'far off' from God but has come 'near' to God.[3] To raise scholastically pointed questions, which the controversial theology of exegesis finds indispensible, such as : 'What is the relation of justification to reconciliation in Paul? or of forgiveness to redemption?' is to break the strings of the harp and to twist them into a tangle that it is hopeless to unravel. Such questions have surely no more value than if we were to ask, what is the relation of an accused person to an enemy or of a debtor to a slave, and while they

---

[1] Cf. p. 71, above.

[2] The idea often hinted at in these pages that certain passages from Paul's letters ought to be read (or listened to) like verses from the Psalms, is no modern invention. Codex 108 of the Moscow Synodal-Library, which was written in the year 993, has on page 4v the verse

ῥύθμιζε, Παῦλε, τὴν χρυσόστομον λύραν
ψυχὰς μελωδήμασι πιστῶν ἡδύνειν.

(Tune, Paul, thy golden mouthed lyre
To sweeten with its song the souls of the faithful.)

Cf. *Exempla Codicum Græcorum*, vol. i., *Codices Mosquenses*, edd. G. Cereteli et S. Sobolevski Mosquæ, 1911, p. 8.

[3] Eph. ii. 13, νυνὶ δὲ ἐν Χριστῷ Ἰησοῦ ὑμεῖς οἱ ποτε ὄντες μακρὰν ἐγενήθητε ἐγγὺς ἐν τῷ αἵματι τοῦ Χριστοῦ. (On the last formula see below, Chapter VIII.).

may, perhaps, furnish matter for pamphlets and make examination candidates uneasy, they are no help towards understanding Paul.

It is more profitable to search in Paul himself for utterances in which the harmony of that chord is completed. There can scarcely be found a finer line than the shout of triumph in second Corinthians :[1]

> If any man be in Christ, he is a new creature.

That is the second chapter of the Pauline Genesis, upon the first page of which was written the flash of light at Damascus.[2] Living in Christ, Paul divides his life into two great periods,[3] that of the old Paul and that of the new created Paul. The 'old man'[4] had languished in the dark prison[5] enclosed by the many walls of the seven spheres of evil, 'in' the flesh,[6] 'in' sins,[7] 'in' Adam,[8] 'in' his overhanging fate of death,[9] 'in' the Law,[10] 'in' the world,[11] 'in' sufferings.[12] The 'new man'[13] lives and works 'in' Christ within the sphere of light and holiness,[14] into which all those dark terrors cannot reach :

> Light shall shine out of darkness ![15]
> The old things are passed away
> Behold they are become new.[16]

---

[1] 2 Cor. v. 17, εἴ τις ἐν Χριστῷ, καινὴ κτίσις; cf. Gal. vi. 15.
[2] 2 Cor. iv. 6; cf. above, p. 130.   [3] 2 Cor. v. 17.
[4] Eph. iv. 22; Rom. vi. 6, ὁ παλαιὸς (ἡμῶν) ἄνθρωπος.
[5] Cf. Gal. iii. 23; Rom. vii. 6, 23.   [6] Rom. vii. 5; viii. 8, 9.
[7] 1 Cor. xv. 17.   [8] 1 Cor. xv. 22.
[9] Rom. v. 21; cf. 1 Jn. iii. 14.
[10] Gal. v. 4; Rom. iii. 19; ii. 12.
[11] Eph. ii. 12.   [12] 2 Cor. vi. 4.
[13] Col. iii. 10, τὸν νέον (ἄνθρωπον).
[14] Cf. the diagram below in the Appendix.
[15] 2 Cor. iv. 6.
[16] 2 Cor. v. 17, τὰ ἀρχαῖα παρῆλθεν · ἰδοὺ γέγονεν καινά.

The *flesh* has no power over the new man because as one who belongs to Christ he has ' crucified' it.[1]

As a new creature, Paul, the Christian, is also free from *sin*.[2] He has been loosed from sin. But is he also sinless, is he incapable of sinning? Paul might certainly in theory subscribe to the statement that the Christian does not sin.[3] But the awful experiences of practice would give him cause to doubt. Paul in his cure of souls retained a sober judgment; freedom from sin is not thought of mechanically and magically. Side by side with his numberless moral exhortations to Christians to battle against sin, there are confessions of Paul the Christian himself,[4] testimonies that even one who has experienced the new creation still knows at times the old deep sense of sin. But he has also daily renewed visitations of the grace of God, and daily anew he experiences in the new creation the transforming influence of this grace.

The new Paul is also rid of the fellowship with *Adam* which is a fellowship with *death*.[5] No longer is he 'in' Adam, but 'in' Christ, and 'in' Him no longer 'in' death but 'in' life,[6] he has the guarantee that death has been overcome.[7]

But Paul, the Christian, is also a new creature, because in Christ he is free from the *Law :*

Christ is the end of the Law.[8]

The ' letter ' has been conquered by the 'Spirit.'[9] The problem of the Law was to the former Pharisee an

---

[1] Gal. v. 24, οἱ δὲ τοῦ Χριστοῦ τὴν σάρκα ἐσταύρωσαν.

[2] Rom. vi. 1-14.   [3] Rom. vi. 2, 6, 11.

[4] Especially Rom. vii.

[5] 1 Cor. xv. 22; Rom. v. 12 ff.   [6] Rom. v. 10, 17.

[7] 1 Cor. xv. 22, ὥσπερ γὰρ ἐν τῷ Ἀδὰμ πάντες ἀποθνήσκουσιν, οὕτως καὶ ἐν τῷ Χριστῷ πάντες ζωοποιηθήσονται.

[8] Rom. x. 4, τέλος γὰρ νόμου Χριστός.

[9] Rom. vii. 6 ; 2 Cor. iii. 6.

especially tormenting one, and it occupies a great space
in the letters owing to Paul's polemical position in
regard to the Judaisers. Its practical point was certainly for him, as for the churches whom agitators had
disturbed, the problem of circumcision, and however
easy this might be to solve theoretically, as a problem
concerning ritual and cult it was peculiarly delicate
and painful.[1] But the problem of the Law was not
solved by one single sufficient formula; Paul, the
Benjamite, remained a pious Bible Christian and could
himself quote the words of the Law as authoritative.[2]
The treasured Bible of the Fathers and distant ancestors
with its Thora, Psalter and Prophets, was too deeply
rooted as a part of his religious inheritance in his heart
from childhood onwards, and had no doubt gained too
firm a place in Apostolical Cultus, through the natural
adoption by the earliest Christian congregation of the
Bible-reading as practised by their fathers for generations, to allow the opponent of the Law to develop into
the destroyer of the Law.   Though often a harsh[3] opponent of the Law, he seeks rather to preserve for it a
part of its value.[4] Freedom from the slavery of the
Law is thus in no sense thought of as libertinism;[5]
Like Jesus Himself,[6] Paul proclaimed the words of the
Law regarding love to one's neighbour as the quintessence of the Law.[7]

[1] Cf. above, pp. 96-97. In all questions in dispute concerning
the history of religion (even in those which appear only theoretical) we
ought first to ask, if we desire to grasp their real profundity, how far
they directly or indirectly affect the cult. It is through their dependence on the cult that they in most cases first receive their pointed-
ness and passionate explosiveness.

[2] See above, p. 101.

[3] The strongest instance is probably his polemic against Moses,
2 Cor. iii. 13 ff.

[4] Cf. especially Gal. iii. 21 ff.

[5] Gal. v. 13, μόνον μὴ τὴν ἐλευθερίαν εἰς ἀφορμὴν τῇ σαρκί.

[6] Matt. xxii. 39 and parallels.   [7] Gal. v. 14 ; Rom. xiii. 8.

How high the new Paul felt himself to be raised above the *world* and its satanic-demonic powers is shown by many powerful words, which derive their force from being combined with Christ. The mightiest song of triumph is surely that in the letter to the Romans : [1]

> Who shall separate us from the love of Christ?
> Shall tribulation, or anguish, or persecution?
> Or famine, or nakedness?
> Or peril, or sword?
> Even as it is written :
> ' For thy sake we are killed all the day long,
> ' We are accounted as sheep for the slaughter.'
> Nay in all these things we are more than conquerors
> Through Him that loved us.
>
> For I am persuaded,
> That neither death, nor life,
> Nor angels, nor principalities,
> Nor things present, nor things to come,
> Nor powers, nor height, nor depth,
> Nor any other creature
> Shall be able to separate us from the love of God,
> Which is in Christ Jesus,
> Our Lord.

Finally there is one characteristically Pauline conviction, little regarded by the doctrinaire students who are more interested in the theories of Primitive Christianity than in its psychic forces, namely, the conviction of being in Christ raised especially above *suffering*. Paul has here given form to one of the profoundest

---

[1] Rom. viii. 35-39, τίς ἡμᾶς χωρίσει ἀπὸ τῆς ἀγάπης τοῦ Χριστοῦ; θλίψις ἢ στενοχωρία ἢ διωγμός; ἢ λιμὸς ἢ γυμνότης; ἢ κίνδυνος ἢ μάχαιρα; (καθὼς γέγραπται, ὅτι ἕνεκεν σοῦ θανατούμεθα ὅλην τὴν ἡμέραν, ἐλογίσθημεν ὡς πρόβατα σφαγῆς.) ἀλλ' ἐν τούτοις πᾶσιν ὑπερνικῶμεν διὰ τοῦ ἀγαπή-σαντος ἡμᾶς. πέπεισμαι γὰρ ὅτι οὔτε θάνατος οὔτε ζωὴ οὔτε ἄγγελοι οὔτε ἀρχαὶ οὔτε ἐνεστῶτα οὔτε μέλλοντα οὔτε δυνάμεις οὔτε ὕψωμα οὔτε βάθος οὔτε τις κτίσις ἑτέρα δυνήσεται ἡμᾶς χωρίσαι ἀπὸ τῆς ἀγάπης τοῦ θεοῦ τῆς ἐν Χριστῷ Ἰησοῦ τῷ κυρίῳ ἡμῶν.

conceptions that we owe to him :[1] since he suffers in
Christ, his sufferings are to him the ' sufferings of Christ,'[2]
or the 'afflictions of Christ.'[3]   It is not the old Paul
who suffers, but the new Paul, who is a member of the
Body of Christ, and who therefore mystically experiences all that that Body experienced and experiences :
he ' suffers with Christ,'[4] is ' crucified with Christ,'[5] 'has
died with Christ,'[6] ' been buried,'[7] 'raised up,'[8] and
' lives[9] with Christ.'   Thus suffering is no anomaly in
Paul's life, but as the 'sufferings of Christ' a normal
part of his state as a Christian ; and a certain fixed
measure of ' afflictions of Christ ' must according to
God's plan be 'filled up' by Paul.[10]

In this Pauline passion-mysticism it is easy to recognise what I have called the undogmatic element in
Paul.   Dogmatic exegesis, which tortures itself over
the problem of interpreting such passages and takes
away from them their original simplicity by introducing
into them an artificially forced '*as it were*,' cannot
express in theological terms the intimacy of this
mystical contemplation of the passion.   But under
the cross of Jesus a suffering man will be able even
to-day to experience for himself the depth of meaning
and the comfort implied by Paul's 'sufferings of
Christ.'   Similarly the ancient Christians were able
easily to understand the mystical meaning of the

[1] Cf. above, p. 163.   On Paul's mysticism of suffering there is good
matter also in Mundle's work (p. 77), mentioned above.

[2] Phil. iii. 10 ; 2 Cor. i. 5.   [3] Col. i. 24.

[4] Rom. viii. 17, συμπάσχομεν.

[5] Gal. ii. 20, Χριστῷ συνεσταύρωμαι.

[6] Rom. vi. 8, ἀπεθάνομεν σὺν Χριστῷ ; cf. Col. ii. 20 ; iii. 3 ; 2 Tim.
ii. 11.

[7] Rom. vi. 4, συνετάφημεν αὐτῷ ; cf. Col. ii. 12.

[8] Col. ii. 12, συνηγέρθητε ; cf. iii. 3 ; Rom. vi. 4 f.

[9] Rom. vi. 8, συνζήσομεν αὐτῷ ; cf. 2 Tim. ii. 11.

[10] Col. i. 24, ἀνταναπληρῶ τὰ ὑστερήματα τῶν θλίψεων τοῦ Χριστοῦ.

several stages of baptism[1] to the death, burial and resurrection with Christ, because having been baptised as adults, they had an indelibly vivid recollection of the ceremony performed upon them by immersion. It is by no means easy for us, brought up in the practice of infant baptism, to realise this vividness. The usages and sentiments attached to other cults of their environment may have rendered the mystical interpretation of their sacrament easier. But that thorough investigation of the Pauline passion-mysticism which is so urgently needed must give the whole problem its right place not only in the general history of religion,[2] but also in the world-wide history of that Christian piety which centres upon the passion, a subject which cannot yet be properly comprehended by any of us, but whose memorials in written word and drama, in music and pictures often give us a wonderfully sympathetic interpretation of Paul's profoundest meaning.

[1] Col. ii. 12 ; Rom. vi. 3 ff.

[2] With this part of the problem cf. Johannes Leipoldt, *Sterbende und auferstehende Götter*, Leipzig and Erlangen, 1923. Ancient material is unfortunately very fragmentary, and many of the fragments are lacking just at the crucial point. It appears to me, however, that a good deal of ancient passion-mysticism with a primitively popular appeal is to be found in the Hussain-cult of the Shi'ites, which can be studied with comparative ease : Ed. Meyer, *Ursprung und Anfänge des Christentums*, iii., p. 570 onwards, deals with this cult.

PAUL THE CHRISTIAN (*Continued*)

CHAPTER VIII

PAUL THE CHRISTIAN (*Continued*)

THE DEVELOPMENT IN CONTEMPLATION OF THE ASSURANCE OF GOD AND CHRIST

PAUL in Christ, Christ in Paul! Paul is full of Christ, and no matter which of his confessions we have considered we have found that it ultimately points to one and the same assurance of salvation, to his normal position with regard to God attained in fellowship with Christ.

Here then would be the place in which, to speak in doctrinaire terms, Paul's 'Theology' and 'Christology' in the narrower sense, that is his 'doctrine' of God and of Christ, should be discussed. It is more correct to speak of the development in contemplation of Paul's convictions concerning God and Christ.

Of his ideas of God Paul never attempts anything that could properly be called a doctrinal statement in the letters which have come down to us. They certainly did not stand in the forefront of any passionate struggle, as did his assurance of Christ, because of its close connection with the problem of the Law. They stand rather in the background, majestically dominating the scene, like the snow-capped peaks of the Taurus range overshadowing the Cilician plain. We can trace them more through the reflection of them in occasional utterances, in the harmonious expressions of contemplation and in words of prayer than in any great doctrinal exposition. But there is quite enough of this indirect

(187)

observation to give us an adequate impression. In this impression there is no indication of any absolutely new features. But Paul's conviction of God had received a new brightness and a new intensity : in Christ it had become to him actual certainty, certainty in the fullest meaning of the word. Paul had found a new position with regard to God, not a new doctrine of God.

The presuppositions of Paul's thoughts of God are to be found in the piety of the Septuagint, in the other living elements of Jewish religion and in the revelations of God given by Jesus. Paul's experience of God is especially closely related to the experience of God which Jesus had as it is reflected in the oldest traditions. That there is here no contrast between Jesus and Paul, receives outward illustration in the fact of cult-usage, that Paul took over into the Hellenistic world the Aramaic word *Abba*,[1] the old Jewish word for Father, which Jesus used as the opening word of prayer.

There are two certainties pervading in equal measure the Gospel words of Jesus and the Pauline letters : God the majestic Lord of heaven and earth, the Holy One, whose demands upon us are infinite, and God, the loving Father who enfolds us with His mercy, helps us, and gladly gives His Grace, even to sinners. In one saying of Paul :[2]

The goodness of God leadeth thee to repentance,

the two are united into the *one* tremendous certainty of the old Gospel : God is holy love.

Here, however, at the centre of all piety there is a difference between Jesus and Paul, a difference not in

---

[1] Gal. iv. 6 ; Rom. viii. 15. Cf. the similar observation on *Marana tha* above, p. 127.

[2] Rom. ii. 4, τὸ χρηστὸν τοῦ θεοῦ εἰς μετάνοιάν σε ἄγει.

the idea of God, but in the independent energy of apprehending God and being apprehended by God.

Jesus in His experience of God is self-supported : He needs no mediation : the Son 'knoweth' the Father.[1] Paul in his experience of God is not self-supported. As a pious Pharisee he used to stand upon the bridge of the Law, hoping with trembling steps to attain to God by aid of his own righteousness. But apart perhaps from rare moments of grace he remained far off from God. The moment near Damascus brought him near to God. Into his weak humanity there flowed the divine power of the living Christ, and through this Christ and in this Christ he received access.[2] Now he can really say ' Abba.' [3]

> I am persuaded :
> Nothing shall be able to separate us from the love of God,
> Which is in Christ Jesus,
> Our Lord.[4]

How great a total impression of His Lord, Christ Jesus, Paul had received, we have already seen.[5] But springing out of fellowship with Christ, this great total impression is transformed into a multitude of separate assurances of Christ. The scattered reflections of these assurances in the letters have been used far too much as material for the Apostle's 'Christology' and thus they have been transposed out of the sphere in which such beautiful and delicate forms of thought were originally alive and powerful, into the vacuum of purely Christological conceptuality. They should rather be allowed to remain in their own sphere, within Christ-mysticism and Christolatry, thereby the more strongly to emphasise the contemplative, edifying and practical character of all that the Apostle had to say Christologically.

[1] Matt. xi. 27.
[2] Eph. iii. 12 ; Rom. v. 2.
[3] Gal. iv. 6 ; Rom. viii. 15.
[4] Rom. viii. 38 f.
[5] Cf. above, p. 136.

No doubt even before Damascus most of the
elements, which later became constitutive for his
'Christology,' were in existence. In particular, powerful suggestions were given to him by the Septuagint
and the traditional idea of the Messiah, by the
testimonies of Jesus about Himself, which occur in the
Gospel tradition, and the primitive apostolical cult-
language, and beyond these by the religious ideas and
metaphors of the non-Jewish world of his environment,
both in the East and the West.

In spite of all this it is not the fact that Paul put
together a mosaic Christology out of the ancient cult-
names and titles of honour, ' Son of God,' 'Spirit of God,'
'Image of God,' 'Anointed,' and 'Judge,' 'Man,' 'Root
of Jesse,' 'Son of David,' 'Slave,' 'One that became
poor,' 'Brother,' 'Crucified,' 'Lord,'[1] and 'Saviour,' etc.,
and that then on the foundation of this Christology the
doctrines of justification, reconciliation, redemption, etc.,
were originated and developed by him. On the contrary, being filled with Christ, daily growing more and
more into Christ, Paul knew that he himself was justified, reconciled, redeemed. And out of this assurance
of salvation in Christ, which is fellowship with Christ
and develops into the Christ-cult, there grew up an
understanding in his contemplative soul of the mysteries
that were hidden in the person of Christ. He whom
Christ has apprehended can only try to express the
meaning of these mysteries with the gleaming words of
ancient cult language. Nor will it be otherwise at the
present day. We must first in some way be taken
possession of by Christ, then the Christology will come
of its own accord. *Tantum Christus cognoscitur, quantum
diligitur*—' Christ is known, as much as He is loved.'

[1] On this point there is plentiful material, if not always correctly
interpreted, in Werner Foerster's *Herr ist Jesus: Herkunft und
Bedeutung des urchristlichen Kyrios-Bekenntnisses*, Gütersloh, 1924.

Christology is not the way to Christ, but the reflection of Christ. A merely intellectual Christology, which does not spring from a religious union with Christ, is of no value. But at the present day every religious Christology will in some form or other be Pauline.

Pauline Christology, as it is called, is by no means mainly intellectual,[1] rather it is contemplative, being most strongly inspired by the mystical experience of Christ and by the Christ-cult.[2] Hence it comes about that Paul's confessions of Christ taken all together do not give the impression of a system patched up out of the motley rags of tradition, but that, though they for the most part make use of old cult-words, they have rather the look of being Paul's own creation.

At the same time we may notice that in the forms of expression in which these confessions of Christ are conveyed anything specifically Jewish is generally rejected by Paul. The Apostle of the world gives us a picture of Christ which is world-wide, instinct with humanity throughout. The fact, so infinitely important to the Jewish Christian, that Jesus was the son of David is for Paul merely something external affecting the flesh.[3] The Jewish Apocalyptic title 'Son of Man' never appears in his letters ; the brilliance of that star is eclipsed by the dawning splendour of the 'Son of God.'[4] Similarly the Jewish title of Messiah falls into the background ; in many, even in most places, the word 'Christ' has already become a proper name to Paul.[5] And that title of honour 'Lord' which Paul

[1] 1 Cor. ii. 9 f.

[2] Further on the essential nature of Paul's contemplation above, p. 105 ff.

[3] Rom. i. 3 f.   [4] Rom. i. 4 and many other places.

[5] With this fact in the history of ideas compare my work (p. 31 ff.), cited above, p. 91, note 6.

particularly loved to apply to Christ, though it was
used by the primitive apostles before Paul, is yet at the
same time world-wide ; [1] indeed it already carries with
it a prophecy of the world-conflict of the Christ-cult and
the Cæsar-cult. [2] It might be urged that 'Lord' as a
title of dignity was indeed world-wide, but only in its
ancient sense : Paul's fundamental certitude that Christ
is 'the Spirit' is formulated not only for all nations but
for all times. [3]

Only in one single point of importance has the
cosmopolitan Apostle's spiritual picture of Christ
preserved its native Jewish characteristics.   Christ
Jesus as the One who is to come, as the One who is
coming to judgment, as the One who is coming for the
fulfilment of the Kingdom of God, as the One to whom
is addressed the prayer [4] *Marana tha*—this Christ Paul
could not give up.   So too the inseparable connection
of the spiritual present Christ with the historical Jesus,
and particularly the identity of the Living with the
Crucified, saved Paul's religious contemplation from
dissipating itself in mythological vagueness. [5]

This Jewish, this historical backbone to the figure of
the spiritual Christ was of great importance to the
popular effect of Paul's gospel.   The religion of the
people does not live on the stuffed specimens of the
dogmatic compendiums, but on the many coloured world
of wonders revealed to observation.

The outlines of the Pauline Christ are perhaps
most clearly recognisable in the second chapter of

[1] Phil. ii. 9 f.

[2] Cf. especially the section 'Christ and the Cæsars,' *Licht vom
Osten*, 4th Ed., p. 287 ff.

[3] Cf. above, p. 136 ff. and p. 155 f.

   1 Cor. xvi. 22.   Cf. above, p. 127.

   Cf. above, p. 123 f.

Philippians.[1] In vigorous lines, but without any show
of mythological phantasies, Paul, the prisoner, seeks to
impress upon the souls of his simple converts the picture
of his adored object. He who had lived eternally with
the Father in divine spiritual glory did not strive to
become equal with God. Instead of ascending a stage
higher, He descended to a lower stage, came down to
earth, became man and slave, humbled Himself, was
obedient to the Father to death, even to death on the
cross, and therefore was highly exalted by God to
heavenly glory, where He lives as Lord of all created
beings and rules to the glory of God :

. . . Who being in the form of God,
Counted not equality with God a prize to be grasped,
But emptied Himself,
Taking the form of a slave ;—
Being made in the likeness of man and being found in fashion as a man,
He humbled Himself, becoming obedient unto death,
Yea, the death of the cross.

Wherefore also God highly exalted Him,
And gave Him the name which is above every name,
That in the name of Jesus every knee should bow,
Of things in heaven and things in earth and things under the earth,
And that every tongue should confess
That Jesus Christ is Lord
To the glory of God the Father.

These lines were not written in the hard tones of a
theological thesis, they are not calculated for discussion
by modern western Kenoticists, nor for fanatics lusting

[1] Phil. ii. 6-11, ὅς ἐν μορφῇ θεοῦ ὑπάρχων οὐχ ἁρπαγμὸν ἡγήσατο τὸ
εἶναι ἴσα θεῷ, ἀλλὰ ἑαυτὸν ἐκένωσεν μορφὴν δούλου λαβών, ἐν ὁμοιώματι
ἀνθρώπων γενόμενος καὶ σχήματι εὑρεθεὶς ὡς ἄνθρωπος· ἐταπείνωσεν ἑαυτὸν
γενόμενος ὑπήκοος μέχρι θανάτου, θανάτου δὲ σταυροῦ. διὸ καὶ ὁ θεὸς αὐτὸν
ὑπερύψωσεν καὶ ἐχαρίσατο αὐτῷ τὸ ὄνομα τὸ ὑπὲρ πᾶν ὄνομα, ἵνα ἐν τῷ
ὀνόματι Ἰησοῦ πᾶν γόνυ κάμψῃ ἐπουρανίων καὶ ἐπιγείων καὶ καταχθονίων καὶ
πᾶσα γλῶσσα ἐξομολογήσεται ὅτι κύριος Ἰησοῦς Χριστός, εἰς δόξαν θεοῦ
πατρός.

for formulæ to promote disunion. The words we have just heard have a soul of their own and that a very different one. They are a confession of the primitive apostolic cult, made by Paul, the prisoner, in order to rally his fellow-worshippers of Jesus Christ round the object of their cult, round a form divine and human and again divine. This Kyrios-confession can be understood only by the pious simplicity of silent devotion. Let us leave all our commentaries on one side and ask an Anatolian Christian to read us the original text of this confession in the soft tones and psalm-like rhythm with which the Christian East is accustomed to hear portions of the Greek Bible read in the twilight gloom of the churches,[1] then a part of the undertones of the old psalm becomes life-like again, we are freed from our pitiful dependence on history, and we come into contact in worship with the poor saints of Macedonia, who were the first possessors of the treasure.

In second Corinthians[2] the confession is simpler, but marked by the same essential lines :—

> Though He was rich, yet for your sakes He became poor,
> That ye through His poverty might become rich.

The eternity of Christ in the past—in doctrinaire terms the pre-existence of Christ—is therefore absolutely beyond question to the Apostle. This certainty,

[1] Roland Schütz, who has a particularly delicate understanding of these things, made a successful experiment of this kind, cf. Z.N.T.W., 21 (1922), p. 183 : 'I remember in a service at the modern Greek Church in Berlin (conducted by the Archimandrite Mawrokordatos) to have heard scarcely a word that sounded like prose. All the texts were recited to music, though one could not call the sound pure singing. They ran on in a swift even flow of sound. We can think of the liturgical worship of the earliest Greek Christians as similar. Through the melodious tone of recital they were removed from the prose of the *koinē*, without the liturgy having to become elaborate.'

[2] 2 Cor. viii. 9, . . . ἐπτώχευσεν πλούσιος ὤν, ἵνα ὑμεῖς τῇ ἐκείνου πτωχείᾳ πλουτήτητε.

however, is only the result of a simple contemplative inference backwards from the fact of the spiritual glory of the present Christ: the Spirit (pneuma) must be and must always have been eternal. The inference is rendered easier by the old Bible sayings about the Spirit [1] and by inherited Jewish teaching concerning the eternity of the most important messengers of revelation. The expression is quite Pauline when later on the second Epistle of Clement [2] tells us that Christ the Lord who saved us, was first spirit and then became flesh; and the celebrated lines of the prologue of John's Gospel [3] concerning the eternity and incarnation of the Word, though somewhat differently formulated, are similarly as regards content thoroughly Pauline.

All further testimonies to the pre-existent Christ spring from this certainty, especially the statements that He took part in the creation of the world,[4] and that He was present with the fathers in the wilderness in the form of the spiritual Rock.[5]

The earthly life of Jesus, then, was appreciated by Paul, at least in the letters that have come down to us, more for its character as a whole, than for its details.[6] True, even in his letters a considerable number of details are referred to: the Davidic descent of Jesus [7] and the fact that he was born as a Jew under the law.[8] Paul himself was acquainted with his brother, James,[9] and the Apostle's celebrated prayer to Christ, thrice

---

[1] E.g. LXX, Gen. i. 2; Job xxxiii. 4.

[2] 2 Clem. ix., Χριστός ὁ κύριος ὁ σώσας ἡμᾶς ὢν μὲν τὸ πρῶτον πνεῦμα ἐγένετο σάρξ.

[3] John i. 1, 14. On the incarnation, cf. Rom. viii. 3.

[4] 1 Cor. viii. 6; Col. i. 15 ff.   [5] 1 Cor. x. 4.

[6] On this whole question cf. especially P. Olaf Moe, *Paulus und die evangelische Geschichte*, Leipzig, 1912.

[7] Rom. i. 3; 2 Tim. ii. 8.

[8] Gal. iv. 4.   [9] Gal. i. 19; ii. 9.

repeated, for the removal of the 'thorn in the flesh '[1]
presupposes a knowledge of the abundant Gospel
tradition concerning the powers of healing possessed
by Jesus. Paul, moreover, mentions the night of the
betrayal,[2] and the Last Supper,[3] along with an exact
quotation of the words of Jesus on that occasion.[4]
Other words of Jesus are also quoted as unimpeachable
authority.[5] The martyr-confession 'before Pontius
Pilate,'[6] the sufferings of Jesus,[7] the death on the cross,[8]
and the burial[9] are of course familiar. One thing is
particularly noticeable : Paul not only knows that the
death of Jesus was brought about by a conflict with the
authorities,[10] but he also, no doubt under the influence
of reports of what occurred at Gethsemane, regards it
as a proof of the obedience of Jesus to the Father.[11]
That Paul is influenced generally by the tradition of
the words of Jesus, even when he does not expressly
quote them, is shown by the moral exhortations of his
letters,[12] and by other silent adaptations of sayings of
Jesus.[13]

In his oral mission preaching[14] the Apostle no doubt

---

[1] 2 Cor. xii. 8 f.   [2] 1 Cor. xi. 23.
[3] 1 Cor. xi. 23 ff.   [4] 1 Cor. xi. 24 ff.
[5] 1 Thess. iv. 15 ; 1 Cor. vii. 10 ; ix. 14 ; Acts xx. 35 ; 1 Tim. v. 18.
[6] 1 Tim. vi. 13.

[7] Cf. the passages referred to above, pp. 164, 181 ff., on the 'sufferings of Christ,' which no doubt apply to the sufferings of Paul, but are only to be understood because Christ Himself had also suffered.

[8] Numerous passages.

[9] 1 Cor. xv. 4 ; Rom. vi. 4.   [10] 1 Cor. ii. 8.

[11] Phil. ii. 8, $\gamma\epsilon\nu\acute{o}\mu\epsilon\nu\circ\varsigma$ $\dot{\upsilon}\pi\acute{\eta}\kappa\circ\circ\varsigma$ $\mu\acute{\epsilon}\chi\rho\iota$ $\theta\alpha\nu\acute{\alpha}\tau\circ\upsilon$, $\theta\alpha\nu\acute{\alpha}\tau\circ\upsilon$ $\delta\grave{\epsilon}$ $\sigma\tau\alpha\upsilon\rho\circ\hat{\upsilon}$; cf. above, p. 67 f.

[12] Gal. v. 14 ; 1 Cor. vi.'7 ; Rom. xii. 14 ; xiii. 8 f. ; xvi. 19.

[13] 1 Thess. v. 2 f. ; 1 Cor. xiii. 2 ; 2 Cor. i. 17 ff. ; Gal. iv. 6 ; Rom. viii. 15.

[14] It is generally overlooked, often under the indirect influence of the theory of mechanical inspiration, that Paul's letters, regarded as a source for his teaching, are only fragments of Paul, that their *testimonium e silentio* must therefore be used only with caution. We

made a still more ample use of the words of Jesus than was necessary in letters directed to Christians. Paul can assume a certain acquaintance with the sayings of Jesus in his churches.[1]   And even that total impression that Paul had of the earthly life of Jesus as one of humiliation, poverty and slavery[2] is itself dominated by the Gospel tradition.[3] How greatly this 'poor' man Jesus must have gripped the souls of the insignificant many, is shown by the success of Paul's missionary labours.

At the commanding centre, however, of Paul's contemplation of Christ stands the Living One, who is also the Crucified, or the Crucified who is also alive. The death on the cross and the resurrection of Christ cannot in Paul be isolated as two distinct facts : rather in his view they are inseparably united. Here we see in Paul probably one of the strongest examples of that law of mysticism and cult-religion that the past is thought of as still present.[4] Even linguistically this can be seen ; the Greek perfect participle for 'crucified,' which might be rendered

He who is the Crucified,[5]

ought to be very sparing in using the formula, ' Paul is unacquainted with . . .' The argument from silence appears in its most objectionable form in the books of noisy writers who have nothing to say themselves. Neither the theologians (this applies even to the critical school) nor the amateurs who lose their bearings and found new religions, without having understood the old, have really freed themselves inwardly as well as outwardly of the theory of mechanical inspiration. It is still an obstacle to right thinking methodologically.

[1] Thess. v. 1 f.   [2] Cf. above, pp. 193 f.

[3] Matt. viii. 20 (Lk. ix. 58) ; Mk. x. 45 (Matt. xx. 28) ; Lk. xxii. 27.

[4] Cf. above, pp. 121 and 143. The 'work of Christ' spoken of in the past tense by dogmatic theology and isolated, is in Paul almost always thought of in the present tense as Christ ' working.'

[5] ἐσταυρωμένος, Gal. iii. 1 ; 1 Cor. i. 23 ; ii. 2. Also Mk. xvi. 6 (Matt. xxviii. 5) is spoken in cult-speech.

goes a great deal further than the Aorist

He who was crucified,[1]

which Paul in his letters does not apply to Christ.[2]
The perfect participle no doubt indicates that the cross
is not a bare fact of the past, but that its influence reaches
into the present. 'The Crucified' is a reality that can
be experienced daily, and the Johannine picture[3] of
the Living One who still bears in Himself the wounds
of the Crucified, is as much Pauline as is the double
meaning in John of the word 'lift up,'[4] which suggests
at one and the same time the death on the lofty cross
and the 'exaltation' to spiritual glory in the sense of
the passage in Philippians.[5]

Another observation akin to this may be added.
The use which Paul makes of the cult-phrase 'the blood
of Christ' corresponds with his conviction of the identity
of the Living One with the Crucified.[6] By the 'blood
of Christ' is to be understood, at least in many places,
not the physical blood, shed long ago in the historic
martyrdom, but the expression is a vivid way of realis-
ing the Living One who is also the Crucified, and with
whom we live in mystical-spiritual 'fellowship of blood.'[7]
We need only recall the Apostle's conviction that he
stands in a fellowship of suffering, a fellowship of the

---

[1] σταυρωθείς.

[2] He only once uses the indicative of the Aorist ἐσταυρώθη (2 Cor.
xiii. 4), but in this case he is not speaking of the present power of
blessing that comes from the crucifixion. Christ was (in the past)
crucified in weakness. The crude materialism of later generations is
shown in the watchword of the Theopaschite controversy 'God who
was crucified' (θεὸς ὁ σταυρωθείς).

[3] John xx. 27.   [4] John xii. 32, 33; iii. 14; viii. 28.

[5] Phil. ii. 9.

[6] On what follows see Otto Schmitz, *Die Opferanschauung des
späteren Judentums und die Opferaussagen des Neuen Testaments*,
Tübingen, 1910, p. 214 ff.

[7] 1 Cor. x. 16, κοινωνία τοῦ αἵματος τοῦ Χριστοῦ.

cross and a fellowship of life with the spiritual Christ.[1]
In many passages in particular the formula 'in the blood
of Christ' borders upon the formula 'in Christ' and
may be translated appropriately :

'in the fellowship of the blood of Christ.'[2]

If it were possible to consider the death on the cross
and the resurrection as two separable events in Paul's
view, then we should certainly have to say : the central
fact to the Apostle is the resurrection of Christ, or
expressed more psychologically the certainty revealed
to him at Damascus that Christ was alive. Then and
not till then the cross became transfigured to him.
Without the Living One the cross would be a stumbling-
block : the Living One makes the cross stand out in the
brightest morning splendour of transfiguration.

It is possible to collect quite a number of Pauline
passages in which the raising of Jesus from the dead is
described as of central significance amongst God's acts.[3]
And after our strong insistence on the mystical character
of Paul's religion this stands in no need of explanation,
for all Christ-mysticism is founded upon the conviction
that Christ is alive.

The following are Paul's convictions about the resurrection of Jesus. In them old Biblical and Pharisaic
beliefs have amalgamated with the apostolical tradition[4] under the influence of his personal experience at
Damascus. It was the miraculous act of God and took

[1] Cf. above, p. 181 f. and 164.
[2] Rom. iii. 25 (cf. with Eph. i. 9); Rom. v. 9; (cf. with v. 10);
Eph. ii. 13. Quite rightly Martin Dibelius (in *Lietzmanns Handbuch*,
iii., 2nd Ed., 1912, p. 104) says on Eph. ii. 13 'ἐν τῷ αἵματι τοῦ Χριστοῦ
is probably simply the repetition of ἐν Χριστῷ Ἰησοῦ.'
[3] 1 Cor. xv. 14, 17; 2 Cor. xiii. 4; Rom. i. 4; iv. 25; v. 10;
vi. 10; viii. 34.
[4] 1 Cor. xv. 3.

place 'according to the scriptures' on the third day ;[1] it
was identical with the exaltation and was the resump-
tion of the spiritual life of Jesus in glory with the
Father.[2] It was not fleshly,[3] but it gave to the Living
One, probably by a process of transformation,[4] a spiritual
heavenly body.[5] It was the conquest of death,[6] and it
did away with the puzzle of the cross.[7]

Thus we have gained the standpoint from which we
can understand the Apostle's tremendous utterances
about the cross. The noble fervour with which he
hymns the solemn praises of the Crucified with ever new
variation and modulation, stirring most profoundly the
souls of the people by the popular force of his words,
is psychologically intelligible as the reaction from his
former blasphemies against the Crucified.[8] A reminis-
cence of his old Pharisaic polemic against the cross is
the statement of first Corinthians that the Crucified was
'to the Jews a stumbling-block.'[9] Since Christ has
now become to him the Living One, Paul can annul
these old slanders by the confession that the Crucified
is the 'miracle of God' and the 'wisdom of God.'[10]

Paul did not attempt and could not have attempted
to express this miracle of God in one poor doctrinal
formula. We make it impossible for ourselves ever to
understand his position at the foot of the cross if we

[1] 1 Cor. xv. 4, ἐγήγερται τῇ ἡμέρᾳ τῇ τρίτῃ κατὰ τὰς γραφάς. No
doubt for this the LXX, Hos. vi. 2, was in the writer's mind : ἐν τῇ
ἡμέρᾳ τῇ τρίτῃ ἐξαναστησόμεθα καὶ ζησόμεθα ἐνώπιον αὐτοῦ (' on the third
day we shall arise and live before him ').

[2] Phil. ii. 9 suggests this.

[3] So one would conclude from 1 Cor. xv. 50.

[4] So one would conclude from 1 Cor. xv. 51.

[5] 1 Cor. xv. 35-51; Phil. iii. 21.   [6] 1 Cor. xv. 54 f.

[7] 1 Cor. xv. 14, 17; 2 Cor. xiii. 4.   [8] 1 Tim. i. 13.

[9] 1 Cor. i. 23, Χριστὸν ἐσταυρωμένον, Ἰουδαίοις μὲν σκάνδαλον; cf.
Gal. v. 11.

[10] 1 Cor. i. 24, Χριστὸν θεοῦ δύναμιν καὶ θεοῦ σοφίαν.

begin by endeavouring to reconstruct 'the' doctrine of Paul concerning the death of Christ, in such a form, for instance, as to assert that 'the' Pauline doctrine of the death of Christ is the idea of sacrifice.

The idea of sacrifice in Paul is far from having the importance which has generally been assigned to it on the basis of a materialistic explanation of passages referring to the blood of Christ, and certain other statements.[1] The metaphor of sacrifice is clearly used in Ephesians,[2] possibly also in first Corinthians,[3] if the passover-lamb there mentioned is thought of by Paul as a sacrificial lamb. But even if the number of passages where sacrifice is clearly mentioned could be increased, we should still have to say, that the thought of sacrifice is one amongst many of the various lines of light which radiate from Paul's contemplation of the cross, and these rays cannot be brought together into a single geometrical figure.

We find, in the first place, simple historical allusions to the death of Jesus. It is an act done in blindness by the rulers of this world,[4] a shameful death,[5] a defeat 'through weakness.'[6]

But it is also a work of God; it is according to Scripture,[7] it cannot have happened in vain,[8] it is a proof of divine love,[9] and came at the right time.[10] On the part of Christ it is a confirmation of His obedience to God,[11] of His love towards us;[12] its result is the discredit

---

[1] Especially statements about justification, reconciliation, redemption, etc., which refer to the spiritual living Christ, and most especially the passage in Rom. iii. 24 ff. For the rest cf. the book by Otto Schmitz referred to above, p. 198.

[2] Eph. v. 2, παρέδωκεν ἑαυτὸν ὑπὲρ ἡμῶν προσφορὰν καὶ θυσίαν τῷ θεῷ εἰς ὀσμὴν εὐωδίας.

[3] 1 Cor. v. 7, καὶ γὰρ τὸ πάσχα ἡμῶν ἐτύθη Χριστός.

[4] 1 Cor. ii. 8.   [5] Phil. ii. 8.   [6] 2 Cor. xiii. 4.

[7] 1 Cor. xv. 3.   [8] Gal. ii. 21.

[9] Rom. v. 8 ff.   [10] Rom. v. 6.

[11] Phil. ii. 8; Rom. v. 19.   [12] Gal. ii. 20; Eph. v. 2.

of sin,[1] and salvation of sinners,[2] even of the individual.[3]
And the cycles of Pauline metaphors, by which salvation
'in' Christ is illustrated,[4] extend also to the contemplation of the cross.   By his death on the accursed tree
Christ has redeemed us from the curse of the Law ; [5]
He has publicly nailed to the cross the bond of debt
which He blotted out ; [6] the enmity between Jews and
Gentiles, like that between them both and God, is
done away in the cross ; [7] reconciliation and peace are
established.[8]

Moreover, from the use which he makes of these
cycles of metaphor we see clearly that in his contemplation of the cross as in other things Paul was undogmatic
and unfettered.   The cross presents itself to the soul of
the redeemed not as a gloomy thing of the past, wooden,
hard and bare, abandoned to the soteriologists and
Christologists, but as a mystery of the present shining
in its own light, which is included for him in the Living
One.

And this is especially clearly seen in the words
already mentioned several times in which the Apostle
treats the sufferings, crucifixion, death, burial, and resurrection of Christ as processes of salvation which he
and other Christians share in ethically and mystically,[9]
not only in baptism but in a continuous fellowship of
suffering, of the cross, of blood and of life with their
transfigured Master.   Of all the religious appreciations
of the cross in Paul these are probably the deepest and
most original : through the certainty of fellowship as a

---

[1] Rom. vi. 10.

[2] Rom. v. 6 ; 1 Cor. xv. 3 ; 2 Cor. v. 14, etc.

[3] Gal. ii. 20 ; 1 Cor. viii. 11 ; Rom. xiv. 15.

[4] Cf. above, p. 167 ff.   [5] Gal. iii. 13.

[6] Col. ii. 14.   [7] Eph. ii. 16.

[8] Col. i. 20 ff. ; Rom. v. 10.

[9] Cf. above, pp. 164 f., 180 f., and 198.

member of Christ the cross has become, instead of a historical conception, altogether a spiritual, mystically realised and living reality. My late father[1] understood Paul when he got Schmitz, the glass-painter of Cologne, to put a window in the Evangelical Church at Erbach, in the wine-growing country of the upper Rheingau, representing the crucified Saviour in conjunction with the Johannine allegory of the vine.[2] The cross has struck root in the earth, and the dead tree of pain[3] has become the living vine. Beneath the out-stretched arms of the Saviour the mystic branches stretch down their bright green leaves and heavy clusters of grapes to the communicants who are united by His sufferings :

> I am the Vine!
> Ye are the branches.

[1] [Adolf Deissmann, 1832-1900, pastor of Erbach and local historian.—L.R.M.S.]

[2] John xv. 1 ff.

[3] This artistic motiv itself, however, is early Christian. Cf. Ludwig von Sybel, Ξύλον ζωῆς, Z.N.T.W., 19 (1919), p. 85 ff. For a later use of this profound thought cf. below, in the appendices 'Santa Croce, Florence' by Otto Crusius.

PAUL THE CHRISTIAN (*Continued*)

CHAPTER IX

PAUL THE CHRISTIAN (*Continued*)

THE LOVE OF CHRIST AND THE HOPE OF CHRIST

It is out of the fellowship with Christ that we can understand all the teaching of Paul that is usually summed up under the headings ' Ethics ' and ' Eschatology.' Here let it at once be said that both these classifications lead to misconceptions.

Paul was neither a teacher of ethics nor an eschatologist. His whole being was fired with a world-conquering ethos, and he thirsted with his whole soul for the coming day of God, but he had no ' ethics ' and no ' eschatology,' if by those terms rationally complete and balanced systematic theories of ethics or eschatology are to be understood. Furthermore, the fragmentary character of his utterances as they have come down to us prevents in this case as in others any attempt at a full and systematic statement.

Therefore we must remain simple here also and not attempt to disfigure plain greatness with doctrinaire Arabesques. So instead of the elaborate modern scholastic terminology we use the popular watchwords coined by the Apostle himself—' the love of Christ ' and ' the hope of Christ.'

The priceless treasure of ethical convictions which Paul brought with him from Judaism into the Hellenistic world [1]—a treasure greatly enriched by the

[1] It would be a task as important as it is stimulating to gather together out of authors, inscriptions, papyri, etc., everything that can

Gospel tradition—received its peculiar brilliance through the experience of Christ which, working from within, renews the entire man. The ethical element in Paul is indeed anchored 'in Christ.' It is here that the energy of his Christ-mysticism, working through the will, is most clearly seen.[1] 'The love of Christ'[2] is the power for good which the individual possesses, and the power for good which permeates the whole organisation of Christendom.

Especially this latter, the social-ethic, is unmistakably religious in tone. Paul is most fond of regarding the community of believers under three aspects—as a family, as a body, as a temple. Each of these metaphors has its centre in the living Christ.

Christians are a family, because God is their Father,[3] and Christ, as the first-born Son of God, is their Brother,[4] whose rights to inheritance they share.[5] Differences of nation, class and sex 'in Christ' are no longer of account :[6]

> There is neither Jew nor Greek,
> There is neither slave nor free,
> There is no male and female :
> For ye are all one man in Christ Jesus.

be called the popular morality of late antiquity. This would be a reconstruction of a but little recognised piece of the great *praeparatio evangelica*. Material of all sorts towards this is given in *Licht vom Osten*, 4th Ed., p. 262 ff.

[1] Cf. above, p. 156 f.

[2] 2 Cor. v. 14; Eph. iii. 19 (Rom. viii. 35?). Cf. on this point Schmitz, *Die Christusgemeinschaft*, p. 134 ff., who tellingly designates 'the love of Christ,' the living power which constantly impels Paul, as 'the outcome of experience which is based upon spiritual unity with the Crucified' (p. 136).

[3] Numerous passages.

[4] Rom. viii. 29.   [5] Rom. viii. 17.

[6] Gal. iii. 28, οὐκ ἔνι Ἰουδαῖος οὐδὲ Ἕλλην, οὐκ ἔνι δοῦλος οὐδὲ ἐλεύθερος, οὐκ ἔνι ἄρσεν καὶ θῆλυ· ἅπαντες γὰρ ὑμεῖς εἷς ἐστε ἐν Χριστῷ Ἰησοῦ.

The religious gulf also between Jews and non-Jews
is bridged over : [1]

> Where there is no Greek and Jew,
> Circumcision and uncircumcision,
> Barbarian, Scythian, slave, freeman,
> But Christ is all and in all.

Yes even the racial hatred between Jew and non-Jew,
the 'enmity' between the nations, is done away in
Christ Jesus. The passage in Ephesians [2] in which
these gigantic certainties tower aloft, shedding their
light about them, is the Magna Charta of the idea of
Christian Internationalism,[3] and a programme for a
divine Millennium, of which we to-day indeed can
scarcely see the very first glint of dawn slowly breaking
out of the gloomy confusion of mankind's awful night.

Paul took the name of brother very seriously :

> The brother for whose sake Christ died,[4]
> Him for whom Christ died.[5]

With such irresistible words he stamps even the most
insignificant brother with a value for eternity and
impresses upon the enlightened indifference of the saints
in Corinth and in Rome the duty of tender brotherly
consideration, making all Christians together collectively
responsible for the mutual care of souls.[6]

---

[1] Col. iii. 11, ὅπου οὐκ ἔνι Ἕλλην καὶ Ἰουδαῖος, περιτομὴ καὶ ἀκρο-
βυστία, βάρβαρος, Σκύθης, δοῦλος, ἐλεύθερος, ἀλλὰ πάντα καὶ ἐν πᾶσιν
Χριστός.

[2] Eph. ii. 11-22.

[3] I have dealt more fully with this subject in an address given at
Whitefield's Central Mission in London to a men's meeting at the
beginning of holy week in 1923 (*The Cross of Christ and the Reconciliation of the Nations*, printed in 'The Christian World Pulpit,'
1923).

[4] 1 Cor. viii. 11, ὁ ἀδελφὸς δι' ὃν Χριστὸς ἀπέθανεν.

[5] Rom. xiv. 15, ἐκείνου, ὑπὲρ οὗ Χριστὸς ἀπέθανεν.

[6] Gal. vi. 1, 2, ἀδελφοί, ἐὰν καὶ προλημφθῇ ἄνθρωπος ἔν τινι παρα-
πτώματι, ὑμεῖς οἱ πνευματικοὶ καταρτίζετε τὸν τοιοῦτον ἐν πνεύματι πραΰτητος,

Brethren, even if a man be overtaken in any trespass, ye which are spiritual, restore such a one in a spirit of meekness; looking to thyself lest thou also be tempted. Bear ye one another's burdens, and so fulfil the law of Christ.

But the most sublime evidence of Paul's sense of brotherhood is the 'way'[1] which he showed to the Corinthians, the Song of Songs on brotherly love :[2]

If I speak with the tongues of men and of angels,
But have not love,
I am become sounding brass
Or a clanging cymbal.

And if I have the gift of prophecy,
And knew all mysteries and all knowledge,
And if I had all faith,
So as to remove mountains,
But have not love,
I am nothing.

σκοπῶν σεαυτὸν μὴ καὶ σὺ πειρασθῇς. ἀλλήλων τὰ βάρη βαστάζετε, καὶ οὕτως ἀναπληρώσετε τὸν νόμον τοῦ Χριστοῦ.

[1] 1 Cor. xii. 31.

[2] 1 Cor. xiii, ἐὰν ταῖς γλώσσαις τῶν ἀνθρώπων λαλῶ καὶ τῶν ἀγγέλων, ἀγάπην δὲ μὴ ἔχω, γέγονα χαλκὸς ἠχῶν ἢ κύμβαλον ἀλαλάζον. καὶ ἐὰν ἔχω προφητείαν καὶ εἰδῶ τὰ μυστήρια πάντα καὶ πᾶσαν τὴν γνῶσιν, καὶ ἐὰν ἔχω πᾶσαν τὴν πίστιν ὥστε ὄρη μεθιστάναι, ἀγάπην δὲ μὴ ἔχω, οὐθέν εἰμι. καὶ ἐὰν ψωμίσω πάντα τὰ ὑπάρχοντά μου, καὶ ἐὰν παραδῶ τὸ σῶμά μου ἵνα καυθήσομαι, ἀγάπην δὲ μὴ ἔχω, οὐθὲν ὠφελοῦμαι. ἡ ἀγάπη μακροθυμεῖ, χρηστεύεται ἡ ἀγάπη, οὐ ζηλοῖ ἡ ἀγάπη, οὐ περπερεύεται, οὐ φυσιοῦται, οὐκ ἀσχημονεῖ, οὐ ζητεῖ τὰ ἑαυτῆς, οὐ παροξύνεται, οὐ λογίζεται τὸν κακόν, οὐ χαίρει ἐπὶ τῇ ἀδικίᾳ, συγχαίρει δὲ τῇ ἀληθείᾳ. πάντα στέγει, πάντα πιστεύει, πάντα ἐλπίζει, πάντα ὑπομένει. ἡ ἀγάπη οὐδέποτε πίπτει. εἴτε δὲ προφη- τεῖαι, καταργηθήσονται· εἴτε γλῶσσαι, παύσονται· εἴτε γνῶσις, καταργη- θήσεται. ἐκ μέρους γὰρ γινώσκομεν καὶ ἐκ μέρους προφητεύομεν. ὅταν δὲ ἔλθῃ τὸ τέλειον, τὸ ἐκ μέρους καταργηθήσεται. ὅτε ἤμην νήπιος, ἐλάλουν ὡς νήπιος, ἐφρόνουν ὡς νήπιος, ἐλογιζόμην ὡς νήπιος· ὅτε γέγονα ἀνήρ, κατήργηκα τὰ τοῦ νηπίου. βλέπομεν γὰρ ἄρτι δι᾽ ἐσόπτρου ἐν αἰνίγματι, τότε δὲ πρόσωπον πρὸς πρόσωπον· ἄρτι γινώσκω ἐκ μέρους· τότε δὲ ἐπιγνώσομαι καθὼς καὶ ἐπεγνώσθην· νυνὶ δὲ μένει πίστις, ἐλπίς, ἀγάπη, τὰ τρία ταῦτα, μείζω δ τούτων ἡ ἀγάπη.

And if I share out all my goods morsel by morsel,
And if I give my body to be burned,
But have not love,
It profiteth me nothing.

Love suffereth long,
Kind is love,
Not envious is love,
It boasteth not,
Is not puffed up,
Is not unseemly.

It seeketh not its own,
Is not provoked,
Taketh no account of evil.
It rejoiceth not in unrighteousness,
But rejoiceth with the truth.
    It covereth all things,
Believeth all things,
Hopeth all things,
Endureth all things.

    Love never faileth.
But whether there be prophecies, they shall be done away;
Whether there be tongues, they shall cease;
Whether there be knowledge, it shall be done away.
For we know in part,
And we prophesy in part:
But when that which is perfect is come,
That which is in part shall be done away.

When I was a child,
I spake as a child,
I felt as a child,
I thought as a child:
Now I am become a man
I have put away childish things.

Yes it is thus: now we see
Only mirror reflections,
Only a riddle—
But then face to face:
Now I know in part;
But then I shall know fully
Even as also I have been fully known.

But now abideth
Faith, hope, love,
These three,
But the greatest of these is love.

Christians are a 'body' and Christ is the head, or
Christ is the body and Christians are the members.[1]
Here Paul has taken a well-known metaphor of which
the ancients were fond, from his Christ-intimacy has
infused it with mystical life, and thereby Christianised
it. His corporative idea, profound in its simplicity, was
passed on by him to assist the progress of the future
Church.

The figure is no less popular when both the individual Christian[2] and the Church[3] are spoken of as
a temple which is still building, and which, though in-
habited by God, requires to be more and more 'edified.'
Paul had seen such unfinished temples in his journeys
in Jerusalem and Asia Minor.[4] The temple of Herod
was only finished in the sixties of the first century, a
short time before its destruction. Like the cathedrals
of the Middle Ages, these ancient temples needed the
work of one generation after another for their building.
This is the explanation of Paul's favourite thought of

[1] 1 Cor. xii. 12 ; Col. i. 18, 24 ; ii. 19 ; Eph. iv. 15 ; v. 23 ; Rom.
xii. 4 ff. Cf. on this point the work of Traugott Schmidt mentioned
above, p. 141.

[2] 1 Cor. vi. 19.

[3] 1 Cor. iii. 16 ff. ; Eph. ii. 20 ff. ; 2 Cor. vi. 16.

[4] When we were in Asia Minor we repeatedly saw in the excavations of ancient temples unfinished stones from those old times,
which had not yet received the final strokes of the mason's hammer.
And on a glorious spring morning (April 18th, 1906) as we were being
taken by boats to the Turkish steamer across the bay of Panormus,
which lies between Miletus and Didyma, we saw in the shallow water
along the coast the gigantic capitals of marble columns, which had been
waiting two thousand years for the team which was to take the building
materials, brought so far by ship, up the hill to their destiny at the
Didymaion.

' edification '—' building up,' which is emphasised particularly in first and second Corinthians. We see the work going forward once more on the site where the new Christian community is being built up : [1]

> According to the grace of God which was given unto me, as a wise master builder I laid a foundation ; and another buildeth thereon. But let each man take care how he buildeth thereon. For other foundation can no man lay than that which is laid, which is Jesus Christ. But if any man buildeth on the foundation gold, silver, costly stones, wood, hay, reed ; each man's work shall be manifest ; for the day [2] shall declare it, because it is revealed in fire ; and the fire shall prove each man's work of what sort it is.[3]

There are incapable persons, who, instead of a temple built of fine squared stones, decorated with gold and silver, can only manage to erect light wooden sheds or even miserable huts of straw and reed.[4] Paul, the city-dweller, who may often have seen in his journeys such

[1] 1 Cor. iii. 10-13, κατὰ τὴν χάριν τοῦ θεοῦ τὴν δοθεῖσάν μοι ὡς σοφὸς ἀρχιτέκτων θεμέλιον ἔθηκα, ἄλλος δὲ ἐποικοδομεῖ. ἕκαστος δὲ βλεπέτω πῶς ἐποικοδομεῖ. θεμέλιον γὰρ ἄλλον οὐδεὶς δύναται θεῖναι παρὰ τὸν κείμενον, ὅς ἐστιν Ἰησοῦς Χριστός. εἰ δέ τις ἐποικοδομεῖ ἐπὶ τὸν θεμέλιον χρυσίον, ἀργύριον, λίθους τιμίους, ξύλα, χόρτον, καλάμην, ἑκάστου τὸ ἔργον φανερὸν γενήσεται · ἡ γὰρ ἡμέρα δηλώσει, ὅτι ἐν πυρὶ ἀποκαλύπτεται, καὶ ἑκάστου τὸ ἔργον ὁποῖόν ἐστιν τὸ πῦρ δοκιμάσει.
We ought to consider here whether the sentence (v. 11) ' another foundation can no man lay . . .' contains a polemical allusion to the Cephas-party at Corinth (1 Cor. i. 12, etc.), who had perhaps raised opposition to Paul by referring to the saying about the foundation applied to Peter, which now stands in Matt. xvi. 18.

[2] The last day.

[3] Otto Eger, *Rechtsgeschichtliches zum Neuen Testament*, Basel, 1919, p. 37 ff., has explained this passage (down to v. 15) wonderfully by means of the customs used in building which have now become known from inscriptions.

[4] Such as Herodotus mentions among the inhabitants of Sardis, such as until a few decades ago were to be found amongst the Yuruks on the plains of Ephesus (*Forschungen in Ephesos veröffentlicht vom Österreichischen Archaeologischen Institute*, Vienna, 1906, vol. i., p. 12 f.), and such as we ourselves also visited on the banks of the Maeander near the ruins of Magnesia.

wretched dwellings reduced to ashes in a moment, does not wish that the churches of Christ should be like them. The solid foundation, the like of which had never been seen, demanded a massive and noble superstructure.

Nevertheless, Paul was far from formulating a fixed 'conception of the Church' which would satisfy a lawyer.[1] The Apostle cannot be called the father of the constitutional Church. His churches were 'assemblies'[2] summoned by God—God's levy. All of them together are spoken of as the 'assembly'[3] and the single assembly sometimes possessed also 'house-assemblies,'[4] that is smaller fellowship-circles meeting for edification in certain houses. Through all these brotherhoods, larger or smaller, breathes the Spirit, perceptible in the wondrous effects produced, and bestowing on every brother the special grace (*charisma*) that the assembly needs. First Corinthians is the classical evidence for this charismatic age before the days of the Church.[5]

The modest beginnings of an external organisation were suggested by the needs themselves, but could also be adopted from the various forms of organisation of associations which existed in antiquity, in particular from the synagogues amongst the Jews and from the religious clubs of the surrounding heathen world.[6]

---

[1] The very valuable study of Karl Holl, *Der Kirchenbegriff des Paulus in seinem Verhältnis zu dem der Urgemeinde*, Sitzungsberichte der Preussischen Akademie der Wissenschaften, 1921, p. 920 ff. (cf. above, p. 122, note 3), has not yet convinced me on all points.

[2] ἐκκλησίαι.

[3] ἡ ἐκκλησία, 1 Cor. x. 32; xii. 28; Col. i. 18, 24, etc.

[4] ἡ κατ' οἶκον ἐκκλησία, 1 Cor. xvi. 19; Col. iv. 15; Philem. 2; Rom. xvi. 5.

[5] Cf. especially 1 Cor. xii. 27 ff., also Rom. xii. 4 ff.

[6] We are indebted to the work of Georg Heinrici for this valuable analogy.

These two analogies with their motley variety of offices and names of offices (very clearly illustrated by inscriptions) are a sufficient hint that we had better not look to find forms of 'constitution,' and names of officers quite uniform in all the Pauline churches. What held together the churches of Paul scattered over the Mediterranean world was in the last resort, not their 'constitution,' but the personality behind them all, which 'burned'[1] with sympathy at their every trouble—the personality of the Apostle. It was his prayer and self-sacrificing manual labour, his messengers, letters and visits, as well as his sharing in the common work of love, which kept the saints together.

His letters are a witness how wide and how manly his ethical ideal was. They are full of detached moral exhortations. Problems of the day in plenty were settled by this great pastor, always on the basis of the certainty of his fellowship with Christ and always in the light of the Gospel. But we should not attempt to make a Pauline 'system of ethics' out of all these scattered sayings, and above all we must avoid the mistake of saying that things which happen not to be mentioned in his letters were 'beyond his ethical horizon.' Here again we have to remember that the letters are fragments.[2] Moreover, Paul is no professed ethical theorist.[3] Like other great spiritual guides, in important questions of ethical principle, he felt no necessity to harmonise his principles with one another : everything comes from God, from Christ, through the Spirit ; yet Paul also believes man is capable of everything. Therefore determinists and indeterminists alike

---

[1] 2 Cor. xi. 29, τίς σκανδαλίζεται, καὶ οὐκ ἐγὼ πυροῦμαι ;

[2] On this point, important for critical method, cf. above, pp. 4 ff. and 196 f.

[3] Cf. above, p. 5 f. and p. 207.

claim his authority: Paul himself was neither one nor the other; to him the oar was as valuable as the sail:

> So then, my beloved, even as ye have always obeyed, work out not in my presence only, but now much more in my absence, your own salvation with fear and trembling. For it is God which worketh in you both to will and to work, for His good pleasure.[1]

Perhaps the greatest thing about this practical ethical ideal is the fact that its energy was in no way paralysed by the mighty hopes that were at work in Paul's soul.

The 'hope in Christ,'[2] the 'hope of Christ,'[3] which we find in Paul is not a comparatively outlying portion of his 'system,' like a section on eschatology which is hurried through at the end of a term's lectures on dogmatics. Rather it is one of the motive forces of his life in Christ. This could be demonstrated merely from the importance he attaches to the ideas of 'testament,' 'promise,' and 'inheritance' which all point to the future. For Paul salvation is not a thing of the past, but of the present and future.

To elaborate Paul's hope systematically as 'eschatology' is to deprive it of its perennial freshness and does not in the end enable one to reconstruct a uniform

---

[1] Phil. ii. 12, 13, ὥστε, ἀγαπητοί μου, καθὼς πάντοτε ὑπηκούσατε, μὴ ὡς ἐν τῇ παρουσίᾳ μου μόνον ἀλλὰ νῦν πολλῷ μᾶλλον ἐν τῇ ἀπουσίᾳ μου, μετὰ φόβου καὶ τρόμου τὴν ἑαυτῶν σωτηρίαν κατεργάζεσθε. θεὸς γάρ ἐστιν ὁ ἐνεργῶν ἐν ὑμῖν καὶ τὸ θέλειν καὶ τὸ ἐνεργεῖν ὑπὲρ τῆς εὐδοκίας. The difficult ὑπὲρ τῆς εὐδοκίας stands, probably like the frequent formula of Egyptian inscriptions of the Imperial period from Tehnéh, ὑπὲρ εὐχαριστίας, indicating that the offering has been made as an expression of 'thanks' to the gods (see Annales du Service des Antiquités, 1905, p. 150 ff.).

[2] 1 Cor. xv. 19, ἐν Χριστῷ ἠλπικότες.

[3] 1 Thess. i. 3, ἡ ἐλπὶς τοῦ κυρίου ἡμῶν Ἰησοῦ Χριστοῦ. Cf. on this point, M. Dibelius in Lietzmanns Handbuch, iii., 2 (1911), p. 3, and O. Schmitz, Die Christus gemeinschaft, p. 140 ff.

system from the fragmentary statements in the letters,
for they are strongly influenced by the writer's mood
and point in different directions.[1] Paul himself said of
the hope that it must not be confused with sight,[2] and
although his own hope reaches a high degree of personal
certainty (' we know,' says Paul when he is hoping [3]), we
see on the whole a marked psychological polarity in
his expectation of the future. I am by no means sure
that we can assume that instead of this polar relation
there was a gradual ' evolution' from one extreme to
the other.

The polarity of Paul's hope of Christ is to be seen
in two points.

Relying implicitly on the prophetic words of Jesus,
the Apostle is certain that the ' coming' [4] of Christ to
complete the Kingdom of God on earth will soon take
place—so certain that he himself hopes to witness the
coming.[5] But alongside this vivid hope, that Christ will
come to us, a hope entirely native Jewish in spirit, there
is also the more tender longing that we may go to
Christ : [6]

'I have the desire to depart and be with Christ.'

This 'with Christ' [7] is a higher stage than the 'in
Christ' which can be experienced here on earth. He
who is united 'with Christ' 'face to face' [8] will have

---

[1] Cf. above, p. 207.

[2] Rom. viii. 24, ἐλπὶς δὲ βλεπομένη οὐκ ἔστιν ἐλπίς.

[3] οἴδαμεν, 2 Cor. v. 1.

[4] Παρουσία. For history of the idea of the Parousia see Licht vom
Osten, 4th. Ed., p. 314 f.

[5] 1 Thess. iv. 17; 1 Cor. xv. 51 f.

[6] Phil. i. 23, τὴν ἐπιθυμίαν ἔχων εἰς τὸ ἀναλῦσαι καὶ σὺν Χριστῷ εἶναι.

[7] σὺν Χριστῷ, 1 Thess. iv. 17; v. 10; Phil. i. 23; 2 Cor. xiii. 4;
Rom. viii. 32; probably also Col. iii. 3.

[8] 1 Cor. xiii. 12, πρόσωπον πρὸς πρόσωπον.

put off all that is fleshly and will possess a spiritual
body,[1] similar to Christ's own body of light.[2] The
Apostle's hope did not however dogmatically fix the
time of this metamorphosis. At one time it tends
towards the more Jewish and Pharisaic conviction of ' the
resurrection ' : the dead will rest for some time in their
graves and will be awakened at the *parousia* of Christ
and along with those who are still alive ' changed ' into
the spiritual.[3] At another time his prophetic gaze is
more Hellenistic and is directed towards the immortality
of the soul :

> For we know :
> If our earthly tent-house be dissolved,
> We have a building from God,
> A house not made with hands,
> Eternal in the heavens.[4]

Thus in Paul there run side by side Eastern (native-
Jewish) and Western (Hellenistic-cosmopolitan) expressions of the hope, and the great popular preacher feels
no necessity to harmonise them theoretically. The
sacred stream which rolls its waters towards eternity
shows for a long time the double colouring due to its
two tributaries. The artless realism of the popular
imagination is shown in the fact that Paul incorporated
in his ' mystery '[5] of hope, as something taken for
granted, features adopted from the ancient popular
expectation of his fathers—the dramatic character of
the events expected, the voice of the archangel,[6] the

---

[1] σῶμα πνευματικόν, 1 Cor. xv. 35 ff.

[2] Phil. iii. 21, σύμμορφον τῷ σώματι τῆς δόξης αὐτοῦ.

[3] 1 Cor. xv. 51 ff.

[4] 2 Cor. v. 1, οἴδαμεν γὰρ ὅτι ἐὰν ἡ ἐπίγειος ἡμῶν οἰκία τοῦ σκήνους
καταλυθῇ, οἰκοδομὴν ἐκ θεοῦ ἔχομεν, οἰκίαν ἀχειροποίητον αἰώνιον ἐν τοῖς
οὐρανοῖς. (See above, p. 60.)

[5] 1 Cor. xv. 51, ἰδοὺ μυστήριον ὑμῖν λέγω.

[6] 1 Thess. iv. 16.

trumpet-blast,[1] the 'descent'[2] of Christ from heaven
and the ascent of the faithful 'into the air,' 'to the
clouds,' 'to meet the Lord,'[3] and the fiery glow of the
last judgment lighting up the whole picture.[4]

The effectual certainties in it all are these : the Last
Judgment by Christ[5] and His saints,[6] the annihilation
of all the Satanic and demonic powers hostile to God,[7]
the conquest of the last enemy, *thanatos*[8] (death), the
reign of Christ,[9] the salvation already experienced on
earth 'in Christ,' finally completed 'with Christ,' that
is to say, in personal fellowship face to face,[10] and at
last the giving up of the Kingdom by the Son to the
Father.[11] But at the remotest distance of the horizon
swept by the Apostle's prophetic vision we still see the
glory of the unfathomable, immeasurable certainty :[12]

God is all in all.

The eye that was privileged to take this last look
was not blinded by the lightning[13] of the day of the
Lord. Paul for himself drew many practical inferences
from the nearness of the end of the world (e.g. that it
was better for him not to marry[14]), but his longing in
Christ for the new world, though enthusiastic and
ardent to an extent that makes the comfortable paper
eschatology of our dogmatic shrivel up to nothing in

[1] 1 Thess. iv. 16 ; 1 Cor. xv. 22.

[2] 1 Thess. iv. 16, καταβήσεται ἀπ᾽ οὐρανοῦ.

[3] 1 Thess. iv. 17, ἁρπαγησόμεθα ἐν νεφέλαις εἰς ἀπάντησιν τοῦ κυρίου
εἰς ἀέρα.

[4] 2 Thess. i. 8 ; 1 Cor. iii. 13 ff.

[5] 2 Cor. v. 10, etc.   [6] 1 Cor. vi. 2 f.

[7] 1 Cor. xv. 24 f.   [8] 1 Cor. xv. 26.

[9] 1 Cor. xv. 25, etc.   [10] Cf. above, p. 217.

[11] 1 Cor. xv. 24, 28.

[12] 1 Cor. xv. 28, ὁ θεὸς τὰ πάντα ἐν πᾶσιν.

[13] Matt. xxiv. 27 (Lk. xvii. 24).

[14] 1 Cor. vii. 7, 8, 26.

comparison, did not degenerate into an unhealthy and barren chiliasm or quietism. On the contrary, it set free moral forces to act on this passing[1] world. Certainly without the hope of Christ Paul would not have become famous in history as the man of action, the Apostle of Christ.

[1] 1 Cor. vii. 31, παράγει γὰρ τὸ σχῆμα τοῦ κόσμου τούτου.

PAUL THE APOSTLE

CHAPTER X

PAUL THE APOSTLE

Born in the borderland between the Hellenistic and
Semitic world, on one of the great international roads
connecting East and West, Saul, the Semitic-Hellenist,
who was also called Paul, felt a vast compelling impulse
to traverse the world from East to West :

Necessity is laid upon me; yea, woe is me if I preach not the
gospel.[1]

From Jerusalem and round about even unto Illyricum I have
fully preached the gospel of Christ.[2]

I must also see Rome.[3]

Whensoever I go unto Spain.[4]

The sick man buffeted by the messenger of Satan,[5]
spent almost a generation in travelling.[6] The Jew, who
came from Cilicia, Jerusalem, and Syria to Ephesus and
Corinth, looked towards Rome and beyond Rome longly
towards the end of the world, to Spain.[7] The mystic,
filled with the Spirit, who, on the coast of Asia Minor,
heard in a vision the voice of the West :[8]

Come over and help us,

[1] 1 Cor. ix. 16, ἀνάγκη γάρ μοι ἐπίκειται · οὐαὶ γὰρ μοί ἐστιν, ἐὰν μὴ
εὐαγγελίζωμαι.

[2] Rom. xv. 19.

[3] Acts xix. 21, δεῖ με καὶ ʿΡώμην ἰδεῖν.

[4] Rom. xv. 24.

[5] 2 Cor. xii. 7.

[6] 2 Cor. xi. 26.

[7] Rom. xv. 22 ff.

[8] Acts xvi. 9, διαβὰς . . . βοήθησον ἡμῖν.

(223)

is a man whose practical performance is almost unparalleled : [1]

I have laboured more abundantly than they all.

He who with prophetic vision saw the coming of
Christ and the new Heaven and the new Earth, had, in
preparing for the coming of the new world, spread over
the old a network of organisation which was destined
to prove effective in the history of the world for
thousands of years.

It was as a missionary that Paul had the most
definite influence upon subsequent history.[2]

This does not mean, of course, that the world contemporary with him observed, or had the remotest conception of the mighty influence vouchsafed to the work
of his life.   His own age saw nothing remarkable in the
travelling tent-maker.[3]   To the Roman official, before
whose tribunal he was brought by the denunciation of
malicious adversaries, he was an obscure Jew, or perhaps a mad enthusiast.[4]

No doubt occasionally, as in Cyprus,[5] Paul made an
impression even on a distinguished Roman, and by the
power of his personality he often had great influence
over simple people.   In the interior of Asia Minor he
was once taken for the god Hermes,[6] another time the

---

[1] 1 Cor. xv. 10, περισσότερον αὐτῶν πάντων ἐκοπίασα.   This statement
can be taken literally and established by statistics.   The map shows
about twenty places where Christianity was established by the primitive Apostles to thirty where it was established by Paul.

[2] Further on the subject of the following paragraphs, cf. the ex-
cellent studies of Paul Wernle, *Paulus als Heidenmissionar*, 2nd Ed.,
Tübingen, 1909, and of Georg Heinrici, *Paulus als Seelsorger*, Gross-
Lichterfelde, 1910, but most of all those profound works, the fruit of
the authors' own work in the mission-field, J. Warneck's *Paulus im
Lichte der heutigen Heidenmission*, 2nd Ed., Berlin, 1914, and Albrecht
Oepke's *Die Missionspredigt des Apostels Paulus*, Leipzig, 1920.

[3] Cf. above, p. 56 and p. 74.   [4] Acts xxvi. 24.
[5] Acts xiii. 12.   [6] Acts xiv. 12.

Anatolians received him as an angel of God, even as
Jesus Christ Himself.[1] So, too, the natives of the
island of Malta, who had at first suspected the prisoner
Paul to be a murderer, afterwards, when they saw him
throw into the fire the poisonous snake that hung on his
hand, were ready to pronounce him a god.[2] And before
that, in the terrible storm which ended in the shipwreck
at Malta, Paul was the only person amongst the 276
people on board the Alexandrian corn-ship who kept
his self-possession and by his exhortation saved the
others from despair.[3]

But on the whole, the leading men of his time,
especially the literary leaders, took no notice of the
traveller, and when he did on occasion, as in Athens,
come into contact with philosophers they either put him
off with the phrases of the worldly wise [4] or abused him [5]
and regarded him as a ridiculous personage : [6]

What has this miserable babbler to say ?

Paul himself felt the distance that separated him
from the leading men of letters. Not from any feeling
of weakness, but with a strong consciousness of superiority, he speaks of himself as a layman and a person

---

[1] Gal. iv. 14.   [2] Acts xxviii. 3-6.

[3] Acts xxvii. 33 ff. This scene has a remarkable parallel in an
experience of Goethe's in May, 1787, at Capri, on the journey back
from Messina : in a calm his ship came into a sea-current and was
threatened with destruction on the rocks of the coast. Then the
worldling encouraged the despairing passengers to pray to the Mother
of God. But the strength and naïveté (and in religion that means
everything) was on the side of the apostolic voyager on the Mediterranean. Cf. also the experience of Albrecht Dürer in December, 1520,
at Arnemuiden (Armuyden) given on p. 71 f. of the book mentioned
above, p. 9, note. The Goethe parallel has now been used by Edward
Meyer in *Ursprung und Anfänge des Christentums*, iii. (1923), p. 35.

[4] *Ibid.*   [5] Acts xvii. 32.

[6] Acts xvii. 18, τί ἂν θέλο ὁ σπερμολόγος οὗτος λέγειν ;

unknown.[1]   To the world at large Paul, the missionary,
was just one of the many travelling speakers who then
went up and down in the world in the service of some
philosophical or religious idea :[2]

A setter forth of strange demons.[3]

We know something of the popular preacher of
philosophy who gathered an audience about him from
the people of the great cities.   In particular the disciples of the Stoa and of the Cynic philosophies were
energetic in itinerant propaganda.

But there was also no lack of religious emissaries.
The age of Paul was an age of missions and that not
simply on account of his work, but also through the
great migration of heathen deities, which transplanted
eastern cults into the West and North and Græco-
Roman cults into the East.

We have important proofs of missionary work
before Paul in the immediate surroundings of Paul
himself.   On the one hand, Judaism in general, and
especially the Pharisees, made propaganda for their
cause.   Jesus said in His controversial utterances
against the Pharisees :[4]

Ye compass sea and land to make one proselyte.

Thus the very tendency in Judaism to which Paul
as a young man gave his adhesion had already given
practical effect to the impulse of expansion and that
gloriously living language of Romans[5] reflects the
Jewish feeling of religious superiority, which was
psychologically the basis of the missionary impulse.

[1] Cf. above, p. 75.
[2] Cf. on this point E. von Dobschütz, *Die Thessalonicher-Briefe*
(Meyer X[7]), Göttingen, 1909, p. 2 ff.
[3] Acts xvii. 18, ξένων δαιμονίων καταγγελεύς.
[4] Matt. xxiii. 15, περιάγετε τὴν θάλασσαν καὶ τὴν ξηρὰν ποιῆσαι ἕνα
προσήλυτον.
[5] Rom. ii. 19 f.   Cf. above, p. 93 f.

On the other hand, we find at the time of Paul's mission in Ephesus a church of twelve Baptists.[1] These Ephesian disciples of John the Baptist surely suggest the conclusion that there had been some sort of Baptist propaganda.

The whole contemporary religious world was thus in a state of vigorous movement even before Paul, and the roads on which Paul the missionary travelled were also trodden by the emissaries of Isis and Serapis,[2] of the God of the Jews and of the Great Mother of Phrygia.

Yet it would surely be impossible to mention any other missionary of that period whose journeys can have led him so far as did Paul's.   Paul's journeys are lines drawn from the most important city centres of culture in the East to the most important centres of commerce in the West.   Any one who, with the map of the Roman Empire before him, merely hears the names of Paul's stopping-places, will be bound to wonder at the world-wide extent of his field of work.   Tarsus, Jerusalem, Damascus, Antioch, Cyprus, Iconium, Galatia, Phrygia, Ephesus, Troas, Philippi, Thessalonica, Athens, Corinth, Illyricum, Rome, perhaps also Crete and Spain—the sower who ploughed the furrows and scattered the seed over this area deserves to have the words of the Master applied to him :

The field is the world. [3]

The cosmopolitan cities were especially his sphere of work.   Paul the city-dweller evangelised in the great cities.   Therefore churches dedicated to St. Paul ought not to be built ' before the walls,' but in the

[1] Acts xix. 1 ff.

[2] Cf. Zoilos the servant of Serapis and his propaganda, above, p. 12.

[3] Matt. xiii. 38.

forum ; where in an ancient city stood the temple of
Hermes,[1] the god whom the people of Lystra took
Paul to be.[2] Amid the bustle and hurry of labour,
there where the waves of the human sea roar and
break, while high in the air the wire of the talking
giant-city vibrate as they link up church tower with
hospital, market hall and Parliament, it is right that
to-day there should be pulpits in churches of St. Paul
from which the Crucified is preached.

The maps of the Roman Empire, being generally on
a small scale, can only indicate the most important
places. Almost without exception the places connected
with Paul are such as are marked on even the smallest
map. Names of villages and small towns such as
appear out of the mists of oblivion in the Gospel
records and cause such terrible annoyance to the
philosophical writers, who at the present day endeavour to prove that Jesus was a myth and never
lived, because their names never occur in the Talmud
or in Tacitus, are almost completely absent from the
records of Paul. The Market of Appius and the Three
Taverns [3] are only mentioned as stations on the road
from Puteoli to Rome.

It is only another way of expressing the same
observation when I add that, since the modernisation
of the means of communication in the Mediterranean
world almost all the important places visited by Paul
can be reached either by steamer or railway or by
both means of communication. Disregarding those
which the Apostle merely touched in passing, the
following places connected with Paul are to-day on the
railway : Tarsus, Jerusalem, Damascus and 'Arabia,'
Iconium (Konieh), Phrygia, Galatia, Ephesus (Ayaso-

[1] Vitruvius i. 7, *Mercurio autem in foro.*
[2] Acts xiv. 12.
[3] Appii Forum and the Three Taverns (A.V.), Acts xxviii. 15.

luk), Laodicea (Gonjeli) with Colossæ and Hierapolis, Beroea (Verria), Rome. We find ports for steamers in Cyprus, Ake Ptolemaïs, Neapolis in Macedonia (Kavala), Nicopolis (Paleo-Prevesa), Crete, Malta. There are approaches by both rail and steamer to Thessalonica (Salonika), Athens-Piræus and Corinth. The only place of first-rate importance in Paul's life which is still wanting on these lists is Antioch on the Orontes; but without doubt this ancient centre will also soon be linked up with the modern lines of communication.

Of course the European companies who invested their capital in these means of communication, did not speculate on the few scholars who might wish to follow the footsteps of Paul, but steamer lines and railways have to obey the geographical conditions which determine the lines of communication, and these are essentially the same as they were when the ancient routes by water and land accommodated themselves to them.

In looking at the evangelist of the great ancient cities, one thing alone seems peculiar, that Paul should never have gone to Egypt, especially to Alexandria the international head-quarters of the Jews of the Dispersion. Apart from voyages in Alexandrian ships [1]— one of which bore the name ' The Dioscuri' [2]—the only connection of which we know between Paul and Alexandria is very indirect. The Alexandrian, Apollus, after Paul had left Corinth, worked in the church there,[3] and Paul thankfully recognised this work as the continuation of his own gardener's work there.[4]

I have no perfectly clear explanation to offer why Paul, who was once taken for an Egyptian,[5] did not go

[1] Acts xxvii. 6; xxviii. 11.   [2] Acts xxviii. 11.
[3] Acts xix. 1.   [4] 1 Cor. iii. 6.   [5] Acts xxi. 38.

as a missionary to Egypt. Did he regard Alexandria—
which would have been 'Egypt' to him just as in the
main Corinth with its environs was 'Achaia'[1] and
Ephesus with its environs was 'Asia'[2]—did he regard
Alexandria on account of its enormous Jewish population, as belonging not to Gentile countries, but to the
'circumcision,'[3] and thus as Peter's mission field?[4]
He is jealously concerned that every missionary should
have his own province and not go beyond it,[5] and in
particular he had no doubt faithfully kept to his com-
pact with the 'pillar apostles.'[6] Or had other Christian
missionaries already been in Egypt at an early date?
Unfortunately we are quite in the dark about the
beginnings of Egyptian Christianity.

The most probable answer seems to me to be as
follows: The Jewish persecutions in Alexandria[7]
which broke out and culminated in a bloody pogrom
in the year 38, just at the time when Paul's missionary
work was beginning, made a mission in Egypt to begin
with an actual impossibility[8] and drove Paul towards

---

[1] 2 Cor. ix. 2, etc.   [2] Rom. xvi. 5.

[3] Gal. ii. 9.   [4] Ibid.

[5] 2 Cor. x. 13 ff.; Rom. xv. 20.   [6] Gal. ii. 9.

[7] Cf. on this point Schürer, Geschichte des jüdischen Volkes, i.,
3rd and 4th Ed. (1901), p. 495 ff.; A. von Premerstein, Zu den
sogenannten alexandrinischen Märtyrerakten, Philologus, Additional
Volume 16, Part II. (1923), pp. 4 f. and 11 f.; and H. I. Bell on
p. 16 ff. of the work mentioned in the next note.

[8] This guess has now risen to be a certainty to me. The newly
discovered letters of the Emperor Claudius to the Alexandrians
(A.D. 41), London, Papyrus No. 1912, 96 f. (published by H. Idris
Bell in Jews and Christians in Egypt, London (1924), p. 25, contains
a direct warning to the Alexandrian Jews, that they were not to ally
with themselves or welcome Jews who came from Syria or Egypt (μηδὲ
ἐπάγεσθαι ἢ προσείεσθαι ἀπὸ Συρίας ἢ Αἰγύπ(τ)ου καταπλέοντας Ἰουδαίους).
This is equivalent to an imperial prohibition of the entry of Syrian
Jews. That it still seemed necessary in the year A.D. 41, shows how
long the dangerous situation in Egypt lasted. Thus Paul had no

the North and West, even if he had intended to do missionary work in the South. Later on, when Egypt was again quiet, no doubt other persons [1] evangelised there.

But even without Egypt Paul's sphere of work is of unparalleled extent.

What was it that drove this man out into the world ?

The experience at Damascus was fundamental for Paul, as a missionary, as for much else. The conversion was not only the transformation of an enemy of Christ into a friend of Christ but also the transformation of an apostle of Pharisaic-Judaism [2] into an apostle of Christ. It was the revulsion not only of a religious consciousness, but also of a special consciousness of a mission, whose content is reflected in the proud words of the Epistle to the Romans to which reference has been already made.[3] Paul himself confided to the Galatians [4] that Damascus had this double meaning for him : the revelation of the living Christ within him, and the obligation to preach that Christ as a gospel to the nations.

Elsewhere too we have numerous proofs of his powerful consciousness of a mission. His language

'open door' (1 Cor. xvi. 9; 2 Cor. ii. 12 [Col. iv. 3]). v. Premerstein, p. 6 f., furthermore thinks that already at that time a passport (which was called the ἀπόστολος !) was required for the outward journey from Alexandria to the sea. Intercourse with Alexandria was in other ways also made difficult for a private person.

[1] It may be concluded from 1 Cor. ix. 6, that Barnabas continued to work as a missionary till the middle of the fifties. The later tradition in the Clementine Homilies makes Barnabas go to Alexandria. Apart from that as a missionary to the heathen he had not much 'place' (Rom. xv. 23).

[2] Cf. above, p. 128 ff.

[3] Rom. ii. 19, 20; cf. above, p. 93 f. and p. 226 f.

[4] Gal. i. 16; cf. Eph. iii. 1-7; 1 Tim. i. 11 f.

becomes solemn with the tone of a religious cult when he speaks of his mission. He is the 'slave'[1] who works in the service of his Master. He is, because of grace given to him,

> a minister of Christ Jesus to the Gentiles, ministering the Gospel of God, that the offering up of the Gentiles might be made acceptable.[2]

He is one of the evangelists of good things foreseen by the prophet whose footsteps are beautiful;[3] he is a 'herald and apostle, a teacher of the Gentiles.'[4] He can even say :

> We are ambassadors therefore on behalf of Christ,
> As though God were intreating by us:
> We beseech you on behalf of Christ,
> Be ye reconciled to God.[5]

Against opponents who attacked his mission he especially defended himself as an apostle who was in no wise behind the others.[6] Even the remorseful thought that he was 'the least of the apostles,' 'not worthy to be called an apostle,' because he persecuted the church of God,[7] could be overcome by the certainty :[8]

> By the grace of God I am what I am.

[1] 1 Cor. iv. 1; ix. 17; Col. i. 23; 2 Cor. v. 18; vi. 4; Rom. i. 1, etc.

[2] Rom. xv. 15 f., διὰ τὴν χάριν τὴν δοθεῖσάν μοι ἀπὸ τοῦ θεοῦ, εἰς τὸ εἶναί με λειτουργὸν Χριστοῦ Ἰησοῦ εἰς τὰ ἔθνη, ἱερουργοῦντα τὸ εὐαγγέλιον τοῦ θεοῦ, ἵνα γένηται ἡ προσφορὰ τῶν ἐθνῶν εὐπρόσδεκτος.

[3] Rom. x. 15 (LXX, Isa. lii. 7), ὡς ὡραῖοι οἱ πόδες τῶν εὐαγγελιζομένων τὰ ἀγαθά.

[4] 1 Tim. ii. 7, ἐγὼ κῆρυξ καὶ ἀπόστολος . . . διδάσκαλος ἐθνῶν. Cf. 2 Tim. i. 11.

[5] 2 Cor. v. 20, ὑπὲρ Χριστοῦ οὖν πρεσβεύομεν, ὡς τοῦ θεοῦ παρακαλοῦντος δι' ἡμῶν. δεόμεθα ὑπὲρ Χριστοῦ · καταλλάγητε τῷ θεῷ.

[6] Especially in Galatians and second Corinthians.

[7] 1 Cor. xv. 9, ἐγὼ γὰρ εἰμι ὁ ἐλάχιστος τῶν ἀποστόλων, ὃς οὐκ εἰμι ἱκανὸς καλεῖσθαι ἀπόστολος, διότι ἐδίωξα τὴν ἐκκλησίαν τοῦ θεοῦ.

[8] 1 Cor. xv. 10, χάριτι δὲ θεοῦ εἰμι ὅ εἰμι.

Most moving of all are those words to the Corinthians : [1]

> Necessity is laid upon me!
> Woe is unto me if I preach not the Gospel.

The Apostle's consciousness of his mission is strengthened by his hope of the end ; the time is short,[2] salvation is at the door ;[3] now is the time to prepare the world for the new state of things.

Nevertheless the 'debtor both to Greeks and to Barbarians, both to the wise and to the foolish'[4] occasionally confesses that he entered a new field of work with anxiety :

> And I was with you in weakness, and in fear, and in much trembling.[5]

And what depth of feeling there is in the picture conjured up by the words

> At Athens alone.[6]

So that even Paul's consciousness of his mission had its ebb and flow.

By combining the occasional references in Paul's letters with the narrative in the Acts we can gain a very incomplete,[7] but in the main trustworthy picture of Paul's missionary labours. Some of the gaps can be filled up from the material for social history furnished by the world of his day, and if we travel in Paul's footsteps to-day we find that in some things this remains still

---

[1] 1 Cor. ix. 16 ; cf. above, p. 223.

[2] 1 Cor. vii. 29.   [3] Rom. xiii. 11 f.

[4] Rom. i. 14, Ἕλλησιν τε καὶ βαρβάροις, σοφοῖς τε καὶ ἀνοήτοις ὀφειλέτης εἰμί.

[5] 1 Cor. ii. 3, κἀγὼ ἐν ἀσθενείᾳ καὶ ἐν φόβῳ καὶ ἐν τρόμῳ πολλῷ ἐγενόμην πρὸς ὑμᾶς.

[6] 1 Thess. iii. 1, ἐν Ἀθήναις μόνοι.

[7] Cf. especially the references in 2 Cor. xi. 23-33 for only a small part of which we have other evidence.

unchanged. Even the apocryphal Acts of Apostles, though often valueless as history, give us material for social history, illustrating the manner of travelling and its difficulties, adventures on the road and at inns—in short, the light and atmosphere of the ancient East. For example, the excellent Acts of John portray in a direct and vivid manner the wandering life of a primitive Christian missionary, and enable the modern traveller, if he possesses a sense of humour, to smile even at the discomforts of the worst night-quarters.

Our knowledge of the Apostle's sea voyages is especially imperfect. The Gospel which first sounded forth on the sunny sea of Gennesareth for fishermen and boatmen, continued to love the rhythm of oars and the wind-filled sail. And where at other times the rude religion of seamen had confided in Asclepius and Serapis or even in the God of Abraham,[1] now the youthful Christ the Lord made hearts strong in the midst of the howling storms of the Mediterranean,[2] and called for the fervent blessing on the hard ship's bread.[3] Paul must often have been on the sea ; even before his last voyage to Jerusalem[4] he was able to look back on three shipwrecks, of which we have no knowledge from other sources. Of so much the more value to us is the one picture of the voyage to Rome in the two last chapters of Acts. With its lively description of what is purely nautical and the wonderful adventures of the ship-wrecked party it is a little apostolic Odyssey, only it is

---

[1] Cf. for instance the fine inscriptions put up by sailors in the 'Harbour of Letters' on the island of Syros, beginning with the Imperial period (*Inscriptiones Græcae*, xii., 5, No. 712). The heathen inscriptions are followed by Jewish and finally by Christian, a unique exhibition of the continuity of ancient religious feeling in the Mediterranean. On Serapis as a rescuer from perils of the sea, cf. also the letter of Apion, a soldier in the marine service, *Licht vom Osten*, 4th Ed., p. 145 ff.

[2] Acts xxvii. 21 ff. [3] Acts xxvii. 35. [4] 2 Cor. xi. 25.

certainly no fiction but the product of real experiences in the soul of a man of the ancient world, a companion of Paul, and for that reason a unique document for the social history of the Roman imperial period.

In describing the experiences of Paul, the missionary, on land the writer of the Acts of the Apostles also shows a happy and as a rule trustworthy touch, although he is less fond of a sober white light than of the play of the seven colours. The popular tumult in the theatre at Ephesus,[1] the events connected with the arrest of Paul at Jerusalem,[2] these and other scenes, in which the crowd was roused to blood-thirsty passions, are set forth in sharp relief when we view them in the light of present-day religious conditions in the Orient. The same fanaticism what once made Paul a persecutor, and afterwards caused him to be stoned himself,[3] has smouldered on there till to-day and breaks out again and again in bloody massacres.

The financial basis of the missionary journeys was the simplest imaginable. Paul had few wants, and the Master's divinely plain words of instruction concerning the equipment of His messengers [4] were doubtless not unknown to him.

Probably he travelled as a rule on foot ;[5] only once

[1] Acts xix. 23 ff.   [2] Acts xxi. 27 ff.
[3] Acts xiv. 19 ; 2 Cor. xi. 25.

[4] Mark vi. 8 ff. and parallels, cf. note 5 below, and as contrast the caravans of the beggar-apostles of the Syrian goddess, *Licht vom Osten.*, 4th Ed., p. 87.

[5] Only once indeed, Acts xx. 13, is it expressly mentioned, cf. below, p. 237. But also it is the natural thing, especially in the light of the words of Jesus at the sending out of the twelve. His command (Matt. x. 14, cf. Lk. ix. 5 ; x. 11), which Paul and Barnabas literally followed after their banishment from Pisidian Antioch (Acts xiii. 51), presupposes that the Apostles went on foot, similarly that they went staff in hand (though the testimony for this is uncertain, Mark vi. 8, against it Matt. x. 10 and Lk. ix. 3). Gregory, the well-remembered,

do our authorities tell us that he rode, namely, when he
was taken from Jerusalem to Cæsarea on the sea-coast.[1]
The painters who were fond of giving an aristocratic air
to primitive Christianity have given Paul—mistakenly
I think—a proud steed in the Damascus scene,[2] just as
on Mar's Hill they delight to depict him clothed in
classical drapery—as though that were necessary. The
real Paul had the simple coat and the rough sandals of
the pedestrian ; if he needed an inn, no roomy caravan-
sary had to open its doors for his hungry saddle horses ;
the simplest shelter sufficed, and the wearied traveller
was thankful if hospitable hands were ready to wash
his dusty feet.[3] He seems even to have preferred going
on foot to travelling by sea : on his last journey to
Jerusalem he left the ship at (Alexandria) Troas and
went on foot to Assos where his travelling companions
then welcomed him on board ship again.[4] His luggage
would be of the smallest ; once indeed he left with a
friend Carpus at (Alexandria) Troas, not only his Bible-
rolls and papers, but also the cloak, which is often so
necessary even for summer nights in Anatolia.[5]

He travelled also without any family. While other
Apostles, including the brothers of Jesus and Peter,
were accompanied on these journeys by their wives,[6]
Paul for his own part, without wishing to impose a

travelled in thoroughly apostolic style (cf. above, p. 29, note 1), as most
visitors to Bible lands have done.

[1] Acts xxiii. 24, 31 f.

[2] The words of the Acts point directly against this. While the
ring of the horse's hoof sounds through the whole (aristocratic) O.T.,
there are no horses in the N.T. (with the exception of the Roman
escort of Paul, Acts xxiii. 23, 32, and the common-place reference in
James iii. 3), but those in the visions of the Revelation of John. Jesus
rode on an ass. On this subject cf. S. Krauss, Revue des études
juives, 63 (1912), p. 67 f. ; correct and incorrect in Origen, cf. von
Harnack, *Texte und Untersuchungen*, 42-3, p. 49.

[3] 1 Tim. v. 10.   [4] Acts xx. 13, 14.
[5] 2 Tim. iv. 13.   [6] 1 Cor. ix. 5.

prohibition on others, renounced marriage,[1] no doubt to some extent under the influence of his hopes of the end of the world.[2] Moreover, he abstained of his own free will from exercising a right that was by others generally admitted[3] and was backed by the authoritative words of Jesus,[4] the right of a missionary to be supported by the churches.[5]

What he needed he earned by his own work as journeyman tent-maker. He was the first artisan missionary, and was proud of his independence :

> It were good for me rather to die, than that any man should make my glorying void.[6]

His churches were poor, and he would not be a burden to them.[7] He retorts with cuttingly sharp sarcasm when his opponents accuse him of basely seeking his own advantage.[8] Only from those who were very near to him did he, making an exception to his rule, receive charitable gifts.[9]

It was through his handicraft, too, that he occasionally gained his first acquaintanceship and perhaps lodging in a strange city. His association at Corinth, and afterwards at Ephesus, with the family of Aquila and Priscilla, tent-makers, is typical.[10] These two apostolic Christians, widely travelled like himself, were of the greatest possible service to Paul, the missionary ; they once rescued him from a most desperate situation at the risk of their own lives.[11]

---

[1] 1 Cor. vii. 8. [2] 1 Cor. vii. 26 ; cf. above, p. 219.
[3] 1 Cor. ix. 4 ff. [4] Matt. x. 10 ; Lk. x. 7 ; also 1 Cor. ix. 14.
[5] 1 Cor. ix. 15. [6] *Ibid.*
[7] 1 Thess. ii. 9 ; 2 Cor. xi. 9, etc.
[8] 2 Cor. xi. 7 ff. ; xii. 13 ff. ; cf. above, p. 68 ff.
[9] Phil. iv. 10, 15, 18 ; 2 Cor. xi. 9.
[10] Acts xviii. 2 ; cf. below in Appendix I.
[11] Rom. xvi. 3 f., cf. on this point, *Licht vom Osten.*, 4th Ed., p. 94 f.

From the house in which he found lodging, Paul no doubt as a rule [1] went on the Sabbath to the synagogue in order to effect something by the spoken word. The Acts of the Apostles, which reports many such visits to the synagogue,[2] is here certainly not incredible. If Paul had not worked within the organisation of the synagogue, how otherwise could the frequent punishments [3] be explained which he suffered at the hands of the synagogue authorities?

In the synagogue Paul found the Septuagint and people who were under the influence of the religion of the Septuagint, Jews, Gentiles and proselytes. The 'Gentiles' whom Paul won over, came no doubt largely from those circles who were already under Jewish influence, from the proselytes or half-proselytes. The alternative which has often been formulated in connection with the question of the composition of his churches: 'Jewish Christians or Gentile Christians,' is too narrow. There were also Gentile Jewish Christians who had been originally Gentiles, then became Jews and finally Christians.

But it was not only in the synagogue that Paul sought for converts. In the streets; in the market-place,[4] in the lecture halls, for example 'in the school of Tyrannus' at Ephesus,[5] and even in prison, 'in bonds,' he on occasion did successful mission work : [6]

The word of God is not bound.[7]

[1] Acts xvii. 2, ' as his custom was.'

[2] Acts xiii. 5 (Salamis in Cyprus), 14 (Antioch in Pisidia); xiv. 1 (Iconium); xvii. 2 (Thessalonica), 10 (Beroea), 17 (Athens); xviii. 4 (Corinth), 19 (Ephesus); xix. 8 (Ephesus).

[3] 2 Cor. xi. 24; cf. above, p. 61 f.

[4] Acts xvii. 17.

[5] Acts xix. 9, ἐν τῇ σχολῇ Τυράννου.

[6] Philem. 10; Phil. i. 12 f.; cf. Acts xvi. 33; and above, p. 19.

[7] 2 Tim. ii. 9, ὁ λόγος τοῦ θεοῦ οὐ δέδεται.

In quiet times he was naturally also at people's
disposal in his dwelling,[1] and he must often enough
have been pressed by business and surrounded with
visitors.[2]   Where he worked for any length of time the
news quickly got about that the preacher of the Gospel
could work miracles : cloths which he had touched
were credited with the power of healing diseases and
driving out demons,[3] and he himself occasionally can
recall acts of power—he calls them 'the signs of an
apostle'[4]—which accredited him as a genuine apostle.[5]

He gathered around himself gradually quite a
number of helpers for his missionary work.   While
his first companion, Barnabas,[6] was at least his equal
in authority, the later associates were distinctly
subordinate to him.   They shared his great work as
fellow travellers (Paul says pleasantly 'companions
abroad'[7]), letter-writers,[8] letter-carriers,[9] personal re-
presentatives,[10] and of course, also as evangelists and
teachers.[11]   In difficult situations he was able to rely
upon them ;   the unreliability of John Mark in Pamphylia[12] or that of Demas, who once, obviously against
the will of the Apostle, went to Thessalonica,[13] was no
doubt a rare exception.   What an attractive personality,

---

[1] Acts xxviii. 30 f.   [2] 2 Cor. xi. 28.   [3] Acts xix. 11 f.

[4] 2 Cor. xii. 12, τὰ σημεῖα τοῦ ἀποστόλου.

[5] In Galatia (Gal. iii. 5), in Corinth (2 Cor. xii. 12 and 1 Cor. ii. 4) ;
generally, Rom. xv. 19.   No doubt the references are to healing of
diseases most especially.

[6] Acts ix.-xv.   [7] 2 Cor. viii. 19, συνέκδημος.

[8] For example Tertius, Rom. xvi. 22.

[9] Titus probably took a letter—now lost—to Corinth (2 Cor. vii.
6-9), probably also our second letter to the Corinthians (2 Cor. viii.
6, 17).

[10] 1 Cor. xvi. 10 ; 2 Cor. viii. 23.

[11] Col. i. 7 ; 2 Cor. i. 19.

[12] Acts xiii. 13 ; xv. 37 ff.   [13] 2 Tim. iv. 10.

for example, is that of Titus, who in a time of passionately strained relations, by his tactful and firm intervention, brought the Corinthian Church back into order after its disturbance by agitators.[1]

Paul was fond of coining expressive names full of personal feeling for these helpers—Timothy, Tychicus, Titus (who has just been mentioned), Silvanus, Aquila and Priscilla, Urbanus, Epaphroditus, Euodia, Syntyche, Clemens, Philemon, Mark, Aristarchus, Demas, Luke the physician, and others. He calls them familiarly ' fellow-workers,'[2] a term borrowed from the workshop ; in a spirit of comradeship the champion of Christ speaks to them as ' fellow-soldiers,'[3] or using a rougher metaphor he calls them 'yokefellows,'[4] with a playful reference perhaps to the words about oxen treading out the corn,[5] which he had applied to the Apostles. Looking to the one Master in common, his helpers are his ' fellow-slaves,'[6] but just because they are in the service of that Master they are to the churches the reflected 'glory of Christ.'[7] The recollection of imprisonment suffered together, causes him to coin the honourable title of ' fellow-captive '[8] for Aristarchus[9] and Epaphras,[10] Andronicus and Junias.[11] Phoebe, the Christian woman of Cenchreæ, the port of Corinth, who had done much for his welfare, is singled out for distinction as his 'patroness,'[12] and the mother of his friend Rufus, he calls his ' mother,'[13] a plain hearty way of showing his respect.

[1] Traces of this are to be seen all through, 2 Cor. ii., vii., viii.

[2] συνεργός, 1 Cor. iii. 9 ; Phil. ii. 25 ; iv. 3 ; Philem. 1, 24 ; 2 Cor. viii. 23 ; Rom. xvi. 3, 9, 21.

[3] συστρατιώτης, Phil. ii. 25 ; Philem. 2.

[4] σύζυγος, Phil. iv. 3.

[5] 1 Cor. ix. 9 f. ; 1 Tim. v. 18 ; cf. above, p. 102.

[6] σύνδουλος, Col. i. 7 ; iv. 7.

[7] δόξα Χριστοῦ, 2 Cor. viii. 23.

[8] συναιχμάλωτος.

[9] Col. iv. 10.

[10] Philem. 23.

[11] Rom. xvi. 7.

[12] προστάτις, Rom. xvi. 2.

[13] Rom. xvi. 13.

What a vast deal lies hidden behind these brief names! How many experiences, how much endurance, how much brotherhood! The emotional strength especially which pulses in these names was one of the magic charms wielded by Paul, the leader of men. His influence upon the common people depended not least on his ability to arouse the slumbering forces in the souls of the simplest by the hearty directness of his appeal as man to man.

All these associates in the Apostle's work were, like himself, men of exceptional activity. If we were to mark on the map the routes of all their journeys which are known to us, the lines would almost make a labyrinth, but we should feel all the more clearly how the Anatolian world was set thrilling by the trumpet blasts of the evangelists :

The word of the Lord runneth. [1]

The people whose souls were moved by the mission of Paul and his faithful companions were—the overwhelming majority at least—men and women from the middle and lower classes :

Not many wise after the flesh,
Not many mighty,
Not many noble !
But the foolish things of the world
Hath God chosen,
To put to shame them that are wise.
And the weak things of the world
Hath God chosen,
To put to shame the things that are strong.
And the base things of the world,
And the things that are despised,
Hath God chosen.
And the things that are not,
To bring to nought the thing that are.

[1] 2 Thess. iii. 1, ἵνα ὁ λόγος τοῦ κυρίου τρέχῃ.

In these lines,[1] ringing like a song of defiance and inspired by the defensive pride which longs for the fray,
Paul sufficiently well described the social structure of
the church of Corinth. It has already been hinted[2]
that even the holes and corners of the slums of this
cosmopolitan   city   had   witnessed   conversions.   It
appears from the scenes at the Lord's Supper depicted[3]
by Paul that some of the poor saints at Corinth
occasionally 'had nothing'[4] at all : instead of sharing
the food which they had brought with them in a
brotherly way, and waiting to eat till all were supplied,
many devoured their own supplies with greedy haste,
and those who had nothing were obliged to go hungry.
The terrible seriousness of Paul's way of dealing with
this desecration of the Lord's Supper[5] enables us to
divine that his sympathy was with the hungry.

Paul also speaks of the 'deep poverty' of the
churches of Macedonia (Philippi, Thessalonica,Berœa).[6]
And the advice he gives to the assemblies of the
Galatian Christians to raise the collection for the
brethren at Jerusalem gradually in small amounts every
Sunday[7] (the touching prototype of the copper collections for missions which have been so richly blessed
amongst us), is a proof that in the interior of Asia
Minor, where money was even rarer than in the coast
cities, in spite of their better earnings, the churches
were still poor.   Even in places where Paul had not per-

---

[1] 1 Cor. i. 26-28, οὐ πολλοὶ σοφοὶ κατὰ σάρκα, οὐ πολλοὶ δυνατοί, οὐ
πολλοὶ εὐγενεῖς· ἀλλὰ τὰ μωρὰ τοῦ κόσμου ἐξελέξατο ὁ θεός, ἵνα καταισχύνῃ
τοὺς σοφούς· καὶ τὰ ἀσθενῆ τοῦ κόσμου ἐξελέξατο ὁ θεός ἵνα καταισχύνῃ τὰ
ἰσχυρά· καὶ τὰ ἀγενῆ τοῦ κόσμου καὶ τὰ ἐξουθενημένα ἐξελέξατο ὁ θεός, τὰ
μὴ ὄντα ἵνα τὰ ὄντα καταργήσῃ. One of Paul's greatest creations, an
echo of Matt. xi. 25.

[2] Above, p. 69.   [3] 1 Cor. xi. 20-22, 33 ff.
[4] 1 Cor. xi. 22, τοὺς μὴ ἔχοντας.   [5] 1 Cor. xi. 20-34.
[6] 2 Cor. viii. 2, ἡ κατὰ βάθους πτωχεία αὐτῶν.
[7] 1 Cor. xvi. 1 f.   Cf. Licht vom Osten, 4th Ed., p. 309.

sonally conducted a mission it is probable that the slave
element, for instance, was more strongly represented
than that of the slave-owning freemen :   In Colosse
and Laodicea 'masters' receive only one short exhortation,[1] while the slaves, on the other hand, have a
whole string of commands and promises ;[2] in this there
is a reflection of the social structure of these churches.[3]

On the other hand, Paul mentions by name certain
fairly well-to-do Christians. Those who possessed a
room so large that 'house churches' could assemble
there for edification as was the case with Aquila at
Ephesus,[4] Nymphas and others at Laodicea,[5] Philemon
at Colosse,[6] cannot have been poor, and Gaius at Corinth
who even offered the hospitality of his house to the
whole church,[7] must, along with his fellow-citizen,
Erastus,[8] the city treasurer, have belonged to the
middle class.   It is noteworthy that several women
whose names are honourably mentioned in connection
with Paul's missionary labours, appear to have been
possessed of means : Chloë apparently in Corinth,[9]
Phœbe at Cenchreæ, the port of Corinth,[10] Lydia in
Philippi, who came from Asia Minor.[11]   Other Macedonian women of the upper clases, considerable numbers
of whom seem at first to have been enthusiastic for the
Gospel (at Thessalonica women of the 'first' circles,[12]
and in Berœa 'Greek women of honourable estate '[13]),
seem later on to have lost their 'first love'[14] ; otherwise

---

[1] Col. iv. 1 ; Eph. vi. 9.

[2] Col. iii. 22-25 ; Eph. vi. 5-8.

[3] On this whole subject cf. my work, *Das Urchristentum und die
unteren Schichten*, Göttingen, 1908.

[4] 1 Cor. xvi. 19 ; Rom. xvi. 5.   [5] Col. iv. 15.

[6] Philem. 2.   [7] Rom. xvi. 23.

[8] *Ibid.*   [9] 1 Cor. i. 11.

[10] Rom. xvi. 1 f. ; cf. above, p. 240.

[11] Acts xvi. 4.   [12] Acts xvii. 4.

[13] Acts xvii. 12.   [14] Rev. ii. 4.

it is difficult to understand the ' deep poverty ' of the
Macedonian churches later on.[1] In Antioch in Pisidia,
it is to be noted, that it was the honourable women
who allowed themselves to be degraded as the instru-
ments of persecution against Paul and Barnabas.[2]

The subject matter of Paul's mission preaching is
Christ exalted on the Cross,[3] the living Christ, the
Crucified,[4] with an especial emphasis on the near
approach of the completed Kingdom of God, and with
strong ethical demands.[5] Everything was presented at
first with the greatest possible simplicity :

> I fed you with milk, not with meat ; for ye were not able to
> bear it.[6]

But then the treasures of those ' riches in Christ '[7] of
which we spoke in an earlier chapter were gradually
opened out, and those unknown people, whom chance
had thrown together in the slums of the cosmopolitan
city, became members of ' the body of Christ,'[8]

> enriched in Him, in all utterance and in all knowledge.[9]

To some extent they appear to have been true
revival churches, zealously held together by Paul, if
necessary by sharp discipline,[10] but also by showing
that he had great confidence in them.[11] A letter sent

---

[1] 2 Cor. viii. 2.　　　　　　　　[2] Acts xiii. 50.

[3] John xii. 32, 33 ; iii. 14 ; viii. 28 ; cf. above, p. 197.

[4] Gal. iii. 1, etc.　　　　　　[5] Cf. Gal. v. 21, προεῖπον.

[6] 1 Cor. iii. 2, γάλα ὑμεῖς ἐπότισα, οὐ βρῶμα· οὔπω γὰρ ἐδύνασθε.

[7] Eph. iii. 8 (cf. above, p. 161 f.).

[8] 1 Cor. xii. 27 (etc.), ὑμεῖς δέ ἐστε σῶμα Χριστοῦ.

[9] 1 Cor. i. 5, ἐν παντὶ ἐπλουτίσθητε ἐν αὐτῷ, ἐν παντὶ λόγῳ καὶ πάσῃ
γνώσει.

[10] Cf. especially 1 Cor. v. 1 ff., devoting the incestuous person to
Satan (Licht vom Osten, 4th Ed., p. 256 ff.), or 2 Cor. xiii. 2, or 1 Cor.
xvi. 22. On the other hand, after he has been very severe Paul
counsels a return to the right path, 2 Cor. ii. 5-11.

[11] Cf. e.g. 1 Thess. iv. 9 ff., the words addressed to those who are
' taught by God ' at Thessalonica.

to Corinth, but now lost, proves what an effect his personal authority had upon them : [1]

> For behold this self-same thing, that ye were made sorry [2] after a godly sort, what earnest care it wrought in you, what clearing of yourselves, yea, what indignation, yea, what fear, yea, what longing, yea, what zeal, yea, what avenging !

One reflects with astonishment, on hearing words like these, so delicate in their psychological discrimination, what extraordinary confidence Paul must have had in the receptiveness and responsiveness of the poor people of Corinth.

In preaching Christ to Jews, no doubt the appeal was made to proof from Scripture (the Septuagint), so to Pagans there was an occasional allusion to the divine wisdom enshrined in the words of the poets : both methods are vouched for by doubtless trustworthy records in the Acts of the Apostles.

The effect of this mission preaching must have been powerful and often even sudden. Paul's own description of the impression made by prophetic utterance upon the hearers [3] undoubtedly reflects the personal experiences of the prophet missionary and revivalist preacher. A stranger, perhaps an unbeliever, comes into the assembly and hears what is being said by the prophet who speaks in the spirit. Suddenly he sees his own inner life, the most secret thoughts of his heart unveiled by the spirit-filled preacher's exhortation to repentance, and as if struck by lightning he falls down before God confessing as he falls :

> God is among you indeed !

[1] 2 Cor. vii. 11, ἰδοὺ γὰρ αὐτὸ τοῦτο τὸ κατὰ θεὸν λυπηθῆναι πόσην κατηργάσατο ὑμῖν σπουδήν, ἀλλὰ ἀπολογίαν, ἀλλὰ ἀγανάκτησιν. ἀλλὰ φόβον, ἀλλὰ ἐπιπόθησιν, ἀλλὰ ζῆλον, ἀλλὰ ἐκδίκησιν. Cf. above, p. 67.

[2] ' Made sorry' by the letter above mentioned.

[3] 1 Cor. xiv. 24 f.

When detained in Galatia by sickness the Apostle's reception had been nothing short of enthusiastic.[1]

On the other hand, Paul encountered the most serious obstacles, chiefly from the agitation stirred up by Jewish-Christian apostles of legalistic bent, who followed him on his journeys and tried to set his churches against him both by personal efforts and by letter.[2] To these 'false brethren,'[3] these 'dogs and evil workers,'[4] who shrank from no malicious action, Paul was indebted for some of his most anxious hours. We are indebted to them for occasioning several of Paul's most valuable letters. But he also suffered much at the hands of Jews whose devotion to the Law led to denunciations and infliction of punishment in the synagogues, and even the business instincts of heathen religion were roused against him, as shown by the riot provoked by Demetrius the silversmith at Ephesus.[5]

The missionary journeys were not anxiously planned out beforehand in every detail.[6] Of course Paul did not travel at haphazard; his aim was naturally the districts opened up by the ancient main roads, and especially the cities with Jewish colonies. He had in his head a map of the Jewish Dispersion. In some cities he had no doubt family[7] or tribal[8] connections and he availed himself of them. But he willingly allowed himself to be turned aside from the regular

[1] Gal. iv. 13 ff.   [2] 2 Thess. ii. 2, 15 ; 2 Cor. iii. 1.

[3] Gal. ii. 4, τοὺς ψευδαδέλφους.

[4] Phil. iii. 2, τοὺς κύνας, τοὺς κακοὺς ἐργάτας.

[5] Acts xix. 23 ff.

[6] Cf. Erich Stange, Paulinische Reisepläne, Gütersloh, 1918.

[7] In Jerusalem Paul had a nephew, Acts xxiii. 16 (cf. above, p. 89 and p. 109).

[8] Cf. the συγγενεῖς Andronicus, Junias, and Herodion in Ephesus, Rom. xvi. 7, 11, and the συγγενεῖς Lucius, Jason, and Sosipater, who were with him in Corinth, Rom. xvi. 21.

route by a sudden inspiration[1] and driven on towards
new goals. No doubt he often experienced what he
bade his faithful followers pray for:[2]

> A great door and effectual is opened[3] unto me!

The great lines of his missionary journeys are comparatively speaking clear.

After the Damascus-experience he first went to
' Arabia.' Whether he actually began his missionary
work there is not certain. That he then sketched out
the system of Paulinism is quite improbable! What is
likely is that he earnestly desired a time of quiet recollection. Then, after a short stay in Jerusalem, he
worked as missionary in Syria and Cilicia, that is for the
most part in Antioch on the Orontes and in his native
city of Tarsus, and after that in company with Barnabas
in Cyprus, in Pamphylia, Pisidia and Lycaonia.

Then there follows, after another short visit to Jerusalem, the most important of his journeys as judged by
its effects : from Antioch on the Orontes via Tarsus
through the Cilician Gates of the Taurus mountains to
Lycaonia, Phrygia, and Galatia. Here in the ancient
country of Galatia, according to my opinion, the churches,
to which the letter to the Galatians was addressed, are
to be located.[4] The intention of evangelising western
Asia Minor and Bithynia, where there was a large Jewish
population, was overruled by the Spirit. The Apostle
felt that he was guided to cross the sea, and he went
from (Alexandria) Troas by ship to Macedonia, where

---

[1] Gal. ii. 2 ; Acts xvi. 6, 7, 9 f. (xvii. 15 ; xix. 1 in Codex D).
[2] Col. iv. 3.   [3] 1 Cor. xvi. 9, cf. 2 Cor. ii. 12.
[4] The account of the origin of the Galatian churches given in Gal.
iv. 13-19 simply does not fit with the data in Acts about the evangelisa-
tion of Antioch in Pisidia, Iconium, Lystra, and Derbe, in which cities
many would place ' the churches of Galatia.' Other data of Acts also
do not fit to this South-Galatian hypothesis. A mention of the foundation of the South-Galatian churches might be expected in Gal. i. 21.

he succeeded in founding churches in Philippi, Thessalonica, and Berœa.   After an unsuccessful attempt at
Athens he came to Corinth,[1] where he secured a success
that is all the more significant.

A sea-voyage took him via Ephesus to Palestine, an
overland journey to Syrian Antioch, and again through
the Cilician Gates into the interior of Asia Minor to
Galatia and Phrygia, till he reached Ephesus, which became for a considerable time the centre of his labours.
We know extremely little of this Ephesian period, but
during that time Paul must have gone through much
more than is recorded in our fragmentary authorities.
Some of his most important letters were written from
Ephesus, some perhaps while he was imprisoned.[2]   From
Ephesus Paul made journeys by land and sea as shown
especially by his letters to Corinth.   At Ephesus he
underwent great suffering for his faith, and he met with
the most loyal and self-sacrificing devotion.

After a journey which led him ' through '[3] Macedonia
to Illyricum there followed a peaceful sojourn in Corinth.   Paul then intended to take with him the collection which he had gathered for the saints in Jerusalem
to the Holy City and from thence to start for Rome and
Spain.   He did indeed journey via Macedonia and Asia
Minor by land and water to Palestine, but was arrested
in Jerusalem, and being taken via Cæsarea and thence by
sea, reached Rome as a prisoner.   Whether Paul after
the two years of work there,[4] actually carried out the
Spanish journey as planned,[5] remains an open question,
but I reckon on the probability of an affirmative answer.

---

[1] This arrival of Paul in Corinth can now, so I believe, be fixed
chronologically with great probability (cf. Appendix I.).

[2] Cf. above, p. 16 f.

[3] When Paul at Ephesus speaks of a journey ' through ' Macedonia
(1 Cor. xvi. 5), we ought in the first instance to think of a journey from
East to West, that is no doubt along the *Via Egnatia*.

[4] Acts xxviii. 30 f.   [5] Rom. xv. 24, 28.

These are, of course, no more than hints. The missionary's own letters and the Acts of the Apostles enable us to illustrate the missionary work of Paul with a series of bright and lively pictures familiar to us all, the church that stands out most realistically being that of Corinth.

I should like to call attention to just three pictures which are comparatively little noticed in the long series.

First the collection for the poor saints of the mother church at Jerusalem. As a cause especially dear to the Apostle it is mentioned repeatedly in several of his letters,[1] and its characteristics become clearer when viewed against the background afforded by the practice of collections in the contemporary world.[2] The warmth of Paul's brotherly affection, his businesslike prudence, his loyal observance of an agreement,[3] and his delicate tact are all revealed in his treatment of this one matter, and so too the readiness of his newly founded churches to take action even at a sacrifice to themselves, appears in the best light.

Next there is the case of the runaway slave, Onesimus,[4] which is treated in the letter to Philemon—a typical instance of the Apostle Paul's care for the individual soul. This one case teaches us better than long investigations could do what the secret of this missionary's influence was. It was the suggestive power of his entirely trustful and entirely brotherly personality which bound people to him.[5]

Finally the little letter to the Christians at Ephesus, preserved in the sixteenth chapter of Romans, shows what Paul, the missionary, made of these people. There he stands amidst his faithful friends, united with them

---

[1] In the two Corinthian letters and in Romans.
[2] Cf. *Licht vom Osten*, 4th Ed., p. 83 ff. and 86 f.
[3] Gal. ii. 10.   [4] Cf. above, p. 19 ff.
[5] Cf. above, p. 239 ff.

in the faith of Christ and in the sufferings of Christ,
knowing each one, and exchanging with all a pressure
of the hand or a friendly look—with men and women—
from the self-sacrificing couple Priscilla and Aquila to
Rufus and his mother, whom the Apostle thankfully
calls his own mother.[1]   In all these unpretentious greetings we feel what is implied though not spoken.   In
these lines the unknown and forgotten inhabitants of
the great city of antiquity, some by their names recognisable as slaves, are striving upwards from the dull,
vegetating multitude, upward to the light, having become personalities, saints in Christ, Christ-intimates
through Paul the missionary.   To such souls with their
unimpaired and sanctified powers the future belongs.

A peculiarly kind fate has preserved for us in the
record a relic of one of these unknown persons.   Paul
had dictated that little letter to his companion Tertius,
and then allowed him to add a line from himself.   The
permission is as characteristic of Paul as of Tertius.
And just as we find in other letters of the ancient
world such lines written by one who is not the sender
—as, for example, in a letter from an Egyptian woman,
Helena, to her brother Petechon,[2] this postscript by her
father :—

> I also, Alexander, your father, salute you much. . . .

So Tertius writes :[3]

> I salute you, I, Tertius, who have written this letter in the
> Lord.

In whatever way we take the words ' in the Lord ' here
appended like a seal—whether we construe it with ' I

---

[1] Cf. above, p. 240.

[2] The Oxyrhynchus Papyri, No. 1067, 3rd century A.D.: κἀγὼ
Ἀλέξανδρος ὁ π[α]τὴρ ὑμῶν ἀσπάζομαι ὑμᾶς πολλά . . .

[3] Rom. xvi. 22, ἀσπάζομαι ὑμᾶς ἐγὼ Τέρτιος ὁ γράψας τὴν ἐπιστολὴν ἐν
κυρίῳ.

salute you '[1] or with 'have written '—in any case this
line of Tertius contains the confession which may
be described as the most fundamental in Paul's
vocabulary :[2]

in the Lord.

It may be called a formula repeated by a pupil—I
am disposed to value more highly the contribution
which Tertius unwittingly made to the New Testament.
I see behind this line, as it were, the impress of the
great man's creative soul on the soul which the great
man had awakened in the insignificant brother.   Tertius
stands before us as a type of the people who were raised
up by Paul, the missionary, out of their dull existence in
the mass to the One exalted upon the Cross, into the
sphere of grace that makes all things new, into the
hallowing fellowship with Jesus Christ the Lord.

It is certain that Paul, the missionary, carried out
his work with the prospect of martyrdom before his
eyes.   Once he allowed his most trusted friends, the
Christians of Philippi, to have a glimpse of his thoughts
about this :[3]

Yea, and if I am poured out as a drink-offering at the
sacrifice which I minister as a priest[4] by the work of your faith,
I joy and rejoice with you all.

The presentiment was fulfilled.   Paul did in fact 'give
his body '[5] as a sacrifice of first-fruits in the great conflict of world history between the Christ-cult and the

[1] That is probably the more likely, cf. 1 Cor. xvi. 19.

[2] Cf. above, p. 140.

[3] Phil. ii. 17, ἀλλὰ εἰ καὶ σπένδομαι ἐπὶ τῇ θυσίᾳ καὶ λειτουργίᾳ τῆς
πίστεως ὑμῶν, χαίρω καὶ συγχαίρω πᾶσιν ὑμῖν.   Cf. 2 Tim. iv. 6, and Rom.
xv. 30 f.

[4] On this cf. Rom. xv. 16 (above, p. 232).

[5] Cor. xiii. 3.

Cæsar-cult,[1] in a martyr's death he finally experienced the literal fulfilment of his fellowship with the sufferings and death of the Crucified.

[1] For the Jewish and apostolic emotional background of this conflict cf. the chapter 'Christus und die Caesaren,' *Licht vom Osten*, pp. 287-324.

PAUL IN THE WORLD'S RELIGIOUS HISTORY

CHAPTER XI

PAUL IN THE WORLD'S RELIGIOUS HISTORY

PAUL the apostle's 'work of Christ'[1] culminates in a martyrdom like Christ's. Recorded with blood in the annals of Christianity, and mirrored to the historian in letters covering only a few pages, what he accomplished in his life irradiates the thought of the patristic and scholastic writers whose folios fill our libraries.

How are we to determine (what he himself never anticipated) his importance for the history of the world?

Behind his enormous work of propagating and organising the Christ-cult, which all eyes can see, we can trace back to Paul these forces that are at work in the world.

Though he was not the founder of the new cult—the origin of the Christ-cult is the secret of the mother church of Palestine—Paul entered into the mystical experience of Christ, which is the psychological precondition for the Christ-cult, in the primitive intensity of its power, and also was practically the creator of far the larger part of its classical forms of expression.

His Christ-mysticism, which was in its origin a reaction to revealed grace, and in its nature Christ-intimacy, a mysticism of fellowship, not of oneness with its object, ethical, not indifferent, but in the highest degree active—this mysticism, though centred in Christ, did not exclude the living God, but rather disclosed

---

[1] Phil. ii. 30, τὸ ἔργον Χριστοῦ.

(255)

Him as Holy Love, and secured access to His
redemptive and re-creative grace.

Paul made this religion of Christ world-wide by
going beyond the old Messianic, that is the specifically
Jewish and national, appreciation of the Person of
Jesus. Christ the Lord, Christ the Spirit—with these
confessions made central by Paul, the ancient Aramaic
reverence for a Messiah, transformed into a cult and at
last separated from the Law, struggles forward to the
position of the world religion of all nations and all
times.

This Christ, the Spirit and the Lord, however,
retains the essential features of the Man Jesus, the
poor, humiliated Jesus of the Gospel tradition, who
served in love, who commanded with power, and at
last obediently suffered and was crucified. With the
eternal wound-prints of His passion the Exalted Christ
is ever present in the Church of His saints, and through
the rich treasure of His living words is powerfully at
work in the individual, in the cult and in propaganda.
Thus was Pauline Christ-intimacy, and through it
Christianity, protected from the excesses of mythological and theosophical imaginings, as well as from
being hardened and deadened by dogmatic speculation.
During well-nigh two thousand years of Christian
thinking upon Christ, the words of Jesus and the cross
of Jesus have constantly been the sign-posts visible
from afar, which have prevented the all-to-subtle
Christologists from completely losing their way. The
identity insisted upon by Paul of the Crucified with the
Living One and of the Living One with the Crucified,
of the earthly with the heavenly and of the heavenly
with the earthly, imparts to Christ-mysticism and the
Christ-cult two things : ethical sobriety and enthusiastic
fervour.

The mere spiritual Christ, so easily liable to become

attenuated to a Christ idea, would have created neither a religion of the people nor a religion of the peoples, but would have remained a rapidly worn out thesis for discussion among a narrow circle of Christologists. The mere historical Jesus would certainly have had greater carrying power as the foundation of the new church, but would have made Christianity retrospective, bound by the Law like Judaism, rigid like Islam. The Pauline Christ-intimacy with its decisive confession to the Christ present and coming, who is the crucified Jesus, made both past and future present. It was capable of creating a cult fellowship both popular and of world-wide historic effect, which, filled with ethical power, was no book religion looking backward to the Law, but a Spiritual religion with face set forward.

In all this Paul united Christian piety inseparably with the Person of Jesus Christ, and that is his achievement in the world's history.

Jesus of Nazareth stood, with His experience of God and with His mighty confidence in the nearness of the Kingdom of God, entirely self-supported. Paul placed himself and mankind, with all their hopes and troubles, where grace alone had placed him, in Christ. Where Jesus in lonely consciousness of His mission stands face to face with the Father, Paul stands before God, and with him stand the others, ' through Christ ' and ' in Christ.'

Was Paul tampering with the old Gospel of Jesus concerning God and the nearness of His Kingdom when he thus incorporated with it religious faith in Christ ?

No! He secured to the many the experience of God which had been the possession of the One.

For the mass of the weary and heavy-laden it is impossible to emulate the heroic independence of the religious experience of Jesus. They need the Paraclete

(Comforter) and the Mediator. Laboriously they climb the heavenly ladder rung by rung hand in hand with their Helper : but over each one of their uncertain steps there is greater joy in heaven than over the titanic knowledge which still thinks itself able to take the firmament by storm, when already its downward plunge has ended in tragic ruin.

The Christ-centred Christianity of Paul is the necessary form in which alone the Master's revelation could be assimilated by mankind, and which alone was capable of fashioning a perennial religion for the people and a religion of the peoples powerful enough to mould the history of the world. Paul did not invent a Christology intellectually adapted to the wisdom of the intellectual. What he did was out of the depths of his own mystical spiritual experience of Christ to bring to the poor and lowly and to those who felt themselves inwardly poor and lowly, the holy figure of the Divine-Human Redeemer—that figure which was folly to earth's wisdom—in order that in fellowship with Him even the poorest and most helpless soul might be granted access to the living God.

The Christ-centred Christianity of Paul is therefore neither a breach with the Gospel of Jesus nor a sophistication of the Gospel of Jesus. It secures for the many the Gospel experience of God which had been the possession of the One, and it does so by anchoring these many souls in the Soul of the One.

APPENDICES

APPENDIX I

THE PROCONSULATE OF L. JUNIUS GALLIO

AN EPIGRAPHICAL STUDY TOWARDS THE ABSOLUTE CHRONOLOGY OF
PAUL. (*See the Photographed Facsimile facing the title page.*)

In my book *Light from the Ancient East,* written in
1909, I used the following sentence :[1]

> No tablets have yet been found to enable us to date exactly
> the years of office of the Procurators Felix and Festus, or of the
> Pro-consul Gallio, which would settle an important problem of
> early Christian history.

The problem of primitive Christianity, which I hoped
might be solved by tablets still resting beneath the
accumulated rubbish of centuries, is the chronology of
the Apostolic age and especially of the Apostle Paul.
We were not in a position to name one tolerably certain
date that would place the relative chronology of Paul,
which is in the main determinable, on a firm basis and
thus bring us nearer to the absolute chronology.[2]   There
always remained a margin of uncertainty amounting to
at least five years.

From the historians of the Imperial period, unless
surprising fresh discoveries of lost texts should be made,
there is scarcely anything to be expected.   Even such

[1] *Light from the Ancient East*, p. 5.

[2] This fact is to be explained from the general character of the
primitive Christian tradition concerning Paul, which has often been
emphasised in the foregoing pages of this book.   Being a popular
tradition it had no interest in fixing facts chronologically.   It is not
calculated for the interests of scholars.   As a whole it is the more
historically trustworthy because so artless.

ingenious combinations of data as Eduard Schwartz [1]
published concerning the years of office of Felix and
Festus are not so convincing as to meet with general
acceptance.   Any real advance is rather to be expected
from unliterary texts.   Should it prove possible, for
instance, to fix the date of the proconsulship of Gallio
in Achaia, which is mentioned in Acts xviii. 12, we
should have gained a starting-point of special importance,
because clear statements of the narrator make it possible
to make further calculations backwards and forwards
from this point.

Let us glance rapidly at the facts narrated in Acts
xviii.   Paul comes to Corinth from Athens.[2]   He finds
there Aquila, the Jewish tent-maker, husband of Priscilla, who had 'lately'[3] come to Corinth from Athens,
having been banished with the other Jews from Rome [4]
in consequence of an edict of Claudius.   Paul is given
lodging and employment in the house of his fellow-
craftsmen.[5]   Every Sabbath he goes out evangelising,
first in the Jewish synagogue before Jews and Greeks,[6]
then after strong opposition from the Jews,[7] in the
house of the proselyte Titius Justus, hard by the synagogue,[8] with the highly successful result that Crispus,
the ruler of the synagogue, with his family and many
Corinthians, came over to the faith and accepted baptism.[9]

[1] *Zur Chronologie des Paulus*, Nachrichten von der Kgl. Gesell-
schaft der Wissenschaften zu Göttingen, philol.-histor. Klasse, 1907,
p. 264 ff.   I mistrust Schwartz's paper partly on exegetical grounds.
Compare now the thorough criticism of his expositions by Eduard
Meyer, *Ursprung und Anfänge des Christentums*, iii., Stuttgart and
Berlin, 1923, p. 42 ff.

[2] Acts xviii. 1.   [3] προσφάτως, Acts xviii. 2.
[4] Acts xviii. 2.   [5] Acts xviii. 3.   [6] Acts xviii. 4 f.
[7] Acts xviii. 6.   It is probably this opposition that Paul himself
alludes to in letters written at Corinth, 1 Thess. ii. 15 f. and 2 Thess.
iii. 2.
[8] Acts xviii. 7.   [9] Acts xviii. 8 ff.

This whole period of missionary work lasted a year and
a half :[1]

> And he dwelt there a year and six months, teaching the word
> of God among them.

After this clear statement of time the narrator continues :[2]

> But when Gallio was proconsul of Achaia, the Jews with one
> accord rose up against Paul, and brought him before the judgment-
> seat, saying : ' This man seduces people to an unlawful religion.'

The proconsul, however, refuses to be drawn into a trial ;
he declares that the dispute is an internal quarrel within
the Jewish community and orders the Jews away from
the tribunal.[3] Enraged by their failure the disappointed
Jews fall upon the ruler of their own synagogue,
Sosthenes, and maltreat him before the tribunal of the
proconsul, who does not interfere.[4] But Paul remains
in Corinth for a considerable number of days[5] after
this episode, and then sails for Syria by way of
Ephesus.[6]

Anyone reading this account for the first time, and
knowing that the governors of the senatorial provinces,
the proconsuls, normally held office for a period of
one year,[7] would arrange the succession of events as
follows :—

1. Edict of Claudius against the Jews : emigration
   of Aquila and Priscilla from Rome to Corinth.
2. Very soon afterwards[8] Paul's arrival in Corinth.
3. One and a half year's missionary work in Corinth.

---

[1] Acts xviii. 11.

[2] Acts xviii. 12 f., Γαλλίωνος δὲ ἀνθυπάτου ὄντος τῆς Ἀχαίας κατεπ-
έστησαν ὁμοθυμαδὸν οἱ Ἰουδαῖοι τῷ Παύλῳ. Gallio was, as is well
known, the brother of Seneca, the philosopher.

[3] Acts xviii. 14 ff.   [4] Acts xviii. 17.

[5] ἡμέρας ἱκανάς.   [6] Acts xviii. 18 f.

[7] Cf. below, p. 278.   [8] Cf. προσφάτως, Acts xviii. 2.

4. Arrival of the proconsul, Gallio, in Corinth.

5. The Jews accuse Paul before Gallio without success.

6. Paul continues his stay in Corinth for a considerable number of days.

7. Departure of Paul for Ephesus and Syria.

The salient point of this series is the fourth. The phrase, ' but when Gallio was proconsul of Achaia,' can only mean, that, as Luke understood, after Paul had evangelised for a year and a half at Corinth, a new proconsul arrived, Gallio, with whom the Jews then tried their luck.[1] The passage has been thus, and rightly I think, explained by H. Lehmann[2] and Oskar Holtzmann,[3] not to mention other authorities.

If Gallio entered upon his proconsulship in the month y of the year x, the arrival of Paul at Corinth is to be dated approximately eighteen months earlier ;[4] still earlier (but not much) would be the arrival of Aquila and Priscilla in Corinth, and the edict of Claudius against the Jews. In the same way we should be able with some certainty to reconstruct the later chronology of Paul's life, starting from this year x.

[1] The case is exactly the same as in Acts xxiv. 27—xxv. 2, where Luke tells us that after two years a new procurator came and the Jews then renewed proceedings against Paul.

[2] *Claudius und Nero und ihre Zeit.* : Vol. I., *Claudius und seine Zeit*, Gotha, 1858, p. 354 : when Gallio ' arrived at Corinth the Jews immediately brought an accusation against Paul who had been working for eighteen months in the city.'

[3] *Neutestamentliche Zeitgeschichte*, 2nd Ed., Tübingen, 1906, p. 132, ' Paul's first residence in Corinth lasted a year and a half (Acts xviii. 11). Towards the end if not after the expiry of this time (Acts xviii. 12 f., 18), Gallio became proconsul of Achaia.'

[4] In making the calculation, of course, we must be generous enough not to insist on the ' eighteen months ' down to the last minute; but we may employ that number as a clear approximate determination.

Now what about this year x? With the aid of a stone found at Delphi we can now calculate it with greater probability than has been possible hitherto.

For my first knowledge of this stone I am indebted to P. Thomsen, who in a bibliography[1] of the year 1909 referred to Joseph Offord's account[2] of the four fragments of a Delphic inscription published by Emile Bourguet.[3] I may as well add at once the other references to the inscription which are known to me. Alexander Nikitsky[4] was, I believe, the first to publish a drawing of a fragment of the stone, but, so far as I can see, without detailed discussion and without gaining any further attention to the fragment. H. Pomtow, however, had already among his papers, which he kindly allowed me to see in December, 1910, for the purposes of the present work, a copy of the main portion of the inscription, with which he had been acquainted for more than twenty years. In the autumn of 1910 he obtained for me, through the kind offices of his collaborator in epigraphy, Dr. Rüsch, an accurate photograph of the published fragments, together with a paper squeeze.[5] Before this

[1] *Mitteilungen und Nachrichten des Deutschen Palästina-Vereins*, 1909, p. 31.

[2] *St. Paul at Corinth*, Palestine Exploration Fund, Quarterly Statement, April, 1908, p. 163 (cf. also January, 1908, p. 5).

[3] *De rebus Delphicis imperatoriæ ætatis capita duo* [Paris Thesis], Montepessulano, 1905, p. 63 f. Bourguet does not go into Pauline chronology; he contented himself with stating Gallio's year of office as A.D. 52, on the authority of the *Prosopographia* (cf. below, p. 281, note 2).

[4] In his Russian work brought to my notice by H. Pomtow on *Epigraphical Studies at Delphi*, I.-VI., Odessa, 1894-1895, Plate VII., No. xlvii. It is the large fragment which stands second in our facsimile.

[5] From which the photographed facsimile (reproduced in Plate I., facing the title-page of the present volume), was made by Albert Frisch in the Art Institute, Berlin, W. 35. In order to secure a sharper reproduction of what has been preserved, the under surface of the squeeze was photographed.

A. J.-Reinach, in his review of Bourguet's work, had
pointed out the importance of this inscription in deter-
mining Paul's chronology, and so far as I can see he
was the first to do so :[1] 'ce texte fixe définitivement
à 52 le séjour de saint Paul à Corinthe.'

Offord, then, in the article already mentioned[2] placed
the entry of Gallio on his proconsulship in the year 52,
the arrival of Paul in Corinth in the autumn of the year
50, his departure from Corinth in the beginning of the
year 53.

Sir W. M. Ramsay[3] calculated on the basis of this
stone that Gallio's proconsulship ran from April, 52, to
April, 53, and that Paul arrived in Corinth in October,
51.

H. Coppieters[4] made no calculation of numbers, but
only remarked that the inscription made it possible to
fix the date of the proconsulship, while Louis Jalabert[5]
described Bourguet's statement (Gallio's year of office,
52) as important for the determination of Pauline chronology.

Carl Clemen,[6] who also adopted Bourguet's date A.D.
52 for Gallio's proconsulship,[7] believed that this date
confirmed his own earlier calculation.[8]

After having for some time been occupied with the
Delphic inscription, in a short notice[9] of Jalabert's ' Epi-

---

[1] Revue des Études grecques, 20 (1907), p. 49. I am indebted to
Louis Jalabert for the reference.

[2] Loc. cit., p. 164.

[3] The Expositor, May, 1909, p. 468 f.

[4] Dictionnaire apologétique de la Foi catholique, Tome I. (Paris,
1910), col. 268.

[5] Ibid., col. 1428 (article ' Épigraphie ').

[6] Theologische Literaturzeitung, 35 (1910), col. 656.

[7] ' . . . that Gallio was proconsul of Achaia in the year 52.'

[8] Paulus, i., p. 396, ' . . . that Gallio arrived at Corinth in the
spring of 52.'

[9] Theologische Literaturzeitung, 35 (1910), col. 796.

graphie' I announced my intention of publishing a closer
investigation of the text.[1]

A few months later there appeared an article written
jointly by E. C. Babut and Alfred Loisy[2] who had no
knowledge of the earlier discussion of the question.[3]
Babut calculated that the proconsulship of Gallio lasted
from the first third of 52 till the first third of 53,[4] and
in accordance with this Loisy, whose hypertrophied
critical mistrust of the above analysed report in the
Acts of the Apostles makes him very suspicious, was of
opinion that the accusation of Paul before Gallio, if historical, must be placed in the year 52 or the beginning
of the year 53.[5]

Finally, William P. Armstrong,[6] who refers to part
at least of the preceding discussion, including Jalabert's
note and my own, reprinted Bourguet's text, and calculated Gallio's time from spring or early summer of 51
to 52, or (and this he thought more probable), from 52
to 53.

The important fact of this whole discussion, apart
from Bourguet's original publication, was the statement
of Babut[7] that since the publication of the four fragments, three new fragments of the Delphic inscription
had been discovered. Just as I was about to have my
own manuscript printed, I received from Babut a photograph of these fragments[8] which he had very kindly sent

---

[1] I finished the main part of my investigation in March, 1911, and
on May 2, 1911, spoke of it in the Archæological Society at Berlin.

[2] *Le proconsul Gallion et saint Paul*, Revue d'histoire et de lit-
térature religieuses, 2 (1911), March-April, 1911, p. 139-144.

[3] Cf. their expression of astonishment that no student of Paul had
noticed the document though it had been published five years (p. 139).

[4] *Loc. cit.*, p. 142. [5] *Ibid.*, p. 144.

[6] The Princeton Theological Review, April, 1911, p. 293-298.

[7] *Loc. cit.*, p. 139.

[8] With a letter dated Montpellier, April 23, 1911.

at my request, and shortly afterwards Bourguet sent me
with the same scholarly courtesy, also at my request, the
squeeze of two of those fragments and a copy of all
three.[1]

On the 30th of April, 1911, Pomtow had very kindly
given me a squeeze which he had made in 1887 of the
middle fragment of the three.[2] This had already been
published by Nikitsky.[3] Even in 1887 Pomtow, as is
clear from his MS. papers, had been led by the similarity of the lettering to compare his fragment with those
which Bourguet afterwards published, as far as they
were accessible. He decided, however, on account of
the differences of spaces between the lines, that it could
not be united with them. Even to-day Pomtow is of
opinion [4] that the ' new ' fragments, while certainly carved
by the same stonemason as the old ones, did not form
part of the text of the same rescript, but were probably
the conclusion of another rescript. In further proof of
this he refers to differences in the height of the letters
in the two groups of fragments.

In Berlin I am not able to decide whether the ' new '
fragments really belong to the old. To do so I should
be obliged in the first place to examine the tablets
myself at Delphi. Pomtow's argument, based on the
spacing and size of the letters, does not entirely convince
me, because the old fragments are in neither respect
quite uniform in their workmanship. Here, however, I
may be content to let the question remain open. For

[1] With a letter dated Athens, May 8, 1911. There were the two
Delphic fragments, Nos. 728 and 500. Bourguet also most kindly
added a new squeeze of the greater part of the old fragments already
published by him.

[2] This is the fragment No. 2311. I have seen squeezes of all
three of the ' new ' fragments.

[3] Plate VII., No. xlvi.

[4] Therefore he published the rescript of Claudius in the third
edition of Dittenberger's *Sylloge* (see below), without these fragments.

however important the 'new' fragments may be for reconstructing the rescript of Claudius, if they are really a part of it, they seem to me to throw no new light so far on our particular chronological problem.

I have respected the wish expressed to me in 1911 by Bourguet that I would use with discretion the unpublished fragments which he sent me. Therefore I did not publish them and refrained from making facsimiles. However, Bourguet told me after he had received my *Paul*[1] that if he could have known how much importance I attached to the rescript of Claudius, he would have begged me to share with him in publishing the 'new' fragments. Thereupon I was able to lend the material to my friend Dr. Plooij (Leiden), who has given in the plate facing the title-page of his *Chronology*[2] a good facsimile of all the seven fragments. Brassac[3] has also previously submitted a facsimile. It is not necessary, therefore, for me to have fresh facsimiles made of the new fragments, but I can at least give a transcription of their text. Parts of it are easily filled out, but it does not appear to me possible to restore the whole at present :—

```
 1.                      ΠΕΣ
 2. . . . . . . . . . ΙΜΕΝΓΑΡΕ . . .
 3. . . . . . . . . . ΤΟΠΟΥΣΚΡ . . .
 4. . . . . . . . . . ΝΠΑΝΤΩΣΕ . . .
 5. . . . . . . . . . ΘΟΙΤΙΝΕ . . . .
 6. . . . . . . . . . ΙΚΑΙΤΟΣΥΝΑ . .
 7. . . . . . . . . . ΕΠΙΤΩ . . . Ν . . .
 8. . . . . . . ΜΕ . . ΟΙΣΜΕΝ . . . . . .
 9. ΛΑΣΕΕΝΤΕΛΛΟΜΑΙ . . . . . . .
10. ΩΝΕΝΑΥΤΩΓΕΓΡΑΜ . . . . . .
```

The literature dealing with this rescript of Claudius which has appeared since the first edition of my *Paul*

---

[1] Letter dated Delphi, August 26th, 1911.
[2] See below, p. 270, note 1.   [3] *Ibid.*

is very considerable. So far as it is known to me I
refer to it in the note below.[1] No doubt it is fragment-

[1] Hans Lietzmann, *Ein neuer Fund zur Chronologie des Paulus*,
Zeitschrift für wissenschaftliche Theologie, 53 (1911), pp.
345-354; Réné Dussaud, Revue de l'histoire des religions, 64 (1911), p. 268; E.
Dubowy, *Paulus und Gallio*, Bibl. Zeitschrift, 10 (1912), pp. 143-153;
Schäfer, *Zur Chronologie des Lebens Pauli*, Der Katholik, 92 (1912),
pp. 149-153; Bares, *Ein interessanter Fund von Delphi*, Pastor Bonus,
24 (1912), pp. 219-223; M. Goguel, Revue de l'histoire des religions, 65
(1912), p. 315; G. Wohlenberg, *Eine Claudius-Inschrift von Delphi in
ihrer Bedeutung für die paulinische Chronologie*, Neue Kirchl. Zeitschrift,
23 (1912), pp. 380-396; Adolf Harnack, *Chronologische Berechnung
des ' Tags von Damaskus,'* Sitzungsberichte der Kgl. Preusz. Ak. d. W.,
1912, phil.-hist. Klasse, pp. 673-682; Ferd. Prat, *La chronologie de l'âge
apostolique, Recherches des sciences religieuses* (Paris), 1912, p. 374 ff.;
Lorenzo Coccolo, *L'anno del proconsolato di Gallione e data della prima
missione di S. Paolo a Corinto*, in the Journal Didascaleion, 1 (1912), pp.
285-294, and *La cronologia paolina*, Didascaleion, 2 (1913), pp. 261-306;
J. Offord, *Archæological notes*, Palestine Exploration Fund, Quarterly
Statement, 1913, pp. 146-149; van der Kar, *Een delphisch opschrift en de
chronologie van St. Paulus*, Ned. Kath. Stemmen, 1913, pp. 282-287; C.
Bruston, *La date du proconsulat de Gallion*, Revue de théologie et de
questions religieuses, 22 (1913), pp. 362-366; A. Brassac, *Une inscription
de Delphes et la chronologie de Saint Paul*, Revue Biblique, 10 (1913),
pp. 36-53 and 207-217; H. Pomtow in Guil. Dittenberger, *Sylloge
Inscriptionum Græcarum*[3], 2, Lipsiae, 1917, No. 801, pp. 492-494; D.
Plooij, *De chronologie van het leven van Paulus*, Leiden, 1918; in
addition Hans Windisch in Theologisch Tijdschrift, 53 (1919), p. 167
ff.; B. W. Bacon, *The Chronological Scheme of Acts*, The Harvard
Theological Review, 14 (1921), pp. 137-166; Adolf Jülicher, Review
of Plooij in *Gött. gel. Anzeigen*, 184 (1922), pp. 200-209; cf. also Theol.
Lit.-Zeitg., 49 (1924), col. 340 f.; [Wilhelm] Larfeld, *Die delphische
Gallioinschrift und die paulinische Chronologie*, Neue kirchl. Zeitschrift,
34 (1923), pp. 638-647; Eduard Meyer, *Ursprung und Anfänge des
Christentums*, iii. (1923), p. 37 f. Luigi Cantarelli, *Gallione proconsole
di Acaia e San Paolo*, Rendiconti of the Reale Accademia Nazionale dei
Lincei, Vol. 32 (1923), pp. 157-175; Otto Stählin, *Die altchristl. griech.
Litteratur (Christ*[6]), München, 1924, p. 1134. In addition the com-
mentaries on Acts and Handbooks and Introductions to the New
Testament, which have appeared since then. Cantarelli cites further
the following works : Pirot, *Actes des apôtres*, pp. 172 and 174; Christ,
Geschichte der Griech Litteratur, II.[5], 2, p. 931 ff.; Omodeo, *Origini
cristiane*, ii., pp. 18 ff., 110, 372 ff.; iii., p. 264.

ary, as the years we have passed through have made any complete knowledge of international literature impossible.

I proceed first to the description and text of the four old fragments. For details of the description I am indebted to Pomtow's MS. papers.

The material is whitish-gray limestone from the Hagios Elias quarries near Delphi. The four fragments now preserved in the Museum at Delphi are numbered in the collection [1] 3883, 2178, 2271,[2] 4001.

Our facsimile [3] gives these four fragments in what is supposed to be their original positions,[4] on a reduced scale of about $1 : 3\frac{2}{5}$. The height of the letters amounts to 18-20 millimetres (i.e. about three-quarters of an inch). Pomtow is confident that the inscription was originally set up on an outer wall of the south side of the temple of Apollo at Delphi.[5]

The text seems to be horribly mutilated and it really is so. But nevertheless, as regards those portions which concern our problem, we may say that chance has for once behaved reasonably and benevolently. Just those passages which are of most importance to us are clearly legible and quite usable.

The length of the lines is, I think, certainly under-estimated by Bourguet, who by restoration brought the first line up to a total of 54 letters. The title of

[1] These numbers are here given in order according to the sequence of the text.

[2] Bourguet, p. 63, gives this as number 59, the number it formerly was known by.

[3] Above, Plate I., facing title-page.

[4] There is no doubt according to the judgment of the archæologists, who have investigated the originals (Pomtow, Bourguet and Rüsch) that the four fragments really all belong to one another.

[5] Bourguet, pp. 59, 67, 69, has already fixed upon the south wall of the temple as the position of the imperial inscription.

pontifex maximus forms part of the full style of Claudius,[1] I have therefore inserted ἀρχιερεὺς μέγιστος, thus making a line of 71 letters. The original line of the inscription must have been about 1·40 metre long (i.e. 55 inches). In the first line the letters seem to be somewhat farther apart than in the following lines.

The text with probable restorations is given opposite.[2]

In ordinary script and with a few additional restorations which I have essayed merely for the sake of illustration,[3] and for which I must refer to the commentary, I would now give the text as follows :—

1. Τιβέρ[ιος Κλαύδιος Κ]αῖσ[αρ Σεβαστ]ὸς Γ[ερμανικός, ἀρχιερεὺς μέ-
    γιστος, δημαρχικῆς ἐξου-]

2. σίας [τὸ ιβ', αὐτοκράτωρ τ]ὸ κϛ', π[ατὴρ π]ατρί[δος, ὕπατος τὸ ε',
    τιμητής, Δελφῶν τῆι πόλει χαίρειν].

3. Πάλ[αι μὲν] τῆι π[όλει τ]ῶν Δελφ[ῶν πρόθ]υμο[ς ἐγενόμην . . . .
    . . . . καὶ εὔνους ἐξ ἀρ-]

4. χῆς, ἀεὶ [δ'] ἐτήρη[σα τὴ]ν θρησκεί[αν τ]οῦ Ἀπό[λλωνος τοῦ Πυθίου
    . . . . ὅσα δὲ]

5. νῦν λέγεται καὶ [πολ]ειτῶν ἔρι[δες ἐ]κεῖναι ω . . . .
    . . . . . . [καθὼς Λούκιος Ἰού-]

6. νιος Γαλλίων ὁ φ[ίλος] μου κα[ὶ ἀνθύ]πατος [τῆς Ἀχαΐας ἔγραψεν
    . . . . διὰ τοῦτο συγχωρῶ ὑμᾶς]

7. ἔτι ἕξειν τὸν πρό[τερ]ο[ν . . . . . .] ‖ ε[. . . . .
    . . . . τῶν ἀλ-]

[1] Groag in Pauly-Wissowa, *Real-Encyclopädie der klassischen Altertumswissenschaft*, 3 (Stuttgart, 1899), col. 2787. For *pontifex maximus* we sometimes find simply ἀρχιερεύς (David Magie, *De Romanorum juris publici sacrique vocabulis solemnibus in Græcum sermonem conversis*, Lipsiae, 1905, p. 64). I have preferred the longer formula, because it seems to preponderate in other inscriptions of Claudius which are known to me. But of course the shorter translation, ἀρχιερεύς alone, is also possible.

[2] The imperfect letters are indicated by dots beneath them ; probable restorations of lacunæ are printed in small type.

[3] Partly after Pomtow and Hiller von Gaertringen in Dittenberger's *Sylloge*.[3]

PLATE IV.

ΤΙΒΕΡ ι ε λ γ κ 5 ο ι ϑ ν α γ κ 5 ο ι ϑ ν α γ κ ΑΙΣ α σ ε β α σ τ ΟΣ ι σ β α σ ι λ ....

ΣΙΑΣ ....

ΠΑΛαι ....

ΧΗΣΑΕ'ΛΕΤΗΡΗσα τη ΝΘΡΗΣΚΕΙαν τΟΓΑΠΟλλωνος τον πυθιον ....

5 ΝΥΝΛΕΓΕΤΑΙΚΑΙπολΕΙΤΩΝΕΡΙδες εΚΕΙΝΑΙΩ

ΝΙΟΣΓΑΛΛΙΩΝΟΦιλος γ' ΜΟΥΚΑ ανϑνΠΑΤΟΣ ι ν ϑ λ ....

ΕΤΙΕΞΕΙΝΤΟΝΠΡΟτεΟυ .... ΙΙ Ε .....

ΛΩΝΠΟΛΕΩΝΙΚΑ

ΑΥΤΟΙΣΕΠΙΤΡΕπω

10 ΦΩΝΩΣΠΟΛΕ

ΤΑΙΜΕΤΩΚΙσα

τ ο ΥΤΟΥ

PROBABLE RESTORATION OF THE TEXT OF THE GALLIO INSCRIPTION.

8. λων πόλεων κα — — — (about 60 letters)
9. αὐτοῖς ἐπιτρέ[πω — — (about 58 letters)
10. φῶν ὡς πολε — — — (about 62 letters)
11. ται μετῴκι[σα — — — (about 62 letters)
12. [το]ύτου — — — — — (about 65 letters)

In commenting on this text we may start from the undoubted fact, that we have here before us one of the imperial letters such as have been preserved by ancient authors and especially by inscriptions.[1] It is no less evident that it is a letter from the Emperor Claudius to the city of Delphi, although the name of the addressee in the præscript has been lost. We may assume from the first—and this is of importance in attempting the restoration of the mutilated text—that the contents of this letter must have been something favourable to Delphi.[2] The Emperor Claudius perhaps guaranteed anew some ancient privileges of the sacred city, just as he confirmed to the Jews of Alexandria their old privileges in a letter written at the beginning of his reign,[3] and in a letter to the authorities of Jerusalem written in the year 45 graciously settled a question that strongly excited the religious sensibilities of the Jews.[4] Other inscriptions, some of them newly

[1] Cf. *Licht vom Osten*, 4th Ed., p. 321 f.

[2] Otherwise the document would hardly have been recorded in stone and set up in the temple of Apollo.

[3] This letter of Claudius has been preserved by Josephus, *Antt.* xix. 5, 2. On the other hand, it must not be overlooked that Claudius even early in his reign sharply reproved the Jews of Alexandria, cf. the newly discovered letter of the year 41 published by Bell, p. 1 ff. (see above p. 230).

[4] This letter of Claudius has also been handed down by Josephus, *Antt.* xx. 1, 2. Further on the letters of Claudius handed down by Josephus, cf. T. Kindlmann, *Utrum litteræ, quæ ad Claudium Tiberium imperatorem apud Josephum referuntur, ad eum referendæ sint nec ne, quæritur*, Cremsirii, 1884.

published by Bourguet,[1] prove that the relations of this very Emperor Claudius to the city of Delphi were of long standing and friendly. Excellent analogies are also furnished by numerous letters from other emperors to the city of Delphi. Recorded, like the letter of Claudius, in the form of an inscription, a good proportion of them have come down to us in considerable fragments.[2]

We come now to details. Line 1 has already been discussed as regards the probable number of letters it contained. The restoration of the name Claudius is certain.

Line 2 is the most important as bearing on our problem because it contains the decisive date. The 12 denoting the number of times Claudius had been invested with the tribunician power ($\delta\eta\mu\alpha\rho\chi\iota\kappa\grave{\eta}$ $\grave{\epsilon}\xi o\upsilon\sigma\acute{\iota}\alpha$) is only restored, but the 26 ($\kappa\varsigma$) denoting the number of times he had been acclaimed imperator ($\alpha\grave{\upsilon}\tau o\kappa\rho\acute{\alpha}\tau\omega\rho$) which is of far greater importance to us, is above all doubt. At my request Hermann Dessau most obligingly put together for me in January, 1911, the materials available for calculating the 26th acclamation of Claudius as imperator. These materials had already mostly been given by Groag[3] :—

'Altogether Claudius was acclaimed imperator 27 times. As *imperator XXVII.* he appears for the first time on a monument of the 12th year of his tribunician

---

[1] *De rebus Delphicis*, p. 62 f. ; cf. Dittenberger, *Sylloge*, 3rd Ed., No. 801, A-C, and Plooij, p. 32.

[2] Cf. Bourguet, p. 59-93.

[3] Cf. Groag, *op. cit.*, col. 2812 f. ; cf. also Ermanno Ferrero in De Ruggiero *Dizionario epigrafico*, ii., p. 297, 300. I give the materials in extenso because hitherto in discussion mistaken statements have repeatedly been made ; in particular the expositions of Cagnat, *Cours d'épigraphie latine, Supplément à la troisième édition*, Paris, 1904, p. 478, have been in part misunderstood by some investigators.

power (which ran from January 25th, A.D. 52, till the
same date in 53) viz., a monumental arch of the Aqua
Claudia at Rome inscribed :—[1]

> Ti. Claudius Drusi f. Caisar Augustus Germanicus pontif.
> maxim., tribunicia potestate XII., cos. V., imperator XXVII.,
> pater patriæ.

'As the aquaduct was dedicated,[2] on August 1st, 52,
the inscription would give the style of Claudius as it
was on August 1st, 52.

'Claudius appears as *imperator XXVI.* in several
inscriptions besides the one from Delphi. To begin
with there is C.I.L. VIII., Suppl. No. 14727 (Africa) and
XIII., No. 254 (Aquitania).[3] The year of his tribunician
power, wanting in both these instances, is given in an
inscription from the Carian city of Cys [4] :—

> Τιβέριον Κλαύδιον Καίσαρα Γερμανικὸν αὐτοκράτορα θεὸν Σεβαστὸν
> ἀρχιερέα μέγιστον, δημαρχικῆς ἐξουσίας τὸ δωδέκατον, ὕπατον τὸ πέμπτον,
> αὐτοκράτορα τὸ εἰκοστὸν καὶ ἔκτον, πατέρα πατρίδος.

'This inscription certainly belongs to the period
between the beginning of the 12th tribunician power
and the first appearance of the 27th imperatorial acclamation, i.e. between January 25th and August 1st., 52.

'It is highly probable that the imperial letter
contained in the Delphi inscription is also to be placed
in this period, although it is not altogether impossible
that Claudius received his 26th imperatorial acclamation during his 11th tribunician power.[5] He certainly

---

[1] *Corpus Inscriptionum Latinarum*, vi., No. 1256 = Dessau, *Inscriptiones selectæ*, No. 218. Only the beginning of the inscription is quoted
above.

[2] Frontinus, *De aquis*, i. 13.

[3] For this passage, which is not mentioned in Dessau's materials,
I am indebted to Lehmann (*Claudius*, Bk. IV., p. 43), who quoted
it from Muratori.

[4] Bulletin de Correspondance Hellénique, 11 (1887), p. 306 f.

[5] We should then have to read τὸ ιαʹ instead of τὸ ιβʹ in line 2 of
the Gallio inscription.

received his 22nd and 24th imperatorial acclamations
during his 11th tribunician year,[1] and, of course, also
his 23rd, though that has not yet been found recorded.
The 25th has also not yet been found but it might fall
likewise in the 11th tribunician year, i.e. before
January 25th, 52. If the 26th also occurred in the
11th year it could only be towards the end of that
year, i.e. at the end of 51 or in January, 52. But
this assumption cannot be regarded as at all probable.'

The small margin of uncertainty in dating the 26th
imperatorial acclamation does not matter as far as our
question is concerned. *Claudius addressed his letter to
Delphi at some time between (the end of 51, or more
probably) the beginning of 52 and August., 52.*

In line 2 I have supplied conjecturally the titles of
consul ($\H{υ}πατος$) and censor ($τιμητής$). The formula
$Δελφῶν τῆι πόλει χαίρειν$ agrees in the order of its words
with the usage of the præscripts in other imperial
letters.[2]

Bourguet in 1905 took line 3 as part of the præ-
script,[3] restoring it thus : $πάλ[ιν\,?\ τ]ῆι π[όλει τ]ῶν Δελφ[ῶν$
$προθ]υμό[τατα\ χαίρειν]$. As regards both form and
contents this restoration seems to me to be open to
grave objection ; $προθυμότατα χαίρειν$ would, I think, be
quite unusual. Bourguet, however, as he informed me
in the letter mentioned above,[4] has since discovered
another restoration : . . . $τῇ παλ[αιοτά]τηι π[όλει τ]ῶν$
$Δελφ[ῶν$, which Baron Hiller von Gaertringen[5] had also
conjectured independently. Attractive as this restoration is, it seems unusual to me if it is to form part of

---

[1] References are given in Groag, col. 2812.

[2] Cf. now also the letter of Claudius written in the year 41, see
Bell, *op. cit.*, p. 23, 15 f. $Ἀλεξανδρέων τῇ πόλει χαίρειν$.

[3] *De rebus Delphicis*, p. 63.   [4] Above, p. 269, note 1.

[5] Letter dated, Westend, April 29th, 1911.

the præscript of the letter; cf. the remarks on line 2
above. For my conjecture πάλαι . . . , which would
be the beginning of the Emperor's reference to his old
feelings of friendly interest in Delphi, cf., for instance,
the beginning of the edict of Gn. Vergilius Capito [1]
(A.D. 48), καὶ πάλαι μὲν ἤκουον.

In line 4, judging from the squeeze taken by Rüsch
in 1911 I thought χησα more probable than Bourguet's
χ . . ισα. The restoration [εὐτύ]χησα which I then
suggested did not fit badly with what one would expect
the thought to be. The Emperor would say with con-
descending hyperbole that it had been his happiness
hitherto to give the city of Delphi signs of his favour.
But I now prefer the restoration given above. An
exact parallel to the sentence which then follows,[2] 'I
have observed the worshipping of Apollo,'[3] is furnished
by a letter of Hadrian to Delphi:[4] καὶ εἰς τὴν
ἀρ[χαιότητα τῆ]ς πόλεως καὶ εἰς τὴν τοῦ κατέχοντος α[ὐτὴν
θεοῦ θρησ]κείαν [5] ἀφορῶν. So, too, Claudius speaks of
the πάτριος θρησκεία in his letter to the Jews of Alexandria [6] and similarly in his letter to the authorities
at Jerusalem.[7]

In lines 5 and 6 I have now adopted the restoration
proposed by Hiller von Gaertringen, ἔρι[δες], although it

---

[1] In the inscription given by Dittenberger, *Orientis Graeci Inscriptiones Selectae*, No. 665, 15.

[2] Hiller von Gaertringen in 1911 attempted a quite different
restoration: ἀπ᾽ ἀρ]χῆς ἀεί[τ᾽ or γ᾽] ἐτηρή[σατε τὴ]ν, etc. But with
Pomtow in Dittenberger's *Sylloge*, 3rd Ed., he decided for ἐτήρη[σα ;
rightly. I have prefered this reconstruction on account of the parallel
from the letter of Hadrian which is about to be mentioned ; in the main
it is Bourguet's.

[3] Instead of τ]οῦ Ἀπό[λλωνος] we might also conjecture θε]οῦ
Ἀπό[λλωνος].

[4] Bourguet, p. 78.

[5] For the genitive after θρησκεία, cf. also Col. ii. 18, θρησκεία τῶν
ἀγγέλων.

[6] Cf. above, p. 273, note 3.   [7] *Ibid.*, note 4.

gives the letter a very peculiar tone, which is certainly
a daring thing to do when making a restoration. The
restored reading ['Ιού]νιος is certain, Λούκιος is probable.[1]

In line 6 ὁ φ[ίλος] μου κα[ὶ ἀνθύ]πατος is also
unexceptionable. 'My dearest friends'[2] is the term
applied to King Agrippa and King Herod by Claudius in
his edict of toleration for the Jews.[3] The expression
'friend' seems to have been in official use with special
reference to provincial governors. Trajan in a letter to
the city of Delphi speaks of [ἀ]νθυπάτῳ καὶ φίλῳ μου
'Ερενν[ί]ῳ Σατορνείνῳ ;[4] and in a letter from Marcus
Aurelius to the Synodus of Smyrna the Proconsul
T. Atilius Maximus is called ὁ κράτιστος ἀνθύπατος καὶ
φίλος ἡμῶν.[5] The whole form of expression tends to
show that Gallio was the Proconsul in office at the
time of the letter.[6]

We may here at once discuss the question of the
dating of his proconsulship.[7] The governors of the
senatorial provinces, the *proconsules* (ἀνθύπατοι), whom
the Senate as a rule appointed by lot, held the office
for a year.[8] It was an exception for a proconsul to
remain longer in office. It is on record that the exception of a proconsulship lasting for two years occurred
in some cases under Claudius.[9] But I consider it very

---

[1] Cf. below, p. 285, the Gallio inscription from Plataea.

[2] On the expression 'friend of the Emperor,' cf. *Licht vom Osten*,
4th Ed., p. 324.

[3] Josephus, *Antt.* xix. 5, 3, τῶν φιλτάτων μοι.   [4] Bourguet, p. 70.

[5] Dittenberger, *Sylloge*, 2nd Ed., No. 406 (= 3rd Ed., No. 851).

[6] Numerous examples of the mention of the proconsul in office in
imperial letters will be found in Léon Lafoscade, *De epistulis* (*aliisque
titulis*) *imperatorum magistratuumque Romanorum* . . . (a Paris
thesis), Insulis, 1902, p. 127, under ἀνθύπατος.

[7] Here, too, I am indebted for kind assistance to Dessau.

[8] Theodor Mommsen, *Römisches Staatsrecht*, i., 3rd Ed., p. 255.

[9] Dio Cassius, lx. 25, 6, καίτοι καὶ ἐπὶ δύο ἔτη τινὰς ἐῶν αὐτῶν ἄρχειν
(A.D. 44-45).

probable that in this particular case of the proconsuls
of Achaia the rule was observed.

In the year 44 the province of Achaia, which had
previously for some time been combined with Macedonia and had been under a *legatus Augusti pro prætore*,
was given back to the Senate by Claudius.[1] Was he
likely, in this special case of a province restored to the
Senate, so soon afterwards to disregard the privilege
of the Senate, which lay in the annual nomination of
the governors of its provinces ? Moreover, there is the
fact that Gallio fell ill with fever in Achaia, and himself
attributed the disease to the climate ;[2] it is therefore not
exactly credible that he should have remained there any
longer than necessary. In any case, however, it seems
to me that in chronological calculations what we have
to do is to take the normal condition of things as our
basis, not the remotely possible exception.[3] We must
assume that the proconsulship of Gallio lasted one year
until it has been proved to have lasted longer.

Now if Gallio, on the evidence of the Delphi inscription, was in office in the period of the 26th imperatorial acclamation of Claudius, it is possible to
calculate with great probability the date of his entry
upon his duties. Gallio's *entry* upon office is the salient
point of the problem. The mistaken notion occurs not
infrequently that the date in the calendar year at which
a proconsulship began was somewhere about April 1st.[4]

[1] Dio Cassius, lx., 24, 1, τήν τε Ἀχαΐαν καὶ τὴν Μακεδονίαν αἱρετοῖς
ἄρχουσιν, ἐξ οὗπερ ὁ Τιβέριος ἦρξε, διδομένας ἀπέδωκεν ὁ Κλαύδιος τότε τῷ
κλήρῳ.

[2] Seneca, *Ep. Mor.*, 104, 1. 'Illud mihi in ore erat domini mei
Gallionis, qui cum in Achaia febrim habere coepisset, protinus navem
adscendit clamitans non corporis esse sed loci morbum.'

[3] This is rightly insisted on by Sir W. M. Ramsay, The Expositor,
May, 1909, p. 469.

[4] For instance, Carl Clemen in his excellent *Paulus*, i., Giessen,
1904, p. 396, says that the office had ' to be entered on before the

A more inconvenient date, however, could hardly be imagined, because it would compel the proconsuls, if their province were at a great distance from Rome, to travel at a most unfavourable time of the year. We possess, moreover, positive information. Tiberius in A.D. 15 had decreed that the officials should leave Rome 'within' the new moon of the month of June;[1] this would point to July 1st as the day of entry upon office, a date that would in many respects be a favourably chosen one. Obviously, however, the time was not exactly ample for reaching some provinces, and it must have been recognised that the date had not been happily chosen. Claudius, therefore—no doubt also because he was annoyed by the length of time that the new dignitaries hung about the Capital—gave orders in A.D. 42 that they must start before the April new moon.[2] In the following year he reduced this very early date to the time before the middle of April.[3]

We may therefore say that the date of the *entry* upon office was about the middle of the calendar year— at any rate sometime in summer.[4] The account in the

beginning of April by a law of Claudius,' and refers to Dio Cassius, lx., 13, 17. But there is no such passage; the reference probably comes from Gustav Hoennicke, *Die Chronologie des Lebens des Apostels Paulus*, Leipzig, 1903, p. 28, where, however, it is said more correctly that by a law of Claudius the new proconsuls had to leave Rome before the beginning of April. The intended reference is to Dio Cassius, lx., 17, 3.

[1] Dio Cassius, lvii., 14, 5, ἐκέλευσέ σφισιν ἐντὸς τῆς τοῦ Ἰουνίου νουμηνίας ἀφορμᾶσθαι. That is, of course, to be understood as the last possible date of departure.

[2] *Ibid.*, lx., 11, 6, κατέδειξε δὲ καὶ τάδε, τούς τε κληρωτοὺς ἄρχοντας πρὸ τῆς τοῦ Ἀπριλίου νουμηνίας, ἐπειδήπερ ἐπὶ πολὺ ἐν τῷ ἄστει ἐνεχρόνιζον, ἀφορμᾶσθαι.

[3] *Ibid.*, lx., 17, 3, πρὸς δ' ἔτι τοῖς ἄρχουσι τοῖς κληρωτοῖς, βραδέως ἔτι καὶ τότε ἐκ τῆς πόλεως ἐξορμωμένοις, προεῖπε πρὶν μεσοῦν τὸν Ἀπρίλιον ἀπαίρειν.

[4] Mommsen, *Staatsrecht*, ii., 3rd Ed., p. 256, assumes July 1st as the normal date.

Acts of the Apostles seems to me to harmonise with this conjecture. If, as seems to me beyond doubt, Acts xviii. 12 speaks of the *new* proconsul, we obtain for Paul's voyage to Syria (Acts xviii. 18 ff.) the very best time of year :—

> about July beginning of the new proconsulship,
> soon after unsuccessful accusation brought by the Jews,
> further residence of Paul in Corinth,
> departure for Syria (say) in August or September of the same year.[1]

If, then, the letter of Claudius to Delphi was written between (the end of 51 or, more probably) the beginning of 52 and August 1st, 52, and Gallio was then[2] in office, *he entered on his proconsulship in the summer (nominally July 1st) of* A.D. 51.[3]

Line 6 f.   The restoration of the remainder of line

[1] There is an interesting parallel in the date at which Festus, the imperial procurator, happened to enter his office. Harnack (*Die Chronologie der altchristlichen Litteratur bis Eusebius*, vol. i., Leipzig, 1897, p. 237) very rightly conjectures, from the statement in the Acts of the Apostles concerning Paul's departure for Rome, that Festus entered on his duties in summer. Of course no decisive weight is to be attached to this parallel, because it is not concerned with a proconsulship lasting for one year.

[2] In the *Prosopographia Imperii Romani*, ii., Berolini, 1897, p. 238, Dessau gave 52 as the date of Gallio's proconsulship, and Bourguet (p. 64), obviously regarded it as an established fact. In 1897, however, it was only a conjecture, though a happy one. 'The fact that the date now proves to be right is no justification for having assumed it then,' Dessau wrote to me on January 20th, 1911.

[3] The purely logical possibility that he entered on his official duties on July 1st, 52, and that the letter of Claudius was written between July 1st and August 1st, 52, suggests itself for a moment, but only to be rejected as altogether improbable. August 1st, 52, is not the day on which Claudius received his 27th imperatorial acclamation, but only the *terminus ad quem* for this title. For a criticism of the above exposition, cf. Cantarelli, p. 14.

6 is of course not certain ; συγχωρῶ is however in any case the technical word for ‘to approve,’[1] especially when referring to the bestowal of imperial favours.[2] The words ἔτι ἔξειν τὸν πρό[τερ]ο[ν] suggest, what was *a priori* probable, that some earlier privileges of Delphi were to be confirmed.

Line 7 f. might of course be restored as [πολ]λῶν πόλεων.[3]

In line 9 I should conjecture with Pomtow [Δελ]φῶν ὡς. Bourguet's [συμ]φώνως is, however, just as well possible.

In line 12 considerations of space make [το]ύτου more probable than Bourguet's [α]ὑτοῦ.

The conclusions as regards the chronology of Paul are easily drawn. If Gallio entered on his office in the middle of the summer of 51, and if the accusation of Paul by the Jews took place soon afterwards, then, *since he had already been working for approximately eighteen months in Corinth, Paul must have come to Corinth in the first months of the year* 50, *and left Corinth in the late summer of the year* 51.

I refrain from comparing this calculation with the more or less divergent results obtained by others above-named who have made use of the Gallio inscription. I have given all the materials, and every one can make this examination for himself. Still less is there any need for me to show seriatim the incorrectness of earlier attempts to find a merely hypothetically possible

---

[1] Cf. the letter of Claudius to the Alexandrians in the year 41, Bell, *op. cit.*, p. 23.32, and 24.46, also that to the authorities of Jerusalem in the year 45, Josephus, *Antt.*, xx. 1, 2.

[2] Cf the letter of Claudius in Josephus, *Antt.*, xix. 5, 3, for Delphi, Trajan's letter in Bourguet, p. 70 (which I assume is rightly restored), and also Lafoscade, p. 110 f.

[3] But cf. ταῖ[ς] ἄλ[λαις] πόλεσιν in a letter of Hadrian's, Bourguet, p. 79.

date, varying from A.D. 48 to A.D. 54 for Gallio's proconsulship. I would rather note that as early as 1858
H. Lehmann,[1] whose knowledge of the sources for the
time of Claudius was very exact, got at the truth (and
at the same time stated the problem in the true way)
when he placed Gallio's *entry* on office in the summer
of 51.

I should like, however, at least to refer to the confirmation which my calculation of the time of Paul's
stay at Corinth receives from a statement which has
often been noted in Orosius. On the authority of
'Josephus,' Orosius says that Claudius in the ninth year
of his reign expelled the Jews from Rome.[2] That
would mean the year which ran from January 25th, 49,
to the same date in 50. And since Paul on arriving at
Corinth met Aquila the tentmaker there, who had
'lately'[3] arrived from Italy after his expulsion from
Rome by the edict of Claudius, from this we could also
conclude that, if the Apostle reached Corinth at the
beginning of the year 50, the year 49 would be approximately the date of the edict of Claudius against the
Jews.

Ramsay,[4] it is true, maintains that Orosius is always
a year behind in his chronology of Claudius ; but that
does not dispose of the remarkable coincidence between
our calculation and Orosius, for in this case Orosius is

[1] *Claudius*, p. 354. It is true, he places the arrival of Paul at
Corinth as early as the end of the year 49 (p. 332) ; but even this is
not impossible.

[2] Orosius, vii., 6, 15, 'Anno eiusdem nono expulsos per Claudium
urbe Iudæos Iosephus refert.' The same statement in Beda, *De
temporum ratione* a. 4007, is certainly taken from Orosius.

[3] Acts xviii. 2, προσφάτως ἐληλυθότα ἀπὸ τῆς Ἰταλίας . . . διὰ τὸ
τεταχέναι Κλαύδιον χωρίζεσθαι πάντας τοὺς Ἰουδαίους ἀπὸ τῆς Ῥώμης.

[4] *St. Paul the Traveller and Roman Citizen*, 11th Ed., pp. 254 and
68 ; The Expositor, May, 1909, p. 468. He therefore places the
expulsion of the Jews 'according to Orosius' in the year 50.

giving not his own chronology but that of his authority,
' Josephus,' and (this is very important to observe) without attaching much importance to Josephus.[1]   In our
texts of Flavius Josephus the statement, it must be
admitted, is wanting.   It is possible that Orosius means
some other ' Josephus,'[2] or that he has made a mistake
in the name of his authority; but the statement itself for
which he does not profess any particular respect ' cannot
be his own invention ' ;[3] that I take to be obvious.[4]

The inscription at Delphi does not exhaust the epigraphical material referring to Gallio.   There is a tablet
from Pompeii[5] inscribed with a receipt which bears on
the question of his consulship, and has often[6] been

---

[1] In vii. 6, 15 he continues : ' Sed me magis Suetonius movet qui
ait hoc modo : Claudius Judæos impulsore Christo adsidue tumultu-
antes Roma expulit.'

[2] This conjecture is not so remote as it may seem at first sight.
In the ancient Church there was current a collection of facts com-
mitted to memory, probably chiefly for catechetical purposes, large
portions of which are preserved in the *Hypomnesticon* of the so-called
' Christian Josephus,' and which is to some extent much older than
the *Hypomnesticon*.   In the list of high priests in this ' Josephus,'
ii. 80 (Migne, Patrologia Græca, 106), which still awaits investigation,
the beginning of the war of the Jews against the Romans is dated
ἔτους ὀγδόου Κλαυδίου, the reference perhaps being to the Jewish re-
bellion under Ventidius Cumanus (Schürer, i., 3rd Ed., p. 568 f. ;
English translation, *History of the Jewish People*, Division I., vol. ii.,
pp. 171-173).   Here it seems is a ' Josephus ' who gives us a date in
the reign of Claudius similar to the one found in Orosius.

[3] Schürer, iii., 4th Ed., p. 62 (passage not in the English translation).   Above in his text he dates the edict ' probably A.D. 49.'

[4] Harnack, *Die Chronologie*, i., p. 236, also considers this statement
worthy of notice.   Cf. also his penetrating remarks in the essay
(mentioned above, p. 270, note 1) *Chronolog. Berechnung*, p. 647 ff.
Eduard Meyer, *Ursprung und Anfänge des Christentums*, p. 38, also
speaks for the notice of Orosius.

[5] *Corpus Inscriptionum Latinarum*, iv., Suppl. No. 45.

[6] E.g. by Hoennicke, *Die Chronologie des Lebens des Apostels
Paulus*, p. 26.

made use of, though it still unfortunately offers some puzzles. Besides this there is a Bœotian inscription[1] which certainly mentions Gallio, but without a date. The inscription is found on a pedestal in an abandoned chapel of Hagios Taxiarches not far from Platæa:[2]

HΠΟΛΙΣΠΛΑΤΑΙΕΩΝΛΟΥΚ/////
ΝΙΟΝΓΑΛΛΙΩΝΑΑΝΙΑΝΟΝ   ///
ΠΑΤΟΝΤΟΝΕΑΥΤΗΣΕΥΕΡ   ///
                                     ΕΙ   ///

It was published by Dittenberger, who thus restored it :

ἡ πόλις Πλαταιέων Λούκ(ιον) ['Ιού]
νιον Γαλλίωνα 'Ανιανόν [3] [ῦ]
πατον, τὸν ἑαυτῆς εὐερ[γ]
            ἐτ[ην]

and referred it to the consulship of Gallio. There is no material impossibility in this view, but is it probable ? When a Greek city erects a statue in honour of Gallio, its benefactor, our first thoughts are of the proconsul of Greece. I should therefore prefer this restoration :

ἡ πόλις Πλαταιέων Λούκ[ιον 'Ιού-]
νιον Γαλλίωνα 'Ανιανὸν [ἀνθύ-]
πατον, τὸν ἑαυτῆς εὐερ[γ-]
            ἐτ[ην].

But I will not deny that Platæa may have shown her gratitude to Gallio after he had been Proconsul and had become Consul.

Whether my restoration is possible can be decided by an inspection of the stone. Even a squeeze would enlighten us as to the length of the lines and the size, etc., of the letters. In 1911 Michael Gasis[4] of Berlin

[1] I am indebted to Dessau for referring me to this inscription.

[2] *Inscriptiones Græcæ*, vii., No. 1676.

[3] See Dittenberger's note at this remarkable form of the name.

[4] Dr. Michael Gasis of Athens was at that time a member of the Berlin University New Testament Seminar and was engaged upon a

very kindly went to some trouble in the matter. At his request M. A. Keramopulos, his brother-in-law, twice (in July and September, 1911) investigated the ruins of the church of Hagios Taxiarches, but without having been able to find the inscription again. One of his workmen told him then that the inhabitants of the neighbouring village, Kapareli, had taken away stones from Hagios Taxiarches about 1900 to build their church of the Transfiguration, and again about 1905 to build their church of Hagios Panteleemon. M. Keramopulos then most kindly investigated both of these new buildings and thoroughly cross-examined the peasants, but without success. (The letter of M. Keramopulos to Gasis is dated 'Eremokastro 29 . 9 . 1911 '). A re-examination planned late in the autumn of 1924 by M. Oikonomos at the request of my friend, Baron Hiller von Gaertringen, had to be given up owing to the unfavourable weather. We must unfortunately reckon with the possibility that the church of Hagios Taxiarches has lost its valuable inheritance from antiquity through the zeal of the Kapareliots for church building.

great work, an interpretation of the New Testament from the standpoint of modern Greek as a living language. After his return home he was not able personally to concern himself about the inscription. He fell in Macedonia fighting for his country in the Balkan War of 1912, an ἀπαρχή (first-fruits) of the European War of 1914-18.

PLATE V.

ALTAR FROM THE SACRED PRECINCTS OF THE TEMPLE OF DEMETER
IN PERGAMUM.

Imperial Period.

(*Front, first dedication.*)

PLATE VI.

ALTAR FROM THE SACRED PRECINCTS OF THE TEMPLE OF DEMETER
IN PERGAMUM.

Imperial Period.

(Left side, second dedication.)

APPENDIX II.

ON THE ALTAR TO THE UNKNOWN GOD
(See the Autotype Plates V. and VI.)

THE Greek inscription which Paul read on an altar at Athens,[1]

To an unknown God,

and which he viewed and interpreted with the eyes of a monotheistic missionary, has often been illustrated by literary evidence culled from Pausanias, Philostratus, and Diogenes Laërtes.[2] We must conclude from this that in Greek antiquity cases were not altogether rare in which 'anonymous' altars[3]

To unknown gods,[4]

or

To the god whom it may concern,[5]

were erected when people were convinced, for example after experiencing some deliverance, that a deity had been gracious to them, but were not certain of the

---

[1] Acts xvii. 23, ἀγνώστῳ Θεῷ. On p. 78, note 8, I have already indicated that I regard the statement of Acts about the Athenian inscription as credible. However tempting it would be to defend this passage against Eduard Norden (*Agnostos Theos*, Leipzig and Berlin, 1913), I must not attempt it here, but refer the reader to Eduard Meyer, who in *Ursprung und Anfänge*, iii., p. 92 ff., says on all the chief questions raised by this great problem very much what I would myself have said. For further literature on Norden's hypothesis see Otto Stählin, *Die altchristl. griech. Literatur*, p. 1179.

[2] Eduard Norden gives the best collection of materials (cf. note 1 above).

[3] βωμοὺς ἀνωνύμους.   [4] ἀγνώστοις θεοῖς.

[5] τῷ προσήκοντι θεῷ (Diogenes Laërtes, i. 110).

deity's name. Altars to 'unknown gods' on the way from Phalerum to Athens,[1] at Athens [2] and at Olympia [3] are specially mentioned by Pausanias (second century A.D.) and Philostratus (third century A.D.).

Hitherto there has been no epigraphical evidence forthcoming to confirm these statements of ancient writers, and I have not infrequently heard the view expressed that their testimony counts for little. Now an inscription from Pergamum has come to light which perhaps gives ground for saying with a little greater probability that Pausanias and Philostratus deserve credence.

On February 1st, 1910, Wilhelm Dörpfeld and two of his collaborators gave a report before the Berlin Archæological Society of the excavations at Pergamum during the autumn of 1909. The most valuable result of a campaign rich in brilliant discoveries was the clearing of the sacred precinct and temple of Demeter, which from about the end of the fourth century B.C. until late in the imperial period must have been an important shrine, as shown by the architectural remains and inscribed stones. The most remarkable epigraphical discovery, next to the inscription recording the foundation of the building, was brought forward at the meeting by Hugo Hepding, and has since been published by him in the report of the excavations,[4] viz., the altar which is reproduced in our plates V. and VI.

[1] Pausanias, i., 1, 14.

[2] Philostratus, *Vita Apollonii*, vi., 3.

[3] Pausanias, v., 14, 8.

[4] Athenische Mitteilungen, 35 (1910), pp. 454-457. Hepding had before this very kindly allowed me to call attention to the inscription in a provisional notice in Die Christliche Welt, 24 (1910), cols. 218 ff. I am also indebted to Hepding for his courtesy in supplying a fellow-student with the photograph of the two sides of the stone. For a detailed description of the altar I refer to the report of the excavations. The most important fact is that the altar was inscribed with

The text of the older votive inscription (Plate V.)
on the altar which is probably of the second century
A.D. is unfortunately mutilated. Hepding thinks it
should be thus restored, in what appears to me also to
be the most probable form :—

$$\theta\epsilon o\hat{\iota}s|\dot{a}\gamma\nu[\acute{\omega}\sigma\tau o\iota s]$$
$$K\alpha\pi\acute{\iota}\tau[\omega\nu]$$
$$\delta\alpha\delta o\hat{\upsilon}\chi o[s].$$

Symmetry requires that about six letters should be
restored at the end of line 1 ; therefore ἀγγ[έλοις] is
not probable, although shown to be a material possibility
by a Latin inscription, *diis angelis*,[1] of the second or
third century A.D. from Viminacium in Serbia. ἀγί[οις],
ἀγι[ωτάτοις], ἀγν[οῖς] are improbable restorations for
material and partly for formal reasons. Hepding[2]
considered it possible that ἀγι[ωτάταις] should be read,
because in a Peloponnesian inscription[3] there is mention
of Demeter and Kore (Persephone) as τοῖν ἀγιωτάτοιν
θεοῖν, and ἡ θεός is often found at Pergamum. But, on
the other hand, he points out that it would be hardly in
keeping with Greek religious feeling to change after a
short time the dedication of an altar to the two chief
deities of the holy precinct—and we know from the
inscription on the left side of the stone, also reproduced
in our Plate VI., that the dedication of this altar was so
changed. It would be less remarkable that an altar to
unknown gods should receive no particular attention
and then should be annexed to another cult. We
should also expect to find on the stone some trace still

a dedication first on the front and then on the left side. The second
dedication [τοῖς 'A]νέμοις Κασίγνητος ἐπιβώμιος, for which I refer to
Hepding, is also reproduced here in autotype (Plate VI.).

[1] Jahreshefte des Oesterreichisch. Archäol. Institutes, 8 (1905),
Supplement, col. 5.

[2] Athenische Mitteilungen, 35 (1910), p. 456. Cf. also Martin
Dibelius, Theol. Lit.-Ztg., 36 (1911), col. 413.

[3] *Corpus Inscriptionum Graecarum*, i., No. 1449.

remaining of the horizontal beginning[1] of the Ω if
ἀγιωτάταις were the original reading. Moreover, the
adoration of 'unknown' gods harmonises well with the
religious thought of the priests of the mysteries of
Demeter at Pergamum in the second century A.D., as
known to us from other inscriptions.[2]

These arguments of Hepding's are illuminating, even
if absolute certainty remains unattainable.[3] I may add,
however, that if Demeter and Persephone were intended
we should expect the definite article and perhaps the
dual, as in the Peloponnesian inscription. The mere
fact that a 'torch-bearer' of Demeter dedicates the
altar does not entitle us to conclude that he must have
dedicated it to Demeter. We have at Pergamum undoubted examples to the contrary,[4] and this very Capito
of our inscription is perhaps identical with the man who
dedicated another altar at Pergamum to Zeus Megistos
Soter.[5]

If rightly restored, the inscription

> To unk[nown] Gods
> Capit[on]
> torch-beare[r]

tells us that about a century after the foundation of the
Christian church in Pergamum[6] Capito, a priest of

[1] Cf. in line 2 of the autotype the beginning of the Ω after the T.

[2] Cf. e.g., the dedication to the Pantheion by M. Aurelius Menogenes
a hierophant and prytanis at Pergamum (Hepding, p. 454, and his
remarks, p. 454 ff.).

[3] Hepding's restoration is advocated even more decidedly than by
me also by Otto Weinreich, Deutsche Lit.-Ztg., 34 (1913), col. 2958. f.,
also in his Habilitation Thesis, De dis ignotis, Halis Sax., 1914, p. 29
ff., and by Eduard Meyer, iii., p. 96.

[4] E.g. a dedication to Helios by Cl. Nicomedes, a torch-bearer
(Hepding, p. 453).

[5] Hepding, p. 457.

[6] The earliest evidence of Christianity in Pergamum is the letter
of Christ in Rev. ii. 12 ff. The foundation of the church may very
likely go back to the time of Paul.

Demeter of Pergamum, who officiated as 'torch-bearer' at her mysteries, dedicated the altar to 'unknown' gods. In some way or other—it may easily be imagined from many analogous dedications that a hint had been received in a dream—Capito had become convinced that he was under obligation to gods whose names were not revealed to him.   He showed his appreciation by giving them an 'anonymous' altar.

No doubt the Athenian altar which made so deep an impression on the Apostle Paul also originated in the same sort of way—in gratitude to 'an' unknown god, the gift of an Athenian whose name stood perhaps beneath the line that Paul quoted. The missionary of the ancient world does not of course interpret the words as a modern epigraphist would.[1] He interprets them with a strong interest for their deeper meaning, the same that he afterwards extracts from the poet's words.

For we are also his offspring.

And so that which according to the letter applied to 'an' unknown god becomes to the Apostle an unconscious [2] anticipation of 'the' unknown God.

---

[1] Paul, however, himself hints that the sense he extracts from the inscription was not present to the consciousness of the person (or persons) who had dedicated the altar (Acts xvii. 23b.).

[2] ἀγνοοῦντες, Acts xvii. 23.

APPENDIX III.

SANTA CROCE, FLORENCE.

AMONGST the most gratifying experiences that have come to me as a result of the publication of my *Paul* are letters from my friend Otto Crusius, now long departed, to whom since our time together at Heidelberg I have been bound with the strong bonds of fundamentally similar temperament and thoughts. In particular the importance of the idea of 'originality' was recognised by us. As an illustration of the Cross as a tree of miracle (above, p. 203) Crusius sent me from Oberammergau (31.8.11) the following poem, which he had written when strangely moved by a Florentine fresco. At my request he kindly gave me permission to print it. The subject, as the director of the Institute for the History of Art in Florence, Dr. Walther Heil, informed me, is a wall painting of the school of Giotto, perhaps a product of the studio of Taddeo Gaddi, in the old refectory of the Convent of Santa Croce (now the Museum of Santa Croce). For my part I reminded Crusius of the crucifixion scene in the Convent of the Passionist Fathers at Rome, as depicted in Immermann's *Epigonen,* so different yet of equal value for the understanding of the Crucified who is also the Living One.

> Before the Altar kneeled the saint in prayer,
> Fixed on the Crucified his steadfast gaze—
> How hard his way with danger and contempt!
> Sudden, with rapture thrilled, his heart beat stayed.
> Was it a miracle or but a dream?
> The chapel walls dissolved and heav'n appeared,
> The cross of shame became a growing tree,
> Raising its branches sun-ward fair and tall—
> See how each twig is weighted down with fruit!
> The close air of the church no more he breathes—
> A gentle breeze bears scents of summer fruit.
> He sees the Glorified with arms outstretched,
> ' Thou in a holy hour hast gazed on Heaven.
> Thy dream is true.   This earthly life is dream,
> The holy cross, it is the tree of life.'
> Now God be praised for pain that veiled His face.

APPENDIX IV.

DIAGRAMS.

IT will strike many people as a strange idea to
attempt to make Paul's teaching understandable by
means of diagrams. This will especially be so in the
case of those who fail to recognise along what simple
and vigorous lines Pauline thought moves. When first I
thought over the synonymity of early Christian ideas,
in setting forth (above, pp. 166-178) somewhat fully Paul's
central convictions, I did not, it is true, give diagrams,
but I described them clearly in order to explain the
various methods of regarding the subject.[1] In every
instance I then said, when endeavouring to represent
this synonymity, the circle which is to enclose the related
ideas must first be drawn ; and the radii, which within
each circle separate those related ideas from one
another, must be drawn afterwards. The next question
was whether one should make the line of the circle or
that of the radii the heavier. The dogmatic method
which isolated the ' concepts ' would draw the radial
lines thick and the circumference thin. The psychological method, which emphasises the close relationship in meaning of religious metaphor, would make the
circumference heavy and the radii light.

[1] Cf. my preface to Heinrich Werner's translation of Trench's New
Testament Synonyms (*Synonyma des Neuen Testaments, ausgewählt
und übersetzt,* von H. Werner, Tübingen, 1907), p. iv. f. and before
that in Theol. Lit.-Ztg., 25 (1900), col. 74 ff. In his able essay, *Zeit
und Raum im Denken des Urchristentums* (Journal of Biblical Literature, 41, 1922, p. 222), E. von Dobschütz has illustrated a fundamental
idea of the Epistle to the Hebrews by means of a diagram.

On that basis I have very easily shown the difference between the various Pauline conceptions, as is indicated in diagrams 1 and 2 ; with which what is said above on p. 166 ff. should be compared. Here there are set side by side a strongly marked circle, which in spite of several faintly marked radii, is at once recognisable as a simple unity, and a circle with faintly marked circumference, the area of which is divided up by strongly marked radial lines.

This scheme of figures for elucidating our way of looking at Paul's teaching can also be specialised to explain one particular important distinction that comes to light

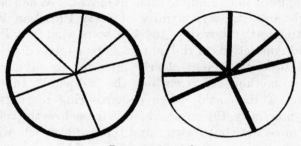

DIAGRAMS 1 AND 2.

through that new view, namely the contrast between Paul's faith in Christ and his so-called 'Christology' (cf. above, p. 165).

The one view is that of lines going out on all sides like rays of light, unlimited and immeasurable, from the one central point of light, the experience of Christ (diagram 3). The other is rather of lines measurable and in some way to be fitted together geometrically, perhaps like a polygon or like the side view of a staircase. This also could be easily portrayed graphically in different ways.

More important than these methodological schemes are the possibilities of making Paul's religious ideas themselves clear by graphic methods. It was very in-

teresting to me to see how Hans Leisegang[1] very cleverly
sought to exhibit the more important lines of the
Apostle's methods of thought in a pictorial scheme.[2]
When I had come to an end of my reflections, I got
to know of that remarkable undertaking 'the graphic
interpretation' of the thought of Angelus Silesius by
Hans Haffenrichter, about which the editor[3] writes as
follows :—

'Hans Haffenrichter (one of the group of expressionist artists "Der Sturm") has made the attempt

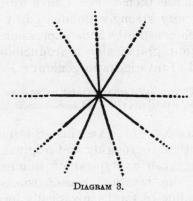

DIAGRAM 3.

to make the thought of the "Cherubinischer Wanders-
mann" visible to the eye by means of graphic representa-
tion. The statement needs no justification that only

[1] *Der Apostel Paulus als Denker*, pp. 9, 18, 22 (cf. also p. 106 n.
3 above).

[2] Leisegang (p. 18) even believes that Augustine himself in his
statement (made after becoming acquainted with Paul), *tanta se mihi
philosophiae facies aperuit*, hints that he had received a pictorial impression of Paul's general scheme of thought. He also holds the
opinion that Augustine's thought itself is similarly capable of being
represented pictorially.

[3] Innenwelt-Büchereii : *Des Angelus Silesius Cherubinischer Wan-
dersmann*, herausg. von Walter Ehrenstein, 2nd Ed., Dresden, 1925,
p. vi.

an expressionist can feel the call to such a task.[1]   The
pictures here produced, which attempt the expression of
such movings of life in the soul, as pass the power of
speech, prove that it has been possible for an artist of
like experience to represent pictorially even the thoughts
of a mystic.'

What I want to do is something less ambitious than
this interpreting by expressionism (which perhaps itself
stands in need of interpretation).   I am satisfied with
the simplest of diagrams.   But I feel strongly that one
has a right to use them.   For Paul's world of thought
on religion is very strongly dominated by the category
of space, which constantly finds expression in metaphor
and is therefore graphically reproducible.[2]   Like the
thought-world of mysticism in general :

> 'I dearly love two little words ; their names are *out* and *in*,
> Out of Babel, out of me : in God and Jesus in.'

This confession of Angelus Silesius,[3] with its
spatial orientation, thoroughly and originally Pauline as
it is, may be taken as typical of unnumbered other
statements of the mystical consciousness in general.
The understanding of Paul's mystically local *in* and its
after effects in classical German mysticism is peculiarly
instructive.

[1] Here I may also indicate that Erich Seeberg, *Zur Frage der
Mystik*, p. 10) not infrequently is reminded of Expressionist art by
the so-called emblematic mysticism (which needs a chapter for itself,
but it is for all that in a certain sense in place in the above consideration).

[2] I cannot here agree with v. Dobschütz, who denies this (*Zeit
und Raum*, p. 221).   Here all turns on the understanding (local interpretation) of ἐν Χριστῷ Ἰησοῦ.   But on the other hand it is just as
clear that Paul is fond of combining the space-category with the time-
category, especially in drawing the contrast between the 'once' and
the 'now' (cf. Eph. ii. 12 f. and many other places).

[3] *Op. cit.*, p. 101.

In place of that doctrinaire misconstruction of the mystically-local *in* in the formulæ 'in God,' 'in Christ Jesus,' and which at one time dominated the commentaries, we are now offered a wonderful and thoroughly sympathetic understanding of it in the light of later mysticism. Without fear of schoolmasterish criticism [1] *mystical* can be used as a grammatical category, and we may speak of a mystical *in*. This mystical *in* (the saint in God or God in the saint) has its greatest influence,

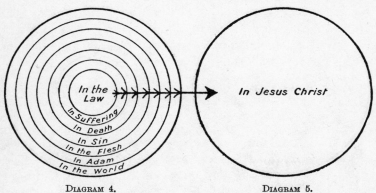

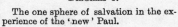

DIAGRAM 4.	DIAGRAM 5.
The seven spheres of evil apart from salvation in the experience of the 'old' Paul.	The one sphere of salvation in the experience of the 'new' Paul.

where, in the technical expressions of German classical mysticism, *in* is used as a prefix.[2]

This 'mystical' *in*, to which the German language owes such a wealth of beautiful creations both in ideas and words, while in origin it is pre-Pauline, has yet through the Pauline *in Christ* become the one great

[1] Cf. above, pp. 163 note 1.

[2] [Here Dr. Deissmann gives a list of such German words compounded with the prefix *in*—drawn from Otto Zirker's *Die Bereicherung des deutschen Wortschatzes durch die spätmittelalterl. Mystik*, Jena, 1923, and points out that many of them are Germanisations of Latin or Greek words similarly compounded.—W. E. W.]

watchword of Christian Mysticism.   And what a wealth
of pictorial imagery also !   Almost all these noble words
(which for us to-day have largely lost their original vivid
pictorial sense) can have their meaning displayed graphically.

But the same is true also of their original prototype,
the Pauline certainty *in Christ*.   All that is essential to
the religion of the Apostle, in so far as it is definable in
that phrase, can be set forth clearly in the contrasting

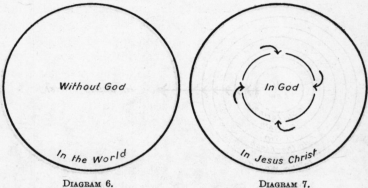

DIAGRAM 6.

Without God in the World !

ἄθεοι ἐν τῷ κόσμῳ !

Separated from Christ, without hope !

DIAGRAM 7.

God-intimacy in Jesus Christ !

ἔνθεοι ἐν Χριστῷ Ἰησοῦ !

Hidden with Christ in God !

diagrams 4 and 5.   Here are the 'old' Paul's seven
spheres of evil, and the 'new' Paul's one sphere of
salvation (cf. also p. 177 f., above).

Here in one glance it can be seen what the essence
of Pauline Christianity is : the certainty that one has
been released from that dark many-walled prison of
the seven [1] spheres of evil, and rescued into the place

---

[1] There is nothing important about the number seven ; but in any
case these seven spheres are mentioned repeatedly in Paul's letters.
The order in which they stand in the diagram could be other than
that here represented ; this also is only a detail not an essential
matter.

of light and freedom, the one sphere of salvation in
Christ.

The greatest of all the concentric spheres of evil,
which surrounds and closes in the others is the cosmic
circle.   When that alone is realised in its naked terror,
the depth of wretchedness enclosed in it is indicated by
the words of Eph. ii. 12 :

Separate from Christ in the world, without Hope, without God !

(Χωρὶς Χριστοῦ . . . ἐλπίδα μὴ ἔχοντες καὶ ἄθεοι ἐν τῷ κόσμῳ.)

When, on the other hand, the one sphere of salvation,
Christ, is realised, all that can be experienced of
Salvation is summed up in the confession ἔνθεοι ἐν
Χριστῷ Ἰησοῦ, or (formulated in Pauline words) 'hid
with Christ in God,' Col. iii. 3.   The normal condition
in the world of being god-forsaken is changed in Christ
in fellowship with God.   The purpose of figures 6 and 7,
(p. 298) is to illustrate this (cf. also pp. 146 and 164,
above).

Diagram 7 also shows how simply for Paul the
immense problem of the relationship of 'Christ-
mysticism' and 'God-mysticism' received its solution.
In Christ we are given 'access' to God (Eph. ii. 13, iii.
12; Rom. v. 2), for the gates of the sanctissimum are
thrown open.   God-intimacy in Christ-intimacy :

> Hier ist ein Ring,
> Der nie anfing.
> Und stille schwebt.
> Sein innrer Punkt.[1]

---

[1] [I have left this in the original German, as in a translation most
of its charm would disappear.   Literally it is : " Here is a ring,
which never began.   And its inner point remains at rest."—W. E. W.]

INDICES

I

PLACES, PERSONS, SUJBECTS

(301)

II

GREEK WORDS

Only a few are noted here ; anyone familiar with the Greek New Testament will easily be able with the help of the other indices to find most of the other Pauline words.

III

PASSAGES CITED

A. FROM GREEK BIBLE

(312)

B. PAPYRI.

C. INSCRIPTIONS.

D. AUTHORS.